To Adam, J
Lucy & Clau

May all your futures
be green & pleasant!

With much love,

Tim & Bran
  x   x

THE FUTURE WILL BE GREEN

The Venerable Anelog
and Brother Sebastien Llewelyn

THE FUTURE
WILL BE
GREEN

Guidelines for the
❀ NEW AGE ❀

With illustrations by the authors
and by Brother Hereward

The Positive Press
LONDON

The Future Will Be Green,
Guidelines for The New Age.

Published by The Positive Press,
10 Lady Somerset Road,
London NW5 1UP
(0171) 485 1646

Set in New Century School Book 10.5pt
and Caslon Open Face 24 pt.

Printed and bound in the UK by
Hartnoll, Bodmin, Cornwall

British Library Cataloguing-in-Publication Data:
A catalogue record for this book is available from
the British Library.

ISBN 0 9529120 0 7

Cover illustration by Brother Hereward

THE FUTURE WILL BE GREEN

by

❧The Venerable Anelog
and Brother Sebastien Llewelyn❧
of the Graigian Society's monastic community.

This book is the result of a unique alliance. That between the Venerable Anelog and 'Green' Brother Sebastien Llewelyn.

The Venerable Anelog (à Nelog), born in 1927, was trained at the Slade School of Art and comes from a gifted family well-known for innovative work in many fields, but also for its defence of humanity, justice and nature, against the aggressive, encroaching forces. Before 1983 he was known as artist and campaigner Tammo de Jongh. He met Brother Sebastien, who was then a child of nearly seven, when the former gave a puppet show at the Keats' Grove Children's Library in Hampstead in 1957. In 1963 Anelog initiated the work of the Camden Civic Society and later worked on the Original Green Manifesto, the Camden carnivals and the building of a Community Centre.

Brother Sebastien was born in 1950 and brought up in an artistic atmosphere. It did not take him long to realise that society generally was going in the *wrong* direction and in 1970, following a 'community holiday' on Mount Anelog he decided to devote his life to alternative ideals. He joined the Venerable Anelog in the old house which was to become, in 1983, the *first* Green Monastery. In 1971 they were already known as the 'Green People'. Together they fought many campaigns to save beautiful old places in England and Wales: Montpelier House, a regency villa in north west London; Sant Pedr, a lovely, idyllically sited neo-Gothic church in North Wales; a genuine country garden in Shropshire and trees everywhere.

They mounted exhibitions of alternative plans, designed by Anelog and Brother Hereward, for the King's Cross Railway Lands. In the last four years they have featured in several television programmes, in both Welsh and English, a 25-minute documentary was made about their lifestyle, and there have been numerous articles in newspapers and magazines about the monastery.

ACKNOWLEDGEMENTS

Jane de Mendelson for the original typescript.

Derek Merrill for help with the 'Devolution' chapter.

Community Press, Islington for enabling us to produce the first extract: a paperback booklet entitled 'The Original Green Manifesto of 1965'. Sadly this press no longer exists. It floundered like many other community-orientated enterprises.

Richard Gardner for introducing us to the mysteries of the Tarot and the original concepts of 'Fire-Consciousness' versus 'Water-Consciousness'.

To all those who helped with the development of 'Natural Psychology' in its early days in the 1960's and 1970's, of which **Kenneth Carter** is the most notable and **Dr. Barry Slater** the most provocative.

Posthumously **Jimmy Adler** for having had the foresight to write the wonderful, inspired, Original Green Manifesto of 1965.

Elsie Magarshack for providing a warm home in which original, inspired, controversial, stimulating, open-hearted, lively ideas and conversation are encouraged.

Hadrian Michell for encouraging us, with advice and the use of a word-processor, to publish the book.

Cheryl Dunn for typing the manuscript onto disk.

Montenegro for the original typesetting.

Mondo Designo for the cover design and finishing the production of the book.

Last, but not least, thanks to MARVELLOUS **Green Brother Hereward** for all his help in preparing the manuscript, for drawing exquisite borders and for many of the illustrations too, suggestions for a few of which came from **Margaret Gullan-Whur.**

CONTENTS

This book is dedicated
to the memory of the late

Jenia Collingwood

without whom we would not have
found Mynydd Anelog (the Hill of
Aiming), nor the basic tenets of the
Green Movement. She was our
guide in 1965 when the new &
necessary political direction for
humanity was too young to be taken
seriously by a pre-occupied &
programmed majority. Let us hope
that *this* time the first 'clarion call'
will bring people together to
recognise what should be done to
STOP the destruction perpetrated by
greedy & un-bridled materialism...
May the Inner prevail!

FOREWORD

N the 16th century a real understanding of the external world came into being. Copernicus discovered that the earth and other planets revolved around the sun; but he hardly dared reveal his insight because popular opinion was against it. People have always preferred a myth or phantasy to reality, that which they have been taught by the official religion, approved by the established authority. During the last hundred years the explorations which took mankind out of itself and into outer space have shown how the Christian church had it wrong. The earth was not flat and the centre of the universe, and the first inhabitants were dinosaurs and not Adam and Eve. God had not made the animals two by two. They had evolved; and it even became questionable whether He really existed. A wide chasm appeared between religion (and with it spirituality) and science. At present popular opinion is on the side of a new authority – mechanistic materialism, which has taught that all is soulless and automatic.

Human beings can talk to each other from one side of the planet to the other and see each other at the same time. Computers can do their mental arithmetics for them and remember an infinite amount of information, fast planes can take them to another continent in a few hours. It is predicted that all this will become faster, smaller and cleverer until mankind will be whirring about like bees around a hive of efficiency.

Something has been left behind, abandoned, neglected and ignored. Inwardly there is pain, suffering, and aching boredom. It is as if below the shining modern edifice there is a dark, dank cellar with a choked spring, clobbered up with rubbish. This is the sub or unconscious, the deeper feelings which have been ignored and abused. The destruction of wild nature, the harm done to the earth show what the insensitivity caused by this neglect has done.

10

THE FUTURE WILL BE GREEN

To save the planet human beings must go back into themselves. Unfortunately as long as everyone is encouraged to play games, compete and be superficial it will be as difficult to make anyone to see the significance of Natural Psychology, a subject which forms part of this book, as it was for Copernicus to get his message across nearly 500 years ago. It requires imagination which can only be had by surrender to it, a poetic, romantic and lyrical frame of mind for which grace and sincerity are required. When the language we use evolved, people still had these qualities, were natural, simple and direct; they expressed what they felt. Nowadays we still say that something is 'airy-fairy' nonsense, someone has 'the blues' or 'is in the pink', a horse can be 'fiery' a man 'earthy' another 'wet'. We talk about each other in this kind of way: 'She has her head in the clouds' but he is 'down to earth'. The boy is a 'firebrand' and the girl a 'soppy date'.

These expressions relate to the 4 elements: earth, air, water and fire and the mixtures they produce. Earth and water, mud: 'stick in the mud'; fire and air, hot air: 'he talks nothing but that'; air and fire, light: 'he saw the light'. The language is full of this and Natural Psychology is based on the understanding this brings by means of objective associations.

In our present time all this is considered meaningless. Natural Psychology is sadly before its time, people sofar had no use for it, like owning a car when there are no roads. The way has to be cleared first.

Brother Hereward♣

11

INTRODUCTION

 s we approach the end of this millennium I, and many people like me, have pondered over the possibility of whether a good future, a *green* future is likely by the year 2000, or soon after. In fact I have been obsessed with that year since the age of 10, the prospect of a new century, a new millennium was so thrilling. Now that alluring advent, that shining star is only 12 years hence.

When I started my apprenticeship in this community in the Summer of 1970 all the ideas now carefully outlined and explained in this book were bright, vivid, excitingly new, like colours straight from an artist's palette. Now, the ideas – the masterplan if you want to call it that – for a new world, a new society are just as rich and beautiful – but thanks to a lot of work, a lot of polishing they have a weight, a maturity, a feeling of rightness and of justice that, perhaps, they lacked before. I believe that manuscripts, just like wine and cheese, actually improve with age, despite the natural desire of the author(s) to see them immediately in print and on the shelves of the bookshops!

This is very much a book written in Britain for British people as a solution to the massive, seemingly insurmountable problems ahead of us. Many people have given up hope – because no-one around them would give them hope. All this is different now, for from today onwards a new hope, a new light is born. This is the astonishing growth of the movement which we founded and initiated on Mynydd Anelog in 1965 – now loosely called the Green Movement. The movement has been given a spiritual dimension by the Graigian Society, which, intends to revive the feminine, Inner, watery and emotional aspect; that which gives life colour,

meaning and beauty. In a society in which the masculine consciousness has ruled for centuries, the other, intuitive and sweet feminine side, out of which the Green Manifesto came in the first place,
did not stand a chance. Someone had to make the environmental
cause all rational, scientific, and 'realistic' before it could be taken
seriously. Perhaps now the time has come for the Original Green
Manifesto of 1965 and the 'human' way of looking at life which
inspired the authors.

Brother Sebastien Llewelyn ❧
Kentish Town, January 9th 1988.

POLITICS is full of prejudice, on the left it becomes more and more idealistic and woolly as you go further out. On the right it becomes more
fanatically repressive and bigoted. On the one hand there is an impossible notion of equality (in which it is an advantage to belong to one of
the minority groups which are discriminated against by the far right)
and on the other hand there is the all too possible, but frightening
creed of selfishness, chauvinism and total intolerance.

The Original Green Manifesto presents a refreshing view. It is,
although seemingly improbable and romantic, deeply realistic. *Re-*
alistic, because it recognises that mankind has a faculty, or an
organ, which has been unconscious for many centuries and which
can be allowed to see the light of day and become its guide. This is
not at all impossible, all we have to do is to allow men their feminine potential, just as we allow women their masculine side. With
a new spirit abroad people will joyously wish to be opened and
amazing transformations will take place in the *Hallowhalls* (halls
adapted or built for this purpose). Communicators will be there to
give guidance and help where this is needed.

All existing politics, including that of the conventional Green
Party, is 'airy', 'modern', motivated by the masculine consciousness, conducted in tasteless surroundings from the head. Yet here
in this *The Original Green Manifesto of 1965*, the 'watery', romantic, feminine, feeling side is represented *for the first time*. Men feel
often threatened by it, but it is just this syndrome which creates

the environmental problems we now face, destroys anything beautiful and makes for bad relationships. Such is the resistance of the usual businessman who controls the media, that he will reject any attempt to present this artistic, spiritual and psychic *other way of living*, this new political objective to the world. The holistic point of view, the extraordinary discovery of soul types and the nature of our consciousness which are fundamental to a moving and transforming creed are startling in the context of a manifesto which, on the face of it, concerns itself with the environment and its ecology. *The Original Green Manifesto* is concerned, however, also with people, not just with their clothing, food and shelter, but with their *Inner* needs.

This manifesto, the true source of the Green Movement, which came about in 1965 on Mynydd Anelog at the far end of the Lleyn Peninsula in North Wales, had to wait for its second, its wider publication, until now. Much of its content has found its way into the language of the Green Party and other Green Groups. The human aspect had to wait and with it the *Water-Consciousness* which the authors needed to promote. There are so many unhappy people, all they have is external – just the things to keep them alive, comfortable and distracted in a very desultory kind of way, – sadly enough perhaps fifty per cent of the population of this country fall into this category. Inwardly they are dead, however talkative and busy they may seem to be. These people's lives could change dramatically if they were given the possibility of becoming fulfilled through *surrender* to what comes from within themselves.

In order to purify the countryside, the rivers, the lakes and the soil, to get rid of the poisons which are used to intensify the production of food, the souls of men first of all need purification. Once this can be enthusiastically accepted – and anything which is widely and well promoted stands a chance of being accepted with great enthusiasm, look at Punk for instance – the cleaning and clearing operation will begin. There is a growing awareness that all is not well with the farming industry, people who are motivated by their deeper feelings will wish to resurrect the countryside and its traditional skills and crafts which were sacrificed to cupidity and greed.

Brother Sebastien Llewelyn and I have known each other for over 30 years and have worked together for almost 20 in the same house in Kentish Town, north west London. I had been instrumental in formulating the ideas which led to the writing of this first Green Manifesto and have been concerned with the presentation of them ever since. Readers may indeed wonder at the amount of psychology, sexuality and references to things out of the normal orbit of Green politics with its emphasis on matters of anti-pollution, anti-nuclear and conservation of wildlife. As artists, craftsmen, psychologists and monks (we are neither Christian, nor Buddhist, but *Green Monks*, our order and religion is entirely new, just as Buddhists or Franciscans were once a new phenomenon) we feel it to be our duty, our obligation to present the artistic, human and therapeutic fields, which have so far been largely ignored by the Green Movement. If this movement means anything at all, it means being honest and natural. In our Graigian Society, no-one is allowed to get away with any kind of pretentiousness, or a wasteful way of life and bad attitudes. People will always try to justify and rationalise all sorts of bad habits and ideas, but they must learn to *work on themselves*. Part of growing up is defining your own boundaries. This is true on an individual basis – but also on the basis of British society as a whole. Using the analogy of growing up, Britain is going through an extremely painful adolescence!

Anelog

Kentish Town, January 12th, 1988

HERE are four ways in which we can divide our experience of life. These are between:

1: True, Actual, Solid, Substantial, Real, Factual and Untrue, Ethereal, Theoretical, Insubstantial, Unreal, Fictional;

2: Meaningful, Beautiful, Graceful, Lovely, Colourful, Lush and Meaningless, Ugly; Disharmonious, Pedestrian, Drab, Bald;

3: Moving, Lively, Resilient, Active, Warm, Keen and Inert, Lifeless, Sad, Passive, Gold, Dull.

But also more significantly between:

4: Seemly, Aware Light, Knowing, Conscious, Bright and Unseemly, Unaware, Dark, Unknowing, Unconscious, Deep.

This last difference concerns our book. Respectable, middle-class people, who are bound by what they find acceptable and think will fit in with their 'list' see the unconscious, working-class, or peasant world as negative. Irish drunks, winos, prostitutes and the like are abhorrent to them. The laws of our country; the ethics and morals are made for the conscious and 'light' world only. Much of what goes on in 'the dark' is illegal, just as what goes on in our bowels is seen as 'dirty'. Some things can only work in darkness, like night animals, owls and badgers; they shun the light of day. The world of darkness is shy and sensitive as well as unmentionable and immoral. It is basic, with a marvellous and natural simplicity, it holds the truth like our dreams at night. This is the world of 'shadows' and of depth, the undercurrent, related to witchcraft.

Middle class men of the 1990's know nothing at all of all this, they have created a front of what goes for normal in this superficial age, say and do all that is considered trendy and have become unconscious of what is hidden in the cupboards and dark corners behind this respectable facade. In the dark world people *know* their feelings but *can't* articulate them. They just spontaneously *do*, but in the light are theories and incomprehensible, complex, complicated, twisted, tortuous explanations which parade as *profound*. Such people go by ideas, their world is blocked by boundaries; so much can't be said, or done, or worn, or even thought.

People with bourgeois aspirations - which includes 'Working Class' people who have become 'nice' - regard the 'dark' as unseemly and rude, thus they wish to eradicate it. Yet doing away with organic processes will cut us off from the soil which sustains us and we will go mad. This is one of the causes, the constant changes in our immediate environment is another (for example the ripping out of most of the familiar, old, red 'phone boxes), of all the mental illness, the instability and madness and the crime rate associated with it which proliferates in this the last decade of the 20th century. Artificiality replaces Nature at a terrible cost to human sanity.

This book attempts to build a bridge between the *light*, conscious side of life and the *dark*, unconscious side, by bringing that into the light, lovingly, meanwhile abandoning all pretentiousness, attitudes, dogmas, wrong conclusions, faulty analyses and prejudices. The people who live in the conscious, light world, the middle class, the intellectuals and academics have so far been unfree and will have to go through an experience *which blows their minds* before they can relax and allow what has only existed before in darkness. That is why it was so difficult to get our book published. Copernicus, who realized that the Earth was part of a solar-system dared not publish his findings for 30 years for fear of ridicule and controversy. On his death-bed, in 1543, the first copy of his book *On the Revolutions* arrived. It contained an unauthorised preface by a friend explaining that what followed was pure hypothesis and need not be taken too seriously. That is how an understanding we take for granted was received 452 years ago. Now it has been *our* turn to suffer a similar fate, this time for revealing the nature of our consciousness.

This is the content of the *Collective Unconscious* which has been shrouded in darkness; repressed, suppressed, ignored and bypassed, despised and condemned by Church and State, together with Tarot cards, necromancy and witchcraft. Naturally what we have discovered will be seen as 'simplistic'— well Nature *is* simple, isn't it? – and not in keeping with specious, incomprehensibly intricate, fashionable theories which are meant to be meaningful and can be accepted by the intellectual establishment because they are ineffectually untrue. Just as the Earth was deemed to be flat and at the centre of the Sun and planets, so nothing as elementary and basic as the four elements of not only Astrology, but all Medieval and most of Eastern lore, fairy-tales and ancient mythology, could be taken seriously by scientific attitudes. Profound symbolism is no longer understood, modern men and women are unbelievably unimaginative, their minds are full of verbiage and sophistry; nothing can be lovely, or fine, or moving. Nine out of ten people in the groups I teach can't make the connections between Earth and Water: mud and fertile soil in which roots grow and that this is organic life with worms, beetles, rotting wood, microbes etc. and that this connects with expressions like *stick in the mud, stuck in a rut,* and *earthy.* Thus the equation between Earth, Water; Air and Fire and the three states of Solid, Liquid, Gaseous and the energy, or heat, which causes these, may elude a number of our readers.

Dr. C. G. Jung, the psychologist whose work has been generally accepted, and is considered to be an authority, was *mistaken* about psychological types, the way his four functions related to these and the roles of intro and extroversion in defining these functions. Because he failed to see certain connections he did not understand the relations between Archetypes, types and 'functions' and the attraction 'opposite' types feel for each other. In his autobiography, *Memories, Dreams, Reflections,* he recalls a dream which he had around Christmas of 1912 in which he found himself on a gold Renaissance chair in a magnificent Italian loggia:

"In front of me was a table of rare beauty. It was made of green stone, like emerald. There I sat, looking out into the distance, for the loggia was set high up on the tower of a castle. My children were sitting at the table too.

Suddenly a white bird descended, a small sea-gull, or a dove. Gracefully it came to rest on the table and I signed to the children to be still so that they would not frighten away the pretty white bird. Immediately the dove was transformed into a little girl, about eight years of age, with golden blonde hair. She ran off with the children and played with them among the colonnades of the castle.

I remained lost in thought, musing about what I had just experienced: The little girl returned and tenderly placed her arms around my neck. Then the dove was back and spoke slowly in a human voice. 'Only in the first hours of the night can I transform myself into a human being, while the male dove is busy with twelve dead'. Then she flew off into the blue air and I awoke.

The Star of Hope

The 17th card of the Major Arcana in the Tarot represents our aims and aspirations. The maiden pours back the water from her ewers which, like our deeper feelings, is part of a universal pool. It is a celestial sign to light the way within the soul of mankind, showing a need to purify ourselves and reach a new depth of understanding.

The Tarot, used for fortune telling, consists of the familiar pack of cards with the addition of 4 pages and 22 cards bearing symbolic images. The 4 suits have cups (hearts) for water, swords (spades) for fire, 'pentacles' or coins (diamonds) for earth and wands (clubs) for air. The first examples date from the 15th century and our playing cards derive from them.

19

I was greatly stirred. What business would a male dove be having with twelve dead people? In connection with the emerald table the story of the Tabula Smaragdina occurred to me, the emerald table in the alchemical legend of Hermes Trismegistos. He was said to have left behind him a table upon which the basic tenets of alchemical wisdom were engraved in Greek.

I also thought of the twelve apostles, the twelve months of the year, the signs of the zodiac etc. But I could find no solution to the enigma. Finally I had to give it up. All I knew with any certainty was that the dream indicated an unusual activation of the unconscious. But I knew no technique whereby I might get to the bottom of my inner processes; and so there remained nothing for me to do but wait, go on with my life, and to pay close attention to my fantasies."

A group of us began to distinguish the 12 basic Archetypes, 6 masculine and 6 feminine, in 1960, the very year that Jung died, and have by observation for almost 40 years found that these correspond to the 12 natures, one of which each human being has been given by 'Providence' even before birth.

Anelog
At the Monastic Community of the Archangel Michael and All Angels
Kentish Town, London, October 26th 1991.

INTRODUCTION

IT HAS taken a quarter of a century for our original vision, contained in our manifesto of 1965 - be it only in part - to reach people generally and it has included that long, hard road most writers and innovators have to tread of being rejected and misunderstood by practically everyone. This huge slice of time has given *us* the chance to solidify our position, to become a monastery and just as importantly; given the Green Movement *as a whole* the time to become respectable and established with the aid of people like Prince Charles, Jonathon Porrit and Petra Kelly.

We have had the a remarkable amount of media interest in the past few years, but journalists have ONLY been interested in the 'externals', the way we dress, eat and inhabit our two houses, our colourful interiors, our paintings and our pottery - our ACTUAL, GREEN PHILOSOPHY, our ideas on government, devolution, the introduction of a true spiritual life with the teaching of our amazing insights in NATURAL PSYCHOLOGY, integrated in a *new* kind of social services, called by us 'The System of Communication', has not interested them one bit. Put bluntly, very bluntly, we still feel censored! We have appeared on television many times, speaking both English and Welsh, and an *acclaimed* documentary, made by Richard Pawelko, 'The Original Green Men', has been broadcast twice on H.T.V. in Wales.

This book is extremely TIMELY - people on the whole still think 'being Green' just means buying a new kind of washing-up liquid or petrol and using recycled paper envelopes instead of 'Basildon Bond'. Although this green consumerism will obviously benefit the environment, we, as a group of serious-minded individuals are also keen that the deeper, philosophical, psychological, artistic and political issues too get a hearing. The idea for writing 'The Future Will Be Green' came to Anelog and myself, strangely enough, when walking through Green Park towards Picadilly in 1975. Since then a good deal of our material has been rewritten and revised. In a superficial world, centred on computers and motorcars, the idea that human beings have a soul or psyche, what this might be and that this could have a bearing on everyday life is not one which meets with recognition. Sensitive people, who seldom or never are part of important decision-making bodies, are aware that a soulless environment and bad atmospheres have a negative effect on one, cause illness and bad relationships. The encroaching urban environment is very dreary and destructive to the human psyche: this is the reason for the proliferation of crime and mental illness. This message, however, is extremely difficult to put across and to find favour with publishers who rely on fashion and public opinion to sell their books. The threat to our earth from pollution and deforestation is becoming urgent enough to create a greater awareness of it and hopefully interest in the subject of this book. This interest will, probably, influence hundreds of millions of people & the astonishing momentum will carry on not just during the next century... but into the *next millennium* too.

Brother Sebastien Llewelyn
Kentish Town, October 29th 1991

PROLOGUE

EYOND the Mountains of Snowdonia and across the sound from Bardsey Island at the far end of the Llyn peninsula stand the furthest hills of Wales. There are two and the tallest is called Mount Anelog; it commands a wide view across the whole peninsula, towards Snowdon in the east and the hazy coast of Ireland in the west. Nowhere do more noble and untarnished elements combine; the air is fresh and clear, the windswept climate full of changes and the rocks, the sea and soil still hold a magic in between themselves which flowers in the gold of gorse and bright purple of the heather. Sheep roam unheeded on this common land where choughs and ravens build their nests and falcons circle overhead.

In this high and untamed country a stream of water came dancing, crystal clear, through wild and flowering mint and sage and over many-coloured pebbles to the sea. Here a primeval place existed which was disturbed by sheep and seagulls only and by a fisherman who left his boat, together with his lobster-pots and mackerel-baskets on a small and stony beach. Its name is Porth Llanllawen, which means the entry to a happy place, a good name for a secret and enchanted spot, hidden by tall cliffs and guarded by tall rocks.

In the height of Summer, on a sunny day in 1965, a group of friends came clambering down into this gorge and one of them remained there as he had been wonderfully inspired by a vision. After they had swam and sat amongst the rocks to dry themselves, he, joining a companion who was sitting by herself, looked down into the shallow water and there the seaweed parted to reveal a map of England, Wales and Scotland which was clearly visible upon the pebbles. This map then clouded over with black particles and then, in another movement of the water, was purified and shone brilliantly and long, lighting up like precious jewels forming shapes of flowers and of hearts and trumpets. He lost all sense of time and place and found he was naked and alone, unknowing with the simple and untrammelled senses of primeval man. He forgot where and who he was and played, experimented and discovered in the golden sunlight of the afternoon; yet he was constantly alert and prepared for any danger. It was as if his thoughts and his experiences came to him from outside, as if they came towards him, like birds would fly or pebbles would be tossed at him. In this way it occurred to him that his name, from now, was William and as he climbed the cliff–side to leave this place he looked back and saw a **W** formed by driftwood where he had been picking pebbles in the **W** stream. William seemed to be a carpenter, a builder or some other craftsman and with this idea he came back to his companions in the cottage on the mountain, carrying a large bunch of flowers which he had picked, walking on bare feet on a jagged, thorny, stone-studded earth-wall. Not one scratch did he receive, so cautiously and carefully aware had he moved about.

This was the beginning, the first phase of a period of miracles and extraordinary events during which the very first emergence of a 'green philosophy', ideals which were both economic and political, came to life. Most of these ideals were intuitively *received*, but they seemed both sound and sensible. They aimed basically towards creating those conditions which make distinction between needs and gluttony possible and which promote the health, happiness and spiritual well-being of the individual.

When these become the aims of our society instead of material gain and glamour, the emergence of a more natural and inwardly satisfying state will be inevitable. Instead, therefore, of the production of material goods continuing to go on increasing and adding to the existing glut, consumers would be encouraged to accept decrease and to adopt a more conscious and careful lifestyle. To this end a kind of conversion, in a way similar to that brought about by Christian missionaries in the 7th Century would be necessary. People should be made to realise that the natural world is being depleted, spoilt, polluted and disfigured and that it needs protecting and conserving. That we need to eat conscientiously and plan our requirements for transport and for shelter in a con-

PROLOGUE

Mount Anelog, one of the few remaining places on the British Isles to keep its original wildness saw the birth of the Green Movement in the summer of 1965. The fields around Y Graig, a small farm on the far right of the drawing, are still covered in wild flowers during the spring.

siderate and satisfying way. Through practice and dedication true feeling can realise itself in human endeavour and people can live from what they are actually motivated by, *not* what they want and have been conditioned to believe.

James Adler, a journalist and craftsman who regrettably died in 1970, was moved and inspired by what he heard about the events on Mount Anelog and wrote the manifesto which was printed in the Autumn of 1965 by a magazine called *Positive Approach*. A meeting was held in the walled garden of the house which is now the Graigian Monastery in North-West London, to which 50 people came and which led to a number of other meetings. It was impossible, however, to form a committee which could agree to further the aims which the manifesto proclaimed. There was a division between political and spiritual motivation amongst those who came. Some people wanted gatherings in which participants aimed at greater understanding of themselves and each other and wanted to sit in silence so that they might become aware of their inner feelings; others wished to form a movement which could bring about REAL changes in the everyday, external world.

However, a great number of pamphlets, booklets and thousands of leaflets, printed in green, were issued from that house in North-West London from that period onwards which led to other groups being formed. Firstly there was the Conservation Society, followed in the early 1970's by Friends of the Earth, the Ecology (now Green) Party and Greenpeace. This divergence is, perhaps, regrettable and may be due to egotism. But, most of all, the reason for it might be that there are a number of approaches possible. Some groups rely on confrontation and the publicity this gets, others look for respectability and membership. One clear distinction is between a more emotional, artistic and human, or a scientific and intellectual image.

The Graigian Society, which revives the Positive Movement (the name used by a small pressure group which carried on with the aims of 1965), is trying to bridge this gap. It is led by a spiritual community which, in the 1970's, was able to buy the house in North-West London where the original meetings had taken place. It also owns a small farm *Y Graig**, on Mynydd Anelog, and the minute cottage on the same mountain where the movement started. Here the Society is directly involved in what might be termed *the Battle for the Countryside* and has been instrumental in focusing a great deal of attention on the damage which was (and is) being done there to nature. The Society is in constant touch with the National Trust, which has been able to acquire Mynydd Anelog as well as Porth Llanllawen. This cove, which was mentioned at the beginning of this prologue, although a Site of Special Scientific Interest, on a Heritage Coastline and in an Area of Outstanding Natural Beauty was raped by a previous owner in 1976 who bulldozed a 'road' into it, quite inappropriately, to obtain access to his white, plastic dinghy.

* Pronounced: 'Er Grige' = the rock, the *i* as in eye. Mynydd Anelog (à Nelog) = mount Anelog (from *anelu*, to aim).

By relating to particular areas (in North-West London to get trees listed and in North-West Wales to introduce the idea of *Nature Reclamation* and forming a trust to buy land for this purpose) the Society is bringing down the principles of ecology to a human scale, something ordinary people *can* understand.

'Nature Reclamation' (a term coined by the Society) means restoring land spoilt by factory-farming or other 'industrial' processes, to its original state by planting hedges and trees, by putting back earth-banks and ditches, re-introducing native grasses and wild flowers and removing dumps and scrapped machinery. To this end we beg you to help the Society in any way possible, particularly in encouraging people you know to join our 'national network of nature-lovers'. James Adler's manifesto of 1965 was genuinely quite original when it was written; the ideas and ideals so revolutionary that everyone who came into contact with them felt charged and inspired by them! The message was dead simple and went right against the materialism of the 'Sixties': 'Less, not more of everything!' These ideas were later taken up and developed in Professor Fritz Schumacher's famous book *Small is Beautiful*. Now, nearly 30 years later; a whole new generation of people has grown-up which will, inevitably, grasp the motto of the new 'Aquarian' Age: "Put it Back!"

B ENEATH supperficial differences, every party in Europe, America and the Communist world is united in a common programme of statistical aggrandisement. All claim that their policies will provide, in so many years hence, so many million more cars, houses, technicians, scientists, refrigerators and television sets. Looking a little further into the future these grim planners of abundance worry (though not too seriously) about the depletion of natural resources... including water!, congestion of cities by people, of the countryside by cities and the roads by cars and the mounting flow of rubbish which spews from the volcanic anus of organised acquisitiveness.

Every country is obsessed either by keeping its lead in this rat race or tortured by fears of falling behind. At a time when there has never been so much wealth and an average man can live in more comfort than a Roman emperor, the failure to produce even more seems to spell doom and ruin. The inherent demands of the system for more and more effort to keep it afloat grow yearly more extravagant. Meanwhile the carrot which is dangled at the end of the 'everlasting' road as a reward for this terrible effort looks depressingly unappetising, dry and futile.

We are in the position of men promised a fixed payment every time they bang their heads against a wall. The head-banging is unpleasant, but somehow no one can stop for fear of accumulating less than his neighbour. Stunned, dead to anything worth-while which the money could buy, the head-bangers persist in struggling through a life made tolerable only by repeated satisfaction of ever less real needs.

The Positive Movement believes that this self-inflicted torture must stop before the consequences of its madness destroy us all. The massive resources devoted to keeping this treadmill churning must be diverted to solving the real poverty which exists even in the so-called affluent parts of the world. By poverty we mean not only lack of food, clothing and shelter but the poverty of our surroundings. During the past century hardly a beautiful building and not a single beautiful city have been built.

Our affluence and waste are ugly and to pay for it the underdeveloped countries grow steadily poorer. Cities must again revert to human scale and proportions, stop their plunder of the countryside and become enjoyable and inspiring places in which to live. The countryside must be preserved (and even *extended*) in order to act as a life-restoring *contrast* to the urban values and environment and a retreat from hyper civilisation. Men and women must again draw pleasure from their daily tasks, take a pride in their achievements and be able to appreciate whatever it is they make. Those who are now apathetic *consumers* the Positive Movement would wish to turn into dedicated *producers*.

None of this will be possible until we cease our reckless chase after abundance. The facts are staring us in the face, but no-one dares recognise them. More material goods can only mean more factories needing more workers, more competitive clamour from armies of salesmen and more irreplaceable raw materials to make goods for more and more people. This way can only lead to more congestion, ever larger and more sprawling conurbations fouling more and more of the landscape. The more complex our society becomes, the more administration, paperwork and planning it requires, leading to more bureaucratic control and the increasing separation of decision-taking from the people for whose benefit the decisions are supposed to be taken. Man ceases to feel that he has any control over his destiny or any contact with his fellows and sinks deeper into the selfish acquisitiveness which serves to keep the treadmill moving.

Human values are displaced by those of the computer and the stock-exchange. Technological advance is seen as all-important.

THE FUTURE WILL BE GREEN

An aircraft which can clip a few minutes off a trans-Atlantic flight is hailed as an achievement (!) as its progress destroys the sleep of millions for the benefit of a few travellers. The stop-watch has perverted the pleasure of sport, our popular music is judged on the sole criterion of the money it earns for its performers and the same idolatry is extended to the 'five minute wonders' of literature, poetry, drama and painting.

Few people are satisfied with this state of affairs and the year 2000 looms ahead like some kind of streamlined nightmare. Today we rear animals by intensive methods, reducing their lives to pure consumption by taking away movement, interest and dignity. Tomorrow it may be the turn of men; already the 'battery' accommodation is rising to blot out the sky. To offer more production as a cure is not only irrelevant but pernicious. Our only hope is a complete reversal of the whole process:

We must produce less... and for fewer people.

We must replace complexity with simplification.

The stimulation of our appetite for material goods by glossy advertising must be replaced by production for need. Better to produce one car that will last for 50 years than five that will last for 10, better not to produce a car at all where a bicycle would be more appropriate, better to meet the need for transport by borrowing from a common stock, as the need arises, rather than encouraging private ownership. Better to let one dedicated engineer build the complete vehicle himself than to have a thousand de-personalised robots throw it together with loathing. If this means bankruptcy... then let it! The materials are to hand still, but money we cannot eat, wear or use to make houses. The time we now waste in mass-producing and selling inferior goods could be enjoyably spent in making for ourselves, by craft-methods, goods that will be treasured and appreciated. We cannot produce less unless we produce for fewer people. At a time when over-population is the most terrifying problem facing the world we still encourage childbearing, both directly by tax benefits and indirectly by misguided romanticism, also by religious principles which survive from a time when there were too few hands available to do all that had to be done.

Animals caged in confined conditions will become irritable and attack each other with savagery. The same is true of men. To turn

30

Pierrot is one of the characters from the 'Commedia del Arte' which became popular 400 years ago. The drawing signifies an innocence and romanticism which belong to a simple, natural, sweet and 'water conscious' way of life. This has always been associated with poverty, humility and a peripheral existence.

the tide we must use every humane method to hand, not excluding progressive taxation of parents who produce more than two children. We must cease hounding the homosexual, he at least does not produce unwanted children and his special qualities could contribute a great deal to the enjoyment of life if only we would stop ridiculing him. We *must* encourage emigration by every *fair* inducement available.

As the population declines we must begin to repair the ravages of more than a century of industrialised madness. The bulldozers must be turned loose in the sprawling suburbs, saving only what is beautiful and useful. Nature must be allowed to reclaim the depressing wastes of ugly buildings which foul our landscape today. Only time will complete the cure, but in the end we should again have a country which gives pleasure rather than pain. In those centres of our towns which are worth saving we must replace the glass coffins of paperwork with living, working people taking a pride in their surroundings and a direct control of their affairs. Towns must again cause their citizens' hearts to swell with pride and affection instead of being choked deserts from which to escape whenever the opportunity offers.

These, then, are the aims of the Positive Movement:

1) Less production instead of more;
2) Communities instead of masses;
3) Quality before quantity;
4) Use instead of abuse;
5) Nurturing instead of exploitation;
6) Value before money;
7) Need not greed.

The alternative is the dreadful 'limbo' projected by the planners, constricted, anxious, artificial and dangerous; negative in its very worst sense. Not even the planners relish the prospects they predict, but they have succeeded in convincing us that it is inevitable. If theirs is not the future we want, the only compelling reasons to make us accept it are apathy, complacency and drift. It is against damnation by default that this positive movement will work. So far, this manifesto has, necessarily, been political in outlook, but the Positive Movement will not fall into the same trap as other

parties in concerning itself exclusively with the material side of life. For many people political action will always be the main method of bringing about their ideals. The ideas expressed so far were arrived at independently from several different approaches. They were travelled by individuals who in their own ways are primarily concerned with such matters as the function of the human personality and psyche and the related worlds of dream-symbolism, religion, ritual, mysticism, community life and philosophy.

To many these worlds are a closed book, in the public areas of our society these matters are suspect and ridiculed, particularly while the statements which issue from them are strident with conflicting opinions. Nevertheless, psychologists and thinkers who have achieved recognition in these spheres all agree that religion (not the dreary futility of present day organised 'Christianity') is of vital importance to human life, that mental ill-health is on the increase and that our civilization imposes intolerable strains on many whom we now incarcerate in mental institutions because they cannot function within the strait-jackets of our limited, prevailing mores.

Regardless of individual interests, which stem directly from individual characteristics, all those working within the Positive Movement are together in a desire to advance on all fronts. All their superficially divergent activities are *inter-related*, because, to rule out any one field of endeavour, is to diminish and cripple the whole. Not every aspect will appeal with equal strength to everyone, but neither will any one aspect interfere with the work of any other, but rather help to further the total advance. All can make that contribution which it is in their essential nature to make.

To the individual reader we would say: Reserve your scorn and outrage which some of these proposals will arouse in you. They are just as important to others as those which win your sympathy are to you. These others are different from yourself and always will be! Reserve your judgement until you have searched deep into that which now appals you; for these areas of disgust, shame and ridicule are a vital clue to your own unconscious and undeveloped aspects.

James Adler
London, October 1965

CHAPTER 1.

RECLAMATION

HEN the Roman legions came to the coast of Britain they brought to a land of forests, fields and wild-flowers, untouched by any urban artificiality, a number of alien attitudes and the legal code of their country. We are accustomed to call this civilization and it so carefully blotted-out the culture which already existed in these islands that hardly a trace of it remains today and practically nothing is still known about it.

The Romans were empire builders who had inherited their attitudes from Alexander the Great, whose empire succeeded those of Persia, Babylon and Assyria. These people knew how to think in a particular way, by means of which they could defend their cities and organise military campaigns. Their laws were designed to further this defensive, aggressive, acquisitive way of thinking and bore no relation to natural, human sensitivity or to the laws of Nature. It fostered a mentality and outlook which we call 'Fire-Consciousness' for it is the use of fire which gives us metal and all things metallic. Fire transforms matter, it alters its chemistry and gives us more power, resilience and speed. It is masculine and fierce and made rockets and bombs possible, firearms and high-rise flats, television-aerials, jet-planes and all the other phallic paraphernalia of our industrial age.

The Roman Empire declined and disintegrated but its attitudes are still with us and have always been the enemy of Nature and have endeavoured to exterminate, ravage and uproot simple, natural life. The countries of Western Europe which sent sailing-ships across the Atlantic Ocean in the 15th, 16th, and 17th centuries to conquer, colonise and Christianise the various parts of Canada, North and South America, followed the Roman example with even greater success and managed to turn an untouched, organic continent into wastes of artificiality and crime.

THE FUTURE WILL BE GREEN

The fate of the so-called Red Indians (these people are neither Indians nor Red!) was sadder, but similar to that of the Ancient Britons. It must be quite clear to enlightened men and women today how these good people, whose culture was wholly part of the cycle of the seasons, who greatly respected their heritage and worshipped Mother Earth, were made out to be savage, cruel and indifferent, just as the Britons were said to sacrifice their kindred to the flames or cut off the heads of their victims in religious rituals. Yet we know for certain that the Roman citizens enjoyed huge spectacles of men killing each other and that the English watched executions with relish, when witches or religious dissidents were fed in public to the flames, or thieves were hanged at crossroads. One can safely call their tales about the nations they subjected to their Fire-Conscious conditions the projections of their own barbarity. It is also interesting how Fire-Consciousness through the ages travelled westward from Babylon to Rome, to London to New York where it found its most ultimate expression in a city made up entirely of verticals, the most brutal and uncompromisingly masculine and therefore criminal place on Earth, which, like its predecessors in their time, is copied everywhere else in the world.

What we mean by Nature is that which, both in human-beings and in their environment exists without any interference from artificially induced plans or schemes, religious dogma or insensitive notions. Therefore a hut or house, or even a temple built without any speculative scheming, coming together organically from indigenous materials, of a truly experienced need and out of feeling, is just as natural and part of the natural order of things as a bird's nest or a rabbit's warren. That which is natural exists only in accord with natural conditions, the type of soil, the weather, climate and its location. It is not 'conditioned' in any other way. Human beings, however, are able to create conditions which go against Nature and thereby alter natural growth: this is what is *un*-natural. A tulip is *unnatural* and a Pekinese dog, a peach tree trained against a garden wall and a pigeon fancier's prize bird. There are degrees of unnaturalness, a plastic tulip (for instance) is more un-natural than a real one. Un-naturalness starts with breeding or cultivating and ends with thwarting, lopping, cropping, training and misdirecting, the deliberate stunting and perverting of natural, human growth, the manufacture of synthetic and artificial substitutes.

In the 18th century there was still a high degree of naturalness left. It had survived in spite of 1000 years of conditioning influences from church and state; in spite of repressive religious doctrines and laws aimed at conformity to a social pattern based on property and class, there were still people in wild country living off

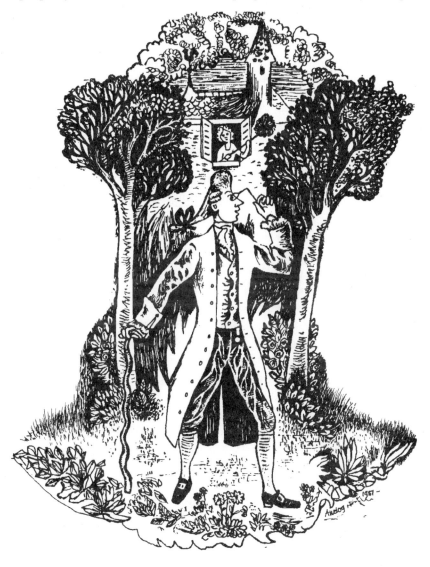

the land, in tune with all that flowered and grew there and there were still craftsmen who made things of iron, clay and wood as they had done since time out of mind. There were still forges, looms and potteries as there had been in the days when whispering trees gave magic incantations and the creaking of wood and the sound of birds were part of the making of a stool or a pot. These simple, humble people preserved a kind of knowledge and a way of life which alone can make us healthy and happy. Out of its magic beauty is born and if we lose it entirely we do so at our peril.

Please understand us: We mean a free, natural and simple life, not slavery, not drudgery. We mean a lot of things which would be considered totally un-important by the urbanised multitude of to-day, like toads, dandelions, elderbushes and the roots of the wild parsnip; all manner of things which happen by chance and many of which have medicinal value*. Woods and thickets grew where there are now suburban houses, places where no-one went, little streams running through these wildernesses, left alone even by gamekeepers and fishermen and although the 18th century mentality was cruel and indifferent to wildlife and indulged in caged birds, trapping and shooting, hunting and cock-fighting, there were not enough people and no machinery to create any sort of impact on nature. A natural way of life, with its natural integrity and natural understanding, its kindness and honesty, its natural beauty– we would now gasp with pleasure and approval at the interior of an ordinary cottage even at the beginning of this century – survived until the great Victorian onslaught of the 1870's when London's first real suburbia spread across the landscape, the lovely River Fleet was made into a sewer and villages like Hampstead and Highgate became part of the Metropolis.

The railways made this urban expansion possible and, later on, the tube trains. There have been four really terrible attacks on Nature by bourgeois, suburban, middle-class, bad taste conventionality; in the 1870's, in the 1900's, in the 1930's and in the 1960's when the new towns were built. Bad taste is an urban, *civilized*, Fire-Conscious, artificial phenomenon. It never existed in the country where there was *only* simplicity *or* nobility. This urban, respectable outlook on life is most anti-nature and has now become gen

---

*In recent years comfrey has become famous for its therapeutic uses.

erally accepted as the only one, or 'normality'. This, from a natural point of view, is totally terrifying. It is a kind of death, it is frightful, frightening because it is so far removed from what is in our hearts. It is inhuman and now threatens to sacrifice all our heritage of wild, singing country, enchanting lanes, hedgerows, land of pure sound, to the roar of engines, the smell of petrol and the tedium of tinted cement slabs and tea-roses in so many un-beautiful front gardens! It wishes to impose un-natural conditions upon us everywhere.

In the 1870's an immense industrial 'growth' made the Midlands black with smoke and Birmingham big*. The factories and houses of that period, now the smoke has risen and the fog no longer falls, have acquired a certain charm, they possess a solidity, an earthiness which endears them to us in our airy age. We live in a house of that period ourselves and we have become fond of it.

This first massive assault on the countryside depended on the steam-engine and the locomotive. With the second assault came gas, gasometers and acres of fussy Edwardian terraced houses in Putney and Ealing, tiled tube stations and soulless monotony which, in regions like Acton and Kensal Rise, can be sickening: areas around the docks of that period in East  London are so desolate that limbo must be Paradise in comparison. The third assault was an electric one and it created what are still the outskirts of London: Huge, horrible, 1930's suburbia which stretches for miles and is so unutterably tasteless and boring; not gloomy like the developments of 1870, not mean or soulless or drab like those of the 1900's, but tasteless, insipid like uncooked pastry or weak tea. They are a pretence that Nature is still there with primulas in front gardens, a few weeping willows and the old, little stream still running behind the back-gardens and cement paths.

What has happened since the Second World War is worse, where tower-blocks and motorways clutter the periphery of our towns

*The word 'growth' has been misused; growth is a natural phenomenon, industry 'expands'.

and the countryside itself has been perverted to make agriculture into an industry and farms into factories. Whatever is left of the natural places which in the 1930's still survived these terrifying offences - just think of yourself as a wild animal to understand what this civilization means - is now threatened by every kind of suburban 'new town' development, by 'industrial growth' and the 'tourist industry'. Nothing can expand indefinitely and if this process of despoliation continues then we will cut ourselves off totally from our roots.

Forces, thankfully, have been at work since the early 1960's to counteract the progress of urbanization and redevelopment, industrialisation and exploitation of natural resources. The success of the Green Movement with groups such as Greenpeace, Friends of the Earth and the Green Party shows a general feeling amongst thinking people, who are becoming alarmed, that we must save what is left and be careful about our resources.

It seems to us that as the population of this country is declining in numbers (or is at least stable) and with the greatest possible encouragement of such a decline in all sorts of ways, a retracting society becomes possible. This will be a society which is on the side of Nature because people have become less 'conditioned' and are free to develop naturally. Such people would want to live in organic communities and just as so much Georgian and Victorian London was destroyed by ruthless redevelopment, so all that has been built around our towns and villages during this century could be cleared up once it becomes redundant. We could reclaim this land and allow wildlife to return.

It all depends on how people generally are, how natural they are, how free to experience their natural feelings, their identity. There are again trends in our society which reflect a desire for this freedom: Organisations for the liberation of women and of homosexuality, spiritual and self realisation groups, often originating in North America or India, are typical examples. Such trends are bound to become stronger, just as a desire for social justice and clean air grew stronger in the first half of this century. Certain things are inevitable. One can say with confidence in this world, that big things started by being small and that what seems important and big today may be in decline tomorrow. A few small mammals in a world full of huge reptiles became the ancestors of a world full of mammals. The streets are now full of motor-cars and they rule our lives, our national economy, international affairs: Yet perhaps in a decade or two (or more) they will be on a scrap-heap and by then we will have some agreeable kinds of omnibus or electric trams. For long distances there might be old-fashioned looking 'community cars' with modern, economical engines and a revival of the railway system. People might even want to travel by barge.

We can create conditions which favour natural and human growth, but to create these conditions there must be a consensus, a climate of understanding which wishes to make them possible. Unfortunately, at a certain point of un-natural conditioning, when habits have hardened and attitudes have crystallised, it is impossible to revert back to an unconditioned state. A tree which has been repeatedly lopped severely, cut back and had its remaining branches twisted into strange shapes, will always, however much you let it grow freely again, retain its weird form. A dog which has been chained up and maddened will always be vicious and so it is with people. Most people receive their information from the mass-media and particularly from the television. We all know that the press, radio and television companies want to confirm what the majority of people have already been conditioned to believe in, however false this is.

Fundamentally these beliefs are: That we must all stand up and fight for ourselves, that the world we live in is bad; 'a vale of tears', that we and the world can only be redeemed by God, who helps them who help themselves, who are the admired millionaires. Most people are abysmally ignorant of the nature of things, of cultural values, of what is good and beautiful. To them life is boredom or a bloody struggle which may end with the explosion of an 'H-bomb', or with the environmental catastrophes which are nowadays predicted.

What can be done to fight this ignorance? The established political parties thrive on it and encourage competition and greed. Most people, again, are aware that the fabric of society is disintegrating and are frightened of what may replace it, which is normally thought of as either extremism (communism, fascism) or anarchy, which imply a loss of freedom, of democratic and civil rights, or chaos and the destruction of reliable values. The established political parties, the government and the Christian churches maintain their status by feeding such fears. A wall of prejudice has to be broken down, all manner of idiotic, contradictory, thoughtless, chauvinistic, automatic reactions and subjective opinions have to be brushed aside before it would be possible to reach the majority of people. Why should they not be given a chance to know the truth about concepts such as ecology, conservation, decentralisation and organic-farming? Why should they not be told about wholefoods, the dangers inherent in the continued denial of the human psyche, the ruthless exploitation of natural resources, urban expansion, factory-farming and industrial growth?* This must all be explained in the most elementary, simplest and most amusing way, so that a child of 5 can understand it. Unfortunately at present, the people who know about these things already are much of a minority and disunited because they have no wish to belong to a cohesive organisation which might cramp their creative lifestyle. We are thus in a situation where an ignorant majority is efficient and organised, whereas an enlightened minority is disorganised, haphazard and consequently impotent!

The BBC and its rivals will say that they have reported on these subjects or did feature programmes on them, but we feel that there should be hard-hitting propaganda, as there is for God. For instance it is common knowledge amongst more enlightened people that white bread is not conducive to good health because it is bleached and de-vitalised, but still the majority of people eat this stuff. Real, good, whole-wheat, stone-ground bread is difficult to get and many bakers don't sell it at all. For organic foods which, by common-sense, should be cheaper, because they need not be processed, we have to go to specialised shops, of which there are depressingly few, even in London.

*This, of course, includes the real dangers of nuclear power and waste.

Chickweed, dandelions and tender lime-leaves are all good food, the equivalent of spinach and lettuce, but how many ordinary people know this?

There are four institutions which hinder natural and human growth and they all begin with the letter M: Mindless Marriage, Mechanicality, Money and Monotony. It is these, when they are automatically accepted as inevitable, that keep conventionality going, they are the mainstays of the suburban 'unnatural' mentality and are the cause of what alienates people from themselves and each other: emotional stagnation, repetition, passive consumerism, apathy and artificiality. Many couples get married because they think they ought to, because they are lonely, bored or the girl is pregnant. Such marriages are based on 'normality' on a compulsive obsession with being the same as everyone else – the husband playing his (almost rehearsed) masculine part and the wife her feminine part – and usually break down after a dozen years of keeping up appearances and become either a habitual arrangement, or end in divorce. Many men repress emotional yearnings, or deep true love, to be accepted as 'normal'. What a waste, what a pity and what a terrible loss to nature, to themselves and their inner development! How un-free and un-natural this conditioned duress, this command performance, this boring, unsatisfying yoke endured passively by millions. It is mechanicality which keeps it all going, the automatic repetitions of the same habits, the machinery thundering and rattling in factories and the sprawling industrial 'plants', the engines and labour-saving devices which have become our rulers, without which most people imagine themselves to be helpless. Our medicine is mechanistic, our scientific research, our whole approach to life. People do their work in a mechanical way and secretaries and receptionists talk automatically, like machines.

Many people get trapped in a family situation from which they can not escape. Wives and husbands destroy each other and make any real growth within the relationship impossible. Often it is a stalemate with one of the partners playing 'Dog in the Manger'; blocking the other person's natural development. The failure of many marriages is due to fixed attitudes about what the other person is like and to entrenched habits. Children suffer badly from

43

marital misunderstanding, are prevented from being happy and able to develop freely. Neurotic conditions and guilt are the result and are passed-on because people often repeat the behaviour of their parents.

Money is an institution which has nearly everyone in its terrible grip. Because of money one has to do work one hates, one has to demean oneself and satisfy the boss, the customer, the 'public'. Money is also most mysterious, it is the basis of the economy which suffers depressions, booms, inflations and recessions for reasons which are almost impossible to understand. It is obvious, though, that a great many factories are turning-out goods which are supposed to be desirable, but which nobody has really asked for, whereas the goods one would wish to buy are unobtainable because it is said that there is no demand for them. No-one knows, either, what the value of money is based on, a lot of it appears to be nothing but elaborately printed paper. There is no money for well-made or beautiful things whereas all manner of vulgar rubbish 'makes' money. An artist can not earn money by painting pictures which would inspire people, but can 'make' it by deadening his senses to help advertise, by some revolting means, some really bad stuff. Because of money everyone who works does this for organisations they do not, or seldom, believe in, whereas they are unable to give much of their time or attention to the causes which would gladden their hearts. When it is said by politicians how necessary it is to 'create jobs' this only means that more people must do work for money in which they only work to make more money for 'industry', not to produce anything of value or to find satisfaction in their work.

RECLAMATION

Mindless marriage, mechanicality and money add up to a deadening, a negation of excitement, diversity, life and therefore produce monotony: Thousands of identical streets with identical people in identical rooms eating identical food out of identical tins and repeating, hour after hour, identical phrases like clockwork which they learn from identical men on identical television screens, who all seem to be wearing identical square spectacles. Phrases like: 'And having said that' or 'At this moment in time' or 'The viability of such a project' or 'In this day and age' or they buy popular newspapers (and videos) which monotonously repeat the same atrocities, sexual sensation and black horror everyday, to titillate their senses numbed by vile impressions and relieve the boredom of a monotonous existence. *None of this has anything to do with real life!*

Real life is ecstatic, exuberant and full, not monotonous mechanicality to make money for mindless marriage. It reveals itself in good relationships (regardless of gender) and sexual intercourse which relates to real, deep, true, guiltless feelings. Such feelings have to be liberated and that can only be done by creating conditions which favour natural and human growth. These depend entirely on the climate of public opinion. People, on the whole, do *not* want to be persecuted and like to be regarded with approval by their neighbours. It was not because of Christian martyrs that Christianity became so successful, but because the Roman Church was well-organised and could capture the attention of the powerful and mighty Roman Emperor. After that people wanted to belong to the Catholic Church because it became the proper thing to do. It was the same with Communism in the 'Eastern Bloc', the majority of people there used to believe in it because this was to be socially acceptable.

How can the climate of public opinion be changed? So far this has only happened through violent means, through war, revolution and conquest. Christianity, Islam – even Buddhism*– were established with the sword, with repressive measures from the conquerors, the government, the powerful elite. It is the same with the leading doctrines of today: Marxism, Private Enterprise, Social

---

*The Emperor Ashoka and his ancestors had made themselves powerful by conquest. Ashoka was able to propagate the teachings of Buddha successfully and effectively because of this.

45

Democracy and all the rest, they all came about through agitation, protest and upheaval. How on earth would it now be possible to make people *want* conditions which favour natural and human growth and what are these conditions anyway?

The first condition is control over the aggressive forces which are dangerous to such growth. Those forces which negate this growth, like greed, exploitation, expansion and competition. If you wish something to grow you must allow it space and time and keep away anyone who might want to trample it down, or put something else in its place. The destructive forces which run loose in this present-day society must be held back, curbed, controlled. What many people mean by 'freedom' is unbridled egoism, everyone for themselves, by themselves and on their own: A race in which one is either a 'success' or a 'failure'. Look around a park, a public library or a café, say Kenwood House (a London art gallery and museum on Hampstead Heath). You see unhappy people often sitting all alone. Loneliness is a big problem! Lonely people need companionship and understanding; to be accepted (just as they are), soothed and calmed. It is a question of bringing individuals together to form a group. It is no use making this compulsory. The group must be so warm, so attractive, so necessary that it does *not* break up after a few weeks. Emotional honesty and variety is essential and therefore the group must have a leader, a co-ordinator, a *communicator* who is thoroughly trained in psychology and can guide the group and help its members.

Provocative and stimulating questions must be asked about society; e.g. what is all this male chauvinism for? What is all this competition and materialism for? What is this bourgeois* conformity in aid of? What kind of world are we making for the future with all these sulphuric factory fumes, untreated swage being poured into the seas and juggernauts belching diesel smoke into the air on ever-widened motorways?

*Bourgeois, in the sense of nylon net curtains and 'keeping up with the Joneses'.

This is the second condition.

The third condition is an organisation which fosters natural and human growth and is able to reach many people with its message, encouraging them to respect wildlife, to join groups and to love nature. Such an organisation would train communicators who are both social workers and teachers of a spiritual way of life. This way of life is based on a new and revolutionary psychology which teaches and distinguishes 12 Archetypes, giving us understanding of our 'Inner Selves', our psyche, how we are motivated and how we function emotionally. Why one soul type (there are 24) is so different from another. It gives us objective insight into our psychic nature, how we naturally are, just as anatomy tells us how we are constructed in a physical way. Some amazing discoveries were made between 1960 and 1970, which have yet to be recognised publicly, based on the work of the Swiss psychologist Carl Gustav Jung. These could have as dramatic an effect on the world as Christianity had and are explained in the course of this book. The organisation is the Graigian Society and the discoveries are called Natural Psychology.

The men (and they are invariably men) who run our Press and broadcasting corporations are not inclined to make knowledge public which they regard as 'idiosyncratic' and which goes against Fire-Consciousness and conditioned notions. That such notions are responsible for an inflammable, dangerous, garish and artificial world does not occur to them.

Fire-Consciousness compartmentalises and dissembles, whereas *Water-Consciousness* relates, integrates and assembles. Water flows, it dissolves and it is soothing, it also washes clean. The knowledge of the 12 Archetypes is basic to Water-Consciousness, it is also the key to symbolism and the interpretation of myths and dreams, a world of misty woods, moonlight and abundant, lush vegetation. Water-Consciousness is the *awareness* of our 'inner' feelings, which have, with most people, become 'sub'- conscious. This subconscious must be freed and brought to consciousness and there are now many techniques for doing this: exercises in relaxation, Deep Massage, Encounter, Gestalt, Rebirthing (Prana Yoga), Group and Art therapy, Reflexology, Co-Counselling, Energy-Releasing, the Latihan, Hatha-Yoga and all sorts of meditation and visualisation.

Education at all levels, from elementary schools onwards, should include Water-Consciousness. Water-Conscious schools are strictly *non*-competitive; children are encouraged to help and love each other, rather than always to claw for the 'top place'. At present children are not at all helped to relate subjects to one another, or to their *own* experience of life. As a result they are very ignorant of nature; children from a large city often do not know you can pick a blackberry and eat it, that butterflies do not sting and that cows are passive. There is also no preparation for life, neither in the emotional sphere nor in the practical one. Because children have to compete at school to gain qualifications they are not encouraged to help others and thereby gain compassion and a conscience. A few progressive, liberal or 'Waldorf' (Rudolf Steiner) schools may be different but, as a whole, children are still seriously misunderstood and given the wrong stimulation and values. An un-natural, repressive or unhappy education can ruin a person for life.

The fourth condition is *respect* for all that is whole-somely, positively female and feminine and total contempt for brutish, or arrogant masculinity. The male chauvinist must be made to feel ashamed of himself, his violence, his destructive and egoistic behaviour, his lack of compassion and sensitivity. Only if what is intrinsically feminine is liberated in both men and women and no longer repressed, scorned and persecuted, will timid boys find

enough moral courage and emotional honesty to express their true feelings, their feminine side, their sensibility and intui- tion. At the moment vandals and 'yobbos' are still en- couraged, by all they see and hear, to go on proving themselves to be 'hard men', to react against any- thing that is in the least vulner- able, to do damage to buildings, public services and trees. This vandalism, football hooliganism and crime is a manifestation of blind boredom and an anti-life attitude: Homosexual feelings, violently repressed, are a contributory factor.

Many men are *voy*, or feminine types: i.e. types whose behaviour may not be feminine, but who need the friendship of a *dard*, or masculine type man, who is self-confident and independent, to give them emotional security and guidance. Many women are *dard* types who need to develop and realise their masculine side, but it is nonsense to say that a voy man should 'ipso facto' find a dard (masculine type) woman. He may be much happier with a man. Happiness should be our only criterion. To summarise, these are the Four Conditions which favour natural and human growth:

1) Controls on behaviour destructive to Nature (which includes characterful, old buildings). This means control over roads and traffic, building, planning, population-growth, commerce and industry (which now seems to include everything from 'Take-Aways' to agriculture).

2) Groups led by 'Communicators' who can alleviate suffering and hardship. Ultimately these Communicators could serve in a very small area, like a parish, or locality, or ward, the functions of nurse, priest/ess, local government official and adviser. These are very broad-minded, friendly people, often girls and young men, who have a spiritual vocation and have been specially trained for several years.

3) An organisation which trains Communicators and Inter-Communicators who, for instance, help to take a sick cat to a veterinary clinic, deal with a hysterical person, or organise a club for lonely people, which is ideally in a converted corner-shop doubling as an open air café. Their function is *not* to preach at people but disseminate kindness, sympathy and understanding. Communicators and Inter-Communicators are skilled at dealing with almost any kind of person and situation; they are Healers in the broadest sense of the word.

4) Respect for all that is feminine, really allowing anything that should happen naturally. Most religion has been, or still is, sexually repressive and wishes to impose mental strait-jackets, this has led to a dreadful taboo on natural love between people. Boys particularly need to be put at ease and made to accept themselves as they really, deeply are.

The majority of people in the world today, who have adopted the West European 'civilization', are brought up with un-natural attitudes. They attach shame to nakedness for instance, have negative attitudes to 'dirt', no longer see themselves as part of nature and lack a sense of belonging to it. They have, as a result, no integrity and do not realise what is fitting or satisfying, what is safe and good for them. Only with *this* sense is it possible to experience how things really are, their quality, goodness or badness, their wholesomeness, or unwholesomeness. Animals use it all the time, to safeguard themselves, to find their way and their food. It is in the smell of the air, in the atmosphere, in the shadows that are cast and in the shades of colour around. Unnatural people make their gardens neat and trim, use weed-killer and concrete inappropriately and do not know what it is to appreciate different textures: that of soil crumbling between their fingers, or of various stones or of wood. Farming has become an abuse of nature and farmers see themselves as industrialists running factories for the 'farming industry.' Such farming is a gross form of exploitation and encourages further unnatural behaviour. It looks upon animals and plants as if these were *things*, not mammals like ourselves, or birds, or living organisms.

Everything industry does to satisfy the so-called demand (created by advertising) of the 'mass-market' is ugly! Until the Second

RECLAMATION

World War one was at least spared this ugliness in the country-side. The 'farming industry' is now making sure that ugliness is so universal that people will forget what it is to love; that nothing of beauty remains to be seen. A cynical trickster mentality is in charge and has made insensitivity and superficiality the rule. Nuclear accidents and pollution will finally bring this home to everyone.

The Christian religion has propagated the assumption that human nature is intrinsically wicked; it has, by its implication that this world does not matter, aided the destruction of our environment and in the course of its intolerant history has encouraged various forms of un-natural repression. These have impaired sensibility and caused sexual, emotional and spiritual problems which have crippled many people's lives. We must return to our source, the place where we were once innocent. Instead of using churches to worship a male deity who has always been represented as unearthly, we should make them into shrines for Mother Earth, the lovely planet on which we live. Unless we instil respect and love for all that lives and grows, for what is vulnerable, venerable and old, for what we feel and see smell and hear in lovely, unspoilt places, the fate of our world will be an unhappy one. Without integrity there will be more crime, aimlessness, boredom and mental illness. Life will be not worth living, for we will have no safety, the hotels in our resorts will go up in flames, our trains and planes will crash or be 'hi-jacked', our streets will be full of criminals with knives and guns. There will be no lovely places to escape to, all love will have disappeared in a world of supermarkets, 'industrial growth', automation and nuclear reactors.

We must create an organisation which can reach people and use our, often redundant, churches for 'opening' them. Everybody *should be opened*, just as everybody was, at one time, baptized. There should be no exceptions to this, everybody must become part of Nature, of a natural, new religion. To be *Opened* is to become receptive, to become aware of feelings, positive emotions and vibrations – to become sensitive to atmospheres, to start growing or developing inwardly. This *Opening* occurs by relaxing properly, calming-down and becoming still to allow a natural and purifying movement from within. Communicators will be able to give talks on Water-Consciousness and on Natural Psychology and reach their audience of receptive, open people. This would indeed be a positive use for a church, which would, again, become part of nature, surrounded by *abundant*, natural, lush growth; a lovely wild garden to feel uplifted by.

Everybody in our present society is forced, compelled, coerced and commandeered to pay income tax and rates (which have been given a different name twice, but in effect are still the same thing) for which they get, apart from nuclear missiles, a noisy and brutal refuse collection, orange (!) street-lighting, the sight of familiar houses being torn down to make way for ugly, impersonal housing estates and high speed rail or motor ways, concrete subways with obscene graffiti sprayed over the monotonous mosaic, a Department of the Environment which gives grants for suburbanising old farmhouses and cottages, a Ministry of Agriculture and county councils responsible for the ripping out of hedges to add to the concentration-camp image of farming, more roads with roundabouts, mechanical means whereby the verges of pavements and lanes are kept trim and sterile, a cumbersome and inept civil administration and numerous other things for which they have not asked. Yet everybody, more or less, accepts that this should be so. The idea, however, that we should make *everybody* more open, more receptive might seem to be an unbearable imposition on those who spend their time being compelled to do work they dislike (or even hate) for organisations they don't believe in, to pay rates and taxes for things they do not want. Why continue with this blindness? Would it not be much better if the majority of people were free to use their senses properly, could thereby enjoy their lives and make the kind of decisions and choices which enriched them spiritually, rather than continue with an unconscious copying of bad examples? Would it not be marvellous if millions of people became aware of the senselessness of their existence and the ugliness of their surroundings? Would it not be wonderful if everybody could be sensitised?

We must reclaim both souls and land for Nature! We must allow wildlife and wild-flowers to return to the places where they once were; we must make our environment good for human and natural growth.

Let us examine these two things: 1) the meaning of reclamation

•RURAL IDYLL•

and 2) that of integrity and what these imply. To reclaim a built-up, or industrialised area for nature implies the demolition of buildings and installations there, the sorting out (and possible recycling) of all materials which have to be removed and the covering over, and filling in of pits and trenches with soil or any other suitable fertile covering (e.g. refuse, manure, wood-ash, sawdust or compost) so that natural, indigenous vegetation can be re-introduced. This, in turn, will create a habitat for various birds, insects, mammals, reptiles, amphibians and fish (if there are ponds) plus all the other forms of life in them which help create a balance. A pool, or pond, which is not overshadowed and has the right kind of weeds, snails and water-bugs, fish and so on will remain fresh, clear and self-regulating. Both for psychological and ecological reasons the indigenous flora and fauna should be maintained and protected. There will be, as a result of this policy, a return of those amazing, wild, free, unkempt stretches of 'Magic Country' which have, in most places, been built on or are municipalized or industrialized.

We mean places where the giant hogweed grows 12 feet tall and swallows build their nest in an abandoned shed, where ox-eyed daisies grow high and the rusty, old kettle lies forgotten in the tall grass, where nothing is interfered with and all things are allowed to be, we mean places full of delight and surprises, including *natural* dumps of *natural* objects. Such places are vital, necessary

53

and valuable, they are not 'economic', but we should have them. *Why*? Because this is what any natural person loves, what naturally appeals and what would generate life, vitality, energy, the energy which would never be in short supply, which could cause no crisis because it has exhausted no deposits of oil, coal or uranium.

It is important to realize that we feed from natural impressions which stimulate us positively and that this food enables us, in turn, to create things of beauty: pots, rugs or paintings. If these impressions are bad our psyche will become polluted, much as the garden pond which is overshadowed by a lime tree, or the river which has rubbish and effluents put into it. With impressions we mean that which makes up the atmosphere of a place, the way it smells, the feeling of it, sounds, shadows, movements as well as colours and shapes. Even when we can not recognise anything and we are faced with strange objects, or curious plants, or animals we have

not seen before, even before we know what plants and animals are, will we be impressed by them. Impressions are *vitally important*, but totally disregarded in our 'civilization'.

It will be seen, in years to come, that our psychic existence is just as important as our physical survival, that most illness is psycho-somatic and that our present day, mechanical conditions are providing the wrong kind of food for our senses. A hundred years ago hygiene had not been heard of and people ate and drank contaminated food and water. Operations were performed without sterilisation. We are now still doing exactly the same thing in a psychic sense. We are contaminating the psychic system of anyone living in the industrialized world. Because the body is treated by the physician and the surgeon and the mind by the psycho-analyst or psychiatrist, people have been encouraged to think of themselves in a DIVIDED way. Complementary/Alternative medicine is gaining support because it treats the patient as a TOTAL entity.

RECLAMATION

It is a matter of psychic or mental and emotional significance to reclaim contaminated and abused land, to abolish silage, put back hedges, trees and earth-walls, to allow wild flowers and wildlife to return to meadows and fields and to cultivate crops only in an organic and sensitive way. It is impossible to love places which are devastated for the sake of cupidity and the energy supplied by love is far greater than any intensive production can supply. There *is* enough land to feed everyone in the world organically and no justification for industrial methods. An inspiring example of Nature Reclamation, given the right publicity, would be the very best way to bring home the message of this book.

Almost 10 years ago (1985) a marvellous opportunity presented itself. A 'factory-farm' at the tip of the Llŷn (or Lleyn) peninsula of Gwynedd in north-west Wales came up for sale. Part of it was a 'monster field' of 63 acres known as 'Bron Orion'. Originally, this prairie consisted of 20 small fields, divided by a beautiful spider's web pattern of stone-studded earth-banks and ditches, the traditional family smallholding of land for sheep and cattle grazing, which dates far back into the mists of time. How far, one can not be sure, perhaps the early Iron Age (circa VII century B.C.) according to archaeological evidence from Castell Odo* which was once a fort on Mynedd Ystum, a small hill overlooking Bron Orion in the heart of the Vale of Anelog**. The Graigian Society's brave intention was to raise the money to buy this desecrated and raped land and with donations, publicity and voluntary help restore the earth-bank and ditch system with the aid of maps and photographs. The Society has a thick file of letters to and from influential, national bodies and a great deal of interest and concern generated, even the Secretary of State for Wales was alerted. Given unlimited time we probably could have raised the exorbitant price asked for it! The land was owned by an English businessman and it was our sworn intention to let it to young, local smallholders (at nominal rents) in order to perpetuate the traditional land use. The owner of Bron Orion had tried potatoes and cereal crops as part of the modern

*Please read: 'Wales: An Archaeological Guide' by Christopher Houlder, Faber and Faber Ltd. 1978 ISBN 0-571-11243-9.

**Please Note! Anelog is three syllables and in Welsh words the penultimate syllable is stressed - in this case 'e'.

'industry' which we call 'EEC Granticulture'! It's a merciful release he never tried pigs – everyone would have had to leave the area! Although we lost the 'battle' of Bron Orion and the campaign cost the Society a lot, we have no regrets, for we instigated a process which eventually will give farmers a conscience if they have none. The Graigian Society, in common with other nature conservation organisations, fights constantly for more effective and wide-ranging legislation to protect our countryside from erosion.

Mynydd Ystum is the name of the hill on which Castell Odo stood and it means the mountain of shape, posture or grimace – a strange name. It is a rather 'magical' hill and being in the centre of the vale commands an enormous panorama. When we (the authors of this book) wrote our historic 'Save the Vale of Anelog' pamphlet – of which we distributed, free of charge, over a thousand copies – we declared that one day we would build, from local stone, a tiny shrine or chapel, with 12 stained-glass windows, like an ancient 'beehive' cell of the early Christians atop this prehistoric site. We hope this will come to pass...a building which will represent the spirit of this beautiful part of Wales.

We have said the Graigian Society fought to buy Bron Orion. To be more accurate it would have been the Bron Orion Trust, in time a Welsh-speaking group or committee which would, through grants and pleasant, social fund-raising events have brought a wider cultural awareness as well as reviving traditional and ecological farming methods. But, it is our misfortune to be 20-30 years ahead of current trends and Fate decreed that we should not buy Bron Orion. Nevertheless we shall continue to press central government and Common Market officers to *explain* how these 'travesties of humanity' could happen in a place 'protected' by 3 or 4 official designations. One could be forgiven for thinking these designations not worth the paper they are printed on if they have no 'teeth'!

Obviously we are striving to show the world how farming could again become part of culture; agriculture, or husbandry, to use a lovely, old-fashioned word. It would entail a massive educational programme, the banishment of poisons, so-called fertilizers and heavy machinery plus the stamping-out of that evil of all evils – a veritable cancer – competitiveness. Young people will learn the wonder, the magic of working together, with love, for a common

Harlequin is another character from the 'Commedia del Arte'. In some ways he can represent the fusion of two opposite archetypes: 'Sparklewheel', the Juggler and 'Deeplake', the Soul. He is therefore magical and free. The caravan denotes his itinerant way of life, the mask a somewhat hidden and dramatic aspect

purpose. 'Idealists, dreamers' we hear our readers mutter beneath their breath; yet it is idealists, dreamers, visionaries and poets who have changed the world so far.

At the same time that Bron Orion was raped...the owner of an idyllic cove, designated as a Site of Special Scientific Interest and protected by other laws (it is part of the 'Heritage Coastline' and in an 'Area of Outstanding Natural Beauty'), bulldozed a road into it. Since then this cove has been bought by the National Trust but an unsightly pile of earth still covers the once-lovely stream, described at the beginning of the Prologue to this book. It would be possible to use the earth dumped here to restore the walls on Bron Orion. This excavation and rebuilding would have to be done with great care using volunteers and workers with shovels, wheelbarrows, horse and cart. Surveys could be made of flora and fauna and an exhibition mounted as an example of what can be done to reclaim nature. A pamphlet about Nature Reclamation in Welsh and in English has been distributed by the Graigian Society.

When new houses are no longer built in vast numbers money will be available for land reclamation, starting with farmland and industrial dumps. In time redundant suburbia may be knocked down to make way for wildernesses and allotments. The ecological value of wild, open spaces will, in time, be generally appreciated. Even nettles have their use: They can be made into an excellent shampoo, tender tops can be boiled and taste better than spinach and beautiful butterflies breed on them. There is very little woodland left, many footpaths have been blocked-up or ploughed-under and agricultural land, meadows or fields no longer provide walks in many parts of the country. Two farmers from Bedfordshire, on holiday in London were heard to remark how wonderful it was to go for walks on the grass in Hyde Park! We need areas of woodland and open fields, with footpaths and stiles, around our cities and towns, places like Hampstead Heath or Richmond Park, but wilder, interspersed with gentle farms. There already are places like disused railway cuttings or cemeteries which have become overgrown and mysterious, a haven for wildlife and for the occasional stroller who seeks solitude. Unfortunately such places are constantly interfered with by those who wish to tidy them up and 'open them to the public', to provide 'recreation' and 'leisure facilities'. This advertised, municipal access inevitably destroys their character.

RECLAMATION

To reclaim human integrity would mean, for many people, the shedding of a great many acquired habits, ideas and prejudices; getting rid of conditions (that which has become chronic, whether illnesses or attitudes) and the gradual realization of what is true and honest, what belongs and feels right, what is good and what is sentimental 'eyewash', a bad habit or second-hand idea.

A lot of people would think that integrity meant being honest with money, or punctuality, or realism, but we mean much more than this. We are so used to disjointedness and unrelatedness in present-day society that it would be difficult for a great many of us to see what the opposite is. In the screaming cacophony of modern 'opinions', music, art and rationalising, in all the tinselly shop-fronts, theatre and television-shows, in the nihilism and gormlessness of planning, designing and inventing, in all that people have taken onto themselves, collected and acquired, what we mean by integrity has got lost.

Integrity means relating the parts to the whole, a comprehensive and complete pattern: Not details in isolation. It is seeing the wood and *then* the trees, the mass and then the particles, the general and then the particular, to see things 'in the round', in a three-dimensional way and in context. A person with integrity, like a tree, has roots. He knows where he belongs and where his life is taking him, he does not allow himself to be swayed by fashionable gimmicks or heady talk, he knows what he feels even when everyone else does not, he knows about harmony and synchronism, when to be daring and when to stand back. He/she has *natural, good taste* instinctively.

Synchronism is when two related things happen at the same time: You are talking about someone and at the same moment he is at the front door, you feel joyous and the blackbird begins to sing, you say: "There are dangers" and the fire engine comes hooting past. We often call these things co-incidence, but at certain times they occur in a magical way. Many miracles happen thus: Just when rain needs to fall, it falls, just when the healer touches the sick man, a soft wind passes through the room, a pigeon flutters by and the pain dies down. When we are in tune with ourselves, with nature and the universe, our lives become so full of synchronism that it no longer seems strange to us in any way.

We are now living on a different 'wavelength',
a magical one. With reclamation this wavelength, which had virtually disappeared, becomes available to us again. It is the wavelength
on which a cat or dog can find its old home (even
if this is 100 miles away) and it is the miraculous and wonderful aspect of life which
dismissively is called instinct. When human
beings are instinctive once more, like animals,
when they have reclaimed, re-discovered their
animal part, then there will be no question of
what is good or bad, no opinions about taste, no
quarrelling about how things should be. Then
there will be only one law, the law of Nature.
That this law was disobeyed came from division, the diabolical division of the sexes; men
this women that. Men and women who are not
concerned with such divisions have re-discovered the nature of the human soul with its 12
aspects, the six masculine and the six feminine
'sides' which together create a balanced whole.
All nature knows this balance, as long as it is
not interfered with this balance exists instinctively. Insects are food for birds and birds are
food for foxes, too many insects or too many birds
or too many foxes can only come about through
un-natural circumstances, through human interference. In nature synchronism is part of the
balance and the result of it; only a human being
who is 'in his head' and not 'in his body' finds it
at all extraordinary.

RECLAMATION

Animals accept everything that happens as a matter of course; no animal is 'in its head'. We human beings are possessed by a particular kind of consciousness (in our heads) which makes it possible for us to deny the instinctive awareness in our body. Instinctive awareness is totally unselfconscious and can not use words, it is an inbuilt knowledge of how things are and what is necessary. Ants build their nests that way and it is the marvel of the universe. When a human being can become sufficiently emotionally free he will reach his instinctive self once more - for he was born with it and used it as a baby - and he will have 'reconciled head and body', he will be aware of himself and intuitive in a blissful state. Once more the British Isles will be a land of forests, fields and wild-flowers, Paradise regained; human nature and natural loveliness reclaimed!

CHAPTER 2.
RE-ORIENTATION

NNER Freedom – the freedom to be conscious of and able to express anything the psyche manifests – hardly exists in this country, that is why very few adults wish to remember their childhood, it often was a period of frustration, unhappiness and emotional deprivation. This is a horrible fact. Yet conventional people like what is British best and do not want the things they are used to be changed, however bad these are. Above all they will resist anything which threatens their habitual way of life. This makes re-orientation very difficult. First of all one has to find a way of reaching these people and secondly one would have to overcome their hostility, much as one has to calm down a dog which has been made angry.

The more limited a person is the more he will cling to his prejudices. The majority of people are very limited because their imagination and perception have been stunted and spoiled. This fact may seem to be an exaggeration to some people: We advise them to look at the most popular newspapers, or visit fairs, dog races, football matches, or other places where large, ordinary crowds congregate. This is why re-orientation is so necessary and why a spiritual revival depends on it. We do not mean education, this is associated with a boring rigmarole which has to be gone through. We mean a new direction in life and a new direction for society; from Fire to Water Consciousness, from the family to the community, from the individual to the group, from base, ugly materialism to real feeling, from indifference to an appreciation of what is sacred and actually beautiful, from sentimentality to the recognition of what is false and most difficult of all: from selfishness to compassion and understanding.

People have to be released from negative, bad emotions, from repressions and inhibitions. With this release comes purification, a spiritual flushing-out, not of all sexual fantasies or natural yearnings, but of all the by-products of competition, like envy and malice and all the residue of religious indoctrination of a narrow and intolerant kind.

Repressive, cold, intolerant, religious and official institutions, snobbery, competition and industrial expansion are responsible for ugliness, for all the stultifying beliefs and inhuman conditions which killed real love and magic. With the justification of the conventional way of life, the class-system, poisonous industry and factory-farming, all that was lovely was destroyed. Re-Orientation would mean to really see this, to actually experience the difference between repressive ugliness and liberating beauty. Spiritual guidance, which includes that for an unperverted use of sensibility, to see, smell and hear clearly and thereby distinguish good from bad in the Arts, in music and in everyday things, does not yet exist. Very few churches are lovely, with the exception of old ones and these usually only on the outside. Most religious institutions have a bleak and life-denying atmosphere. People on the whole, those whose reading stops at the daily tabloids, aren't aware of any other values than those of a cash register. They believe and accept any old tripe and their ideas are usually mundane, commonplace and stereotyped, or just plain idiotic. They have been put in a bad, deadening atmosphere, bombarded with disagreeable, hateful or sickening impressions, told a series of untruths or half-truths and fed with de-vitalised food and negative emotions. Good feeling has been sorely lacking.

Re-Orientation is turning towards a different direction, to become open to a new outlook, to experience love. Just as practically everyone in our present society has enough to eat, something which compared to other countries, or another age is quite remarkable, so everyone should now be given what they emotionally crave, to have their Inner hunger satisfied too.

To be made inwardly free means to have one's deepest, most valid feelings confirmed, to be released from the bondage of compulsive habits and false ideas. Very often, what people say about themselves is untrue, they say these things because they are afraid,

they want to feel secure in the acceptance of others, of society and they have buried their deep and sincere longing, their own true yearning, the powerful and soaring emotions they might have felt about someone they could have really loved and what this meant to them, to suit conventionality, in order to be 'normal'. Re-Orientation would mean a process in which fears and anxieties are allayed and in which an alive and unashamed, natural character can be formed: A process of learning about oneself, becoming conscious of one's dreams and desires, learning about other people, their needs, and about relationships. Most people in the external world, the 'outer' society, are concerned with their identity, or image, a mask to hide behind. This is because they were intimidated, told to compete, to prove themselves, to be a 'success', to go up in the World. All this is a strain, it means making artificial efforts, to put on a show, to pretend. To give up this straining and trying hard is a relief, one can begin to relax and to be receptive, to love instead of hating life, oneself and all the things one does naturally, or 'unconsciously'.

In very recent times it has been discovered what human nature really is, how the human psyche consists of 6 'Masculine' and 6 'Feminine' Aspects. These are NOT to be confused with Male and Female, these terms are used here in the sense of the Chinese principles of Yin and Yang; it is *nothing* to do with Astrology, it is something we can observe for ourselves naturally. We all know what it is to feel big or small, distant or close, superior or inferior, ordinary, humble, carefree or concerned. It is these differences which are the key to understanding the human psyche. Before we list them below in two columns we must stress that a complete human being does not deny any of these 12 aspects, but that people usually 'take sides'. In Re-Orientation one learns to experience oneself in every one of the following ways:

RE-ORIENTATION

Masculine aspects or worlds

1. As expansive, capable, strong, active, courageous, *big.*
3. As resilient, clever, skilful, inventive, witty, *smart.*
5. As independent, detached, calm, objective, factual, *distant.*
7. As knowledgeable, critical, discriminating, exemplary, disciplined, *high minded.*
9. As questioning, precise, conscious, changing, *clear.*

11. As free, generous, wild, forgetful, spontaneous, *fast.*

Feminine aspects or worlds

2. Or, as self-effacing, reflective, gentle, imaginative, kind, *small.*
4. Or, as sensitive, dreamy, truthful, serious, intuitive, *deep.*
6. Or, as emotional, loving, passionate, romantic, responsive, *close.*
8. Or, as ordinary, humble, accepting, warm, relaxed, *lowly.*

10. Or, as settled, simple, resigned, natural, habitual in a good way, 'regular', *restful.*
12. Or, as committed, careful, reliable, methodical, restrained, *slow.*

These represent 12 'worlds' in the sense of the 'Industrial World' (3) or the 'Academic World' (7), the kind of environment and lifestyle associated with a particular aspect of the human psyche. When one identifies with one of these the opposite may become 'un' or 'sub'conscious. Someone's behaviour may, for instance, become more and more expansive until he/she is incapable of any reflective thought and too proud to go back on themselves. Such a person becomes inflated and perhaps dangerous. Another person effaces him/herself until he/she feels they hardly exist and becomes a martyr in their self sacrifice. Girls and boys tend(ed) to be conditioned to identify with the aspects or 'worlds' thought to be appropriate to their physical sex. Once young people begin to re-discover their real and natural selves, lost during adolescence, they can be open to beneficial influences and make choices from their 'inner and truthful feeling', a different and happy, caring society will come into being.

It is also possible that someone experiences conflicting aspects (worlds), that for instance at times he/she feels free and generous and behaves in a wild, forgetful way and at other times is careful, restrained and held in. Such a person may not be conscious of such inconsistency in his/her character and indeed many people are divided and are in fact as it were, not one but several people. The 6 differences, or conflicts between Masculine and Feminine worlds within one person's psyche, the unconscious polarities, sometimes called the 'Intra-Psychic Conflicts', *can* be reconciled and the understanding of this is called 'Natural Psychology'.

Natural Psychology is an endeavour to discover the truth about normal, healthy, sane and ordinary human beings, the way they function inwardly, what lies behind behaviour patterns and the emotional attraction between close friends and lovers. It shows why one type of man is attracted to another type of man as well as a woman and vice-versa. It also shows the way which leads to the further evolution of humanity. The methods used in 'Self Discovery' and in 'The Awakening' are designed to help people attain a higher level of development. Self-Discovery courses and Awakening groups are part of 'Anelog Work' taught thus far only at the Graigian Monastery.

A total human being has developed his/her masculine and feminine potential. We call such a person a genius; throughout history such exceptional persons have had a profound effect on society and it is remarkable how many of these were homosexual, or attracted to members of both sexes. A long list could be made of such cases, starting with Sappho and Socrates. Jesus Christ according to the gospel of St. John loved one of his disciples and Shakespeare wrote sonnets for Mr W. H. Often this very true and great love has been camouflaged in books written by bigots. What distinguishes a genius from ordinary men and women is their strength of character, their originality and lack of conformity.

Most human beings in a society which has developed the intellect at the expense of natural qualities and in which competition, ingenuity and cleverness are promoted at the expense of feeling, become contrived, unable to resist the conditioning forced upon them, often from birth: Pink for a girl, blue for a boy! Feeling in a great many conventional women is replaced by cloying sentimentality and therefore instead of being able to express or even be conscious of their natural responses, they, like most men, develop what Jung called a 'persona'. Other psychologists have described it by other names. Karen Horney refers to it as the 'ideal self' and Ouspensky as the 'False Personality'.

What would happen naturally to children who are not influenced by the customs of the society in which they are born can only

be judged by the behaviour of unusual individuals who are able to withstand all pressures from outside and develop in their own way. We have already referred to geniuses in this context. The false personality exists entirely for the sake of other people and is largely a product of the imagination, sometimes it is the result of social pressures. In the British Working Class a man is expected to be virile and hard, 'macho' and not a 'poof', such men will often 'put on' a show of these admired qualities, although they themselves may not have any regard for them at all. A shy and sensitive boy at a comprehensive school in Burnham-on-Crouch is bullied because he comes from a free and artistic background. This forces him to speak and act Burnhamese. As a result he develops a kind of 'crust' in his consciousness, below which all that he really feels lies buried. He is not aware of this at all and makes love, friends, music and passes his time in a way which does not give him any joy and has nothing to do with himself, but he is *not even* conscious of the fact that he does all this *only* to be acceptable to his friends. His 'False Personality' tells him that he is being 'normal' and is at one with the fashion.

The behaviour of people in whom such a 'crust' has hardened will have become mechanical, or robotic, and they will not know what it is to live properly and experience real pleasure, contentment or happiness. A very large number of boys, particularly in our society, suffer this fate and therefore criminal activity abounds. Re-Orientation is the only hope for these people and a very special course is designed for them consisting of a variety of exercises which will help break-up the 'crust'. It is also very important that such boys are able to 'get back to themselves' in an environment which understands their needs and allows them to unfold naturally.

THE FUTURE WILL BE GREEN

Not many individuals, particularly in our big cities, are able to express themselves in a natural, uncontrived and spontaneous way. Conventional people can not respond freely and behave unselfconsciously because of fashionable attitudes, class-consciousness and snobbery. They can not be honest and direct and it is this facility which Natural Psychology makes possible because it teaches people about each other's nature. There are 12 Natures, consisting of the 6 Masculine and 6 Feminine Worlds, these natures are basic to 24 types and it is the understanding of these 'psychological' or 'soul' types which will enable people to relate to each other, not only without clothes, but also without pretences and realize that all of us have childish habits, feel pain and are capable of foolishness. The words 'masculine' and 'feminine' are used here *irrespective* of physical sex. Women have masculine characteristics and men have feminine ones, whatever social convention makes out to be. They must get used to each other in uncompetitive, unthreatening and helpful circumstances. With the right kind of guidance in self-observation and self remembering they will begin to discover all kinds of reactions and unreasonable responses which they might have imagined themselves not capable of.

Re-orientation is a change in attitude and direction, a change which will make people think quite differently about entertainment, work and recreation, relationships and values. Work will become the development of oneself, one's awareness and psychic well-being. Many illnesses are psycho-somatic and caused by stress, pressure and tension. A serious artist, someone who leads a creative life, a craftsman, is involved in a process of self-development, of learning and experiencing more and more. Work should be recreation, one's interest or hobby, something one loves to do. Recreation should not be a waste of time but a relaxing and creative aspect of work. Entertainment should be beautiful and moving as well as funny and relationships should be with partners who relate to one's Inner development and with whom there is true love. Value should be placed on the things which have a beneficial effect and are precious. These are spiritual values, which are subtle and fine and create a beautiful and peaceful atmosphere. A spiritual life is devoted to understanding and reconciliation, refinement and purification, it has nothing to do with belief in phantasies, dogmas, religious fanaticism, intolerance or repression.

RE-ORIENTATION

Instead of accepting the industrial society as inevitable, it has to be rejected in favour of a spiritual society. This can become a reality when a spiritual movement has political power, when enough people will unite to acknowledge a spiritual leadership which is able to bring harmony and clearmindedness. Such a direction will be objective as well as receptive and be therefore 'Divinely Inspired', by basing its decisions on an Inner awareness, hardly known to-day: An awareness through goodwill, stillness and reflection. By cool and fair judgement one can see beyond all preconceived ideas, mistaken attitudes and wrong opinions.

In the final decade of the 20th Century a great change will come. Something will catch the popular imagination. A Phoenix, a dragon-bird rising from the flames being driven through our towns and cities and making known the miracle of the 12 Archetypes. These are the opposing forces of the Universe; figures, beings, gods and goddesses, spirits who each have their own colour, mood, temper and state,  each their season and devotees; each one has to be understood to fully appreciate the composition of our psychological life. There are the blood-red Giant, a mighty Warrior, a frightening and angry Hero who comes in the smouldering harvest days of July, a hunter, hard, active, impressive and huge like a volcanic outburst and his opposite the flittering, shimmering, pale, greeny-blue fairy or angel, a fleeting wisp of delicate colour who comes in the misty morning when the catkins are out and the first flowers begin to show in meadows and gardens, in February, sweet and soft, a purifying, kind influence – like the reflections in a drop of water or the glistening dew bejewelling a spider's web. .

There are the ice-cold, glass-green, high, frosty and Divine Father Figure, the ancient King of January, of icicles and snow and his opposite the warm/reddish brown, pliable Mother, a nomad, a primitive tribeswoman, part of the earth and of the herd, a Gypsy, full-bosomed and voluptuous, who comes with the ripening fruit of August.

There are the dry, and barren, parchment-pale Observer of November, and his opposite the purple, excitable Lover, the Queen of April; the shocking-pink Fool of May and his opposite the Wise Old Woman of October who is the colour of the withering leaves, the hazel-nuts and the Autumn sky when it rains.

There are the deep-blue, veiled Goddess, a mysterious lady, the miraculous Madonna whose month is March and her opposite the bright-red Trickster, a clever, skilful talker who comes in June when the air is as hot as his deceptive patter.

Lastly come Mother Nature, the witch, heavy and dark, with all that Autumn brings in September: the decay of wood and vegetation, smelling of the damp soil, toadstools and fallen leaves and her opposite who lives in the brilliant light of his intelligence and who discovers everything but is sure of nothing and comes in the last, long December night at the solstice. A Wizard who by analysis and alchemy can change base metals into gold!

Together these 12 Archetypal Figures express a marvellous totality, a complete understanding of relationships and human psychology, and will precipitate a true and poetic religion, part of the cycle of the seasons in the northern hemisphere, quite different from the Zodiac and nothing to do with birthdays. They are based on natural and objectively associated ideas; the way every child, or a simple, sensitive, uncontaminated person is able to imagine figures which personify the 12 months of the year. These islands have a special quality, a charm which is unique, because the climate here is mild, the ground undulates, there are many rivers and streams and the grass in May is lush and green. If England had not been scarred and polluted by industry and commerce it would be so sweet and fresh, if it had not given birth to so many unhappy, sick and twisted people, so pure and sacred, that it could have been a holy example, a crown, a jewelled sceptre indeed and the rest of the world, too dry, too wet, too high or too flat as it is, would be sustained by this earthly paradise. A wonderful spirit which is neither male nor female and is divine and whole, the totality of all 12 Worlds may yet flower here.

England will change, her population will decrease and her chil-

*Stained-glass window of the Fool archetype (↑ ℧). The design is based
on a Tarot card. The yapping dog signifies the kind of reaction a free
spirit will evoke in those who are bound by convention. The border by
Green Brother Sebastien is of the symbols for the 12 archetypes, replacing the usual combination of 2 elements.*

dren will have souls again, but this time they will be conscious of it and they shall not be suppressed. People will come about who are natural and spontaneous, who will be really happy for the first time in history. There shall be no vomiting, spewing factories, no ugly sprawling industrial developments, they will all have vanished; in the course of the next century they will be demolished. The demons who still burden our lives and who forbid what is lovely will have perished, there will be no more repressive and rapacious men, no more bitter and vindictive women. There will be places, centres like beehives for Inner growth and self-development: Halls which have 12 Chapels, each chapel with a window depicting in glowing colour one of the 12 Archetypes, each window with its own predominant colour and each chapel with its own appropriate ritual. England will have become an agricultural country again where the seasons matter and life is related to the food which is gathered and grown here. A land where poetry is understood again and fairy-tales are alive, where art and music are part of religion and towns and villages are like those in fairy-tales*.

Look at people closely and see what they are really like. We must watch them coming out of a tube station, out of a railway station, out of a cinema or pub. What are they identified with, what motivates them? Most of them follow fashions which fail to make them happy, they are all conscious of class, of status, of their possessions. Few of these possessions have any real value; their status and their class are based on worthless comparisons, on a deprived childhood in one way or another, on one kind of slavery or another, one set of conditions or conventions or another. How on earth could they possibly be liberated from their habits, miserable thoughts, false ideas and negative emotions, their mistaken judgements and wrong attitudes? People deceive themselves to an extraordinary degree. Women spend large sums of money on make-up and clothes of the latest fashion in order to look beautiful and in fact they would look nicer if they didn't bother. Men buy expensive,

*There are two historical periods which inspire the illustrators of fairy tales and the makers of Christmas cards; the time of Chaucer (around 1400) and the Regency period (around 1800), which were both romantic and supremely elegant. Christmas cards particularly feature the decade from 1830-1840.

fast cars to show off their masculinity and no-one is impressed. What a pathetic situation. Pathetic, because if these people could only be *genuinely themselves* they could, in fact, be beautiful, or impressive, influential, loved and all the other things they wish to be.

As long as they are possessed by prejudice, misled by daily papers and propaganda for selfishness and self-indulgence, highly-coloured, glossy advertisements which come with the post and the milkman, they will remain as blinkered as they are. The propaganda they read, their favourite television programmes: 'East Enders', 'Dynasty', could be re-designed to give them some enlightenment, to show them that there are people who live quite differently from themselves, that even people like the authors of this book exist... and that these are sane.

There has to come promotion for 'WORK ON ONESELF', 'SELF-REALIZATION' or 'SELF-DISCOVERY'.

A plane flies overhead: We take this for granted, so much so that we do not even hear the noise. What is its purpose? Why is it necessary for these people, or goods, to travel vast distances so quickly? For thousands of years mankind was quite content to walk, or ride, or sail and our ancestors would have considered our haste and greed a waste, to be undignified and indecent. The sensuous experience of sitting on a horse's back, the awareness of the landscape, the places one passed through, the weather, the simplicity and beauty of it all, the billowing sails, the wooden ships, all this richness is sacrificed to convenience and speed. Critics of our sentiments will say that we are 'Romantics', but we say that there is nothing wrong with that, yet *everything* with 'sleep' (that is to say unawareness of one's true feelings, one's environment and situation) and that our critics should be confronted with the truth about their soulless lives, the destructive dreariness of the way they conduct their business and the ineptitude of their tastes.

Re-Orientation can not come without shocking the sleeping multitude and those shocks must come via the 'media'. This is where we come up against the myth of free speech. A handful of people control the editorials and programmes and anything which is not supposed to sell, or be popular, does not reach the public. There must be many wonderful manuscripts gathering dust in bottom drawers, while the most unspeakable trash is published and advertised everywhere. The British people are, unfortunately, conservative, and will only try something new if it has already been accepted in America. On the other hand because of this extraordinary feature, when a new thing does take root in these islands it is likely to last. When we initiated 'Green Politics' in 1965 we were declared to be idiots and in the 1970's Green organisations were regarded as a joke by the Press. Only when the Green Party in Germany became successful in the 1980's were British journalists able to treat the movement with some respect and take it seriously. The 'human aspect' with which this book deals is still totally disregarded by the media.

It sometimes seems as if there is a conspiracy, a plot, to prevent the televiewers, the radio listeners and newspaper readers from coming into contact with anything that might move them, might improve their understanding of other human beings and inspire them with illuminating thoughts. This plot is not a conscious one, it is a result of the division between the arbiters of all that is fashionable (and its following 'the general public') and a new kind of person who, as yet, has no public influence, but is awake and has a great deal to say. These latter are loosely connected through their interest in the Gurdjieff work, Jungian psychology and esoteric meditation. When a prominent personality is known to be favourably inclined towards these subjects, this affection is ridiculed by the press. It is commonly put about that it is natural to be selfish and greedy. Ordinary people are encouraged to compete, to mistrust everyone else and to be afraid of anything which they are not familiar with. The chance of getting to know an unfamiliar but lovely side of life is denied to them by a vicious-circle in which they have been trapped. Thus an unnatural form of independence has come into being which necessitates everyone to have their own flat or suburban box.

Re-orientation means a new and inspiring social organisation. But first there must be models: Healthy cells, as it were, examples of a new way of life. Here a few places are closed off to ordinary

MOUNT PLEASANT 1892 | MOUNT PLEASANT 1992 | MOUNT PLEASANT 2092

traffic. No cars are allowed, no aeroplanes nor helicopters either. These areas are to revert to a natural, beautiful state. Ugly developments of this century are demolished here and new model communities are made around the central Hall, school and institute. A new name has to be found for such a centre: A *Mentate*, or a *Salubriat*, a *Moonth*, or *Moonthplace*, or a *Hallow Hall* because it is unlike anything else that exists, or has existed. It is possible to close off a peninsula or an isolated valley, but one can also do the same with certain areas in London, or in other large cities. A rural area in open country can be declared sacred and made into such a spiritual place, for instance where a loop in a river creates a barrier and traffic can be diverted. In a town, houses form a natural barrier and one only has to cut off the side roads. Everyone will become familiar with this other, different, peaceful and beautiful life. Here nothing at all bad or disturbing will be able to penetrate; disruptive or malicious influences will be kept out and banished to bad areas where eventually careful discipline will isolate this badness and control it so much that it can not contaminate or hurt. Gradually more and more people will be influenced and follow the good example.

Not everyone needs liberating. Particularly a number of males are possessed of a demonic energy. They are, although unconscious of it, 'devotees' of the Archetypes of fire, the flaming, flickering, malicious 'Trickster' and the roaring, seething, voracious, furious 'Fighter', a devilish deceiver and a dangerous egoist in the denial of their opposites. These demons need restraining and to be intimidated, kept in place and 'schooled'. Just like the fire on the hearth, they need to be confined and supervised. Not in prisons, but in zones, in certain areas of the country where such males receive a special training, are drilled, disciplined and taught according to their age, their ability and soul-type. Those who are really dangerous, like mad bulls, will have to be put into a particular kind of barracks. Some criminals might actually be mad and a study will have to be made of their condition and the reasons for it. The average policeman of today is too one-sidedly masculine to really cope with this problem and a particular kind of social worker called a 'Ranger' should take his place. Rangers could be everywhere in soft-green and russet flowing clothes. Wearing cloaks below their beautiful, long hair and soft hats they would be truly uni-sexual. A new and refreshing attitude towards people, human psychology and human needs will change the treatment of criminal and a-social types dramatically. There are so many factors in the making of a hoodlum which no-one can see, or wishes even to look at, in our present day, so many repressed desires and unconscious, twisted feelings which need sorting out and putting right, that to really know how this could be dealt with in the future would both astonish and shock a great many people, even those who look upon themselves as enlightened.

To begin with certain places would be chosen for 'Community Holidays'. Not a boring binge of self-indulgence, a 'Butlins', or a seaside resort, but lovely and unspoilt countryside where brown or olive-green canvas tents are put up to house groups of people who come together to work, to restore an old, derelict cottage and a barn, to talk and play and do spiritual exercises and learn to live in harmony; to practice Anelog work. Such a Community Holiday can have a wonderful and lasting effect, it can bring about a spirit of co-operation, friendship and openheartedness which starts off larger projects such as the restoration of earth walls and the planting of hedges or the reclamation of a redundant industrial area. How inspiring to see the *Mentate* and the *Salubriat* rising with its

Moonthplaces and *Hallowhall* where there used to be a soulless desert of breezeblock boxes, some terrible, unhappy 1960's, 1970's or 1980's subtopia. These buildings come together out of all kinds of materials: used bricks, old wood, bricks made out of local clay by the community, or local stone, tiles, slates and handblown glass. Everything which goes into the building of it is made with love*. There is the central *Hallowhall* for exercises to get rid of bad feelings and thereby release good energy – spontaneous, unpremeditated, soulful, totally unselfconscious singing and dancing, rituals expressing personal feeling. At other times the Hallowhall is used for meditation, for Yoga or for talks and discussions. A Moonday rite will be held in the Salubriat on Sunday nights (in the Graigian Monastery this is held every Monday morning at 10) when the Moonday bread is divided, and the Moonday cup is shared and the Six Gods and Six Goddesses, the Twelve Archetypes at their *most sacred* and most positive are given full recognition.

The congregation will gaze at an image of the glowing, deep-red one, the Hero – and then his opposite the pale-blue Angel, who inspires worship. Then the purple one, the Lover and then her opposite the parchment-pale Observer, who makes us silent. Then the deep blue Madonna and the vermilion Trickster, the golden yellow Sage and the dark brown Peasant, the ice green King and the chestnut ruddy-faced Servant, the nut brown Spinster and the shocking pink Fool. To courage, creation and the creator: To kindness, surrender and the Angel, to the Lover and the Observer, to the Dreamer and the Player, the Investigator and the Cultivator, the Father and the Mother, the Gatherer and the Scatterer* . A slow masked mime and dance will be performed to exciting music made by a small band on a stage, a lute, a pair of drums and some other curious instruments, some like violins and others like flutes.

* Our design for a *Salubriat* is based on a model made by Bran Collingwood in 1968.

* The king, Father and Patriarch are the same archetype, i.e. God the Father, Father Christmas, Father time, the Pope, Papa or Father. The Servant is the same as Mother Earth, the nurse or cook, she whom sustains us. The nomad or gypsy are likewise the same as this warm 'earthy' archetype of fruitfulness or animal submission. The Spinster is the wise-old woman or Gatherer. A Scatterer is a fool.

THE FUTURE WILL BE GREEN

The moon will reflect in the water around the *Salubriat*, this temple for the Twelve Gods (or Archetypes, for they are not external entities) depicted in the stained glass of the windows. A bell tolls; it is midnight and silence follows, broken after several minutes by the sound of horns. Now it is Monday, the day set aside for our psyche, for self-development and looking inward. Around the Salubriat are the 12 'chapels' (Moonth Places) each with its window and characteristic things, pictures, sculptures relating to the God or Goddess of the month. On the 21st of December it is the feast of Light and the celebration of the God of Light, who is also called the Magician, 'Goldlight' the Sage, the All-Seer and in this chapel or Moonthplace are put holly, mistletoe, branches of fir and incense and candles are lit. On the 21st of January it is the feast of Frost and the celebration of the God of Frost, the King, Frostbeard the Patriarch, the Father and to him are brought snow-white narcissi, jonquils, snowdrops and branches decorated with snowflakes and glass balls. On the 21st of February it is the feast of Reflections and the Dew and the celebration of the Goddess of Dew, the virgin, Dawndew the Angel with catkins, primroses and crocuses. Every month, every Archetype is thus celebrated and in this way they become real and meaningful to every child. Masks and puppets of these Archetypes have been made and can be seen at the Graigian Monastery of the Archangel Michael where the authors of this book live.

The 12 Archetypes represent very real states, 'worlds', energies, atmospheres and ways of being. Each has its own negative as well as positive aspects, each has its own mentality. This can be experienced and understood, everyone should be able to relate to this knowledge. Classes are held in the Mentate, the school attached to the Salubriat; classes which combine art with nature study and psychology in which the symbolism of the 12 Worlds and their Archetypes is explained. In these classes – as indeed in larger meetings in the Hallowhall – everyone sits on the sanded and varnished wooden floor on cushions and rugs around the room and there are low tables for writing, drawing or painting on. Sometimes sessions take place when questions are answered by 'testing' and 'receiving', by intuitively sensing the answers. The people who come here wear long flowing dresses or robes and wash their bare feet in

The Salubriat is the round building at the top of the Highstreet of an unspoilt and restored market town, the Hallow Hall is in the nave of the church and the Mentate is the building in front of the tower. Green Bother Sebastien drew the border for a booklet we designed in 1971 which is about a New Age city in 2001!

a 'vavum', a sort of bathroom with a shallow stone basin set in the floor. Here they leave their shoes, sandals and socks or stockings. The head of this Mentate and also of the Salubriat is the 'Communicator' or the 'Mediator', or higher still the 'Nominator', three spiritual as well as secular ranks. More often than not, this is a woman, a beautiful, sweet and lively girl. She has been specially trained and has dedicated herself to this work. If it is a man, he could be feminine looking, dressed in the striped, green robe and green cloak of a Graigian monk/priest(ess) and with long flowing hair. The Tarot cards are also consulted here and yarrow stalks, which accompany the I Ching, are used for divination, blots are developed with watercolours (pictures are made by seeing things in blots of coloured inks or paints) and dreams and memories analysed.

This is a place for Water-Consciousness, where the imagination is encouraged and dreams are made conscious. It is totally unlike the dreary repressiveness of the patriarchal religious institutions of today, or the fearful hallucinations of people who write radio and television plays about the future. The atmosphere and the design of the future, spiritual Salubriat will inspire people and have a very real effect on them. They will have an air of mystery, be covered in ivy, roses, honeysuckle, buddleia and creepers, surrounded by trees and bushes, elder, lilac and jasmine; there will be a pool, a fountain, tall Lombardy poplars and irises, angelica and other magical herbs. The teachers, the 'Communicators' are above all artists and gardeners, a totally new breed of human being, not limited, but free, awake, tolerant and gifted. The building is on two or three levels, many-sided and with the character which Oriental or Medieval buildings have and which comes from integrity and a deeply felt, cultural unity. The houses of a village cluster around a central building, they are full of surprises, of interest, organically merging with the landscape. They have been built by people who live in them, or have lived in them, but not in a chaotic, careless, haphazard way. There was an overall plan and a great deal of thought and deliberation went into the design and construction. It is characterful, beautiful: Little winding lanes, steps made of used stone, arches and gates, courtyards and arcades have the unselfconsciousness and friendliness of the people who live there. It is all unpretentious, simple and natural.

Just as there is a tonescale with higher and lower notes, so there is a scale of human quality with 7 degrees, levels, or grades. A person's quality, that is to say, their 'presence' or their 'being', the feeling they give you, is not easy to describe. It is nothing to do with quantity, how intelligent, how clever or how energetic they are, but it is something which belongs to their 'Inner Self', the extent to which they are really true to themselves and sincere in their wish to love, to help, to become, or remain, healthy and happy.

At the top of this scale are people who are no longer self-centred, who can really help others to become better or to overcome difficulties, who do not feel any envy but are full of goodwill. These are lovely, smiling people who have 'found themselves', are free and fair, just and discerning, and can, by giving a wonderful example, make others happy. These should be leaders, but in the present-day society such people are still very much in the shade. The 'Nominators', 'Mediators' and 'Communicators' of a future state and religion are like this. At the bottom of the scale are people who are either soulless, or so devoid of any Inner resources that they can not rise above the immediate gratification of self-indulgent passions. Such people are both very stupid and very insensitive, they constantly need help and are unable to overcome bad habits or resist criminal impulses. Left to themselves they are destructive, create appalling conditions and have a bad influence on children, animals and plants which they neglect and starve. Some of these people have no wish to change and improve themselves and need to be restrained and prevented from doing harm. Such people chop down any tree or bush they are able to, steal, rob, hurt or kill without reason and create utter desolation.

81

Above them are the usual materialists, coarse but well meaning people who do not wish to be inwardly disturbed and whose ultimate horizon is that of amusements and games; who are not very imaginative or perceptive and can only appreciate something they are not used to in a limited way. Such people are 'psychostatic' and although not bad are unable to realise anything outside their limited sphere of conventions. They are 'mechanical', that is to say devoid of any originality and therefore wish to be trained and directed, set on a certain track and as it were 'programmed'. On the 5th Level or Degree too are people who can not live without conventions, social rules and commonly accepted mores and turns of phrases, who repeat what others have said and desire to be 'normal' in everything. That is to say they are, although intelligent and perhaps even very clever and able to do difficult work, devoid of any self-awareness and originality, like those of the 6th Degree or Level. It is on the 4th Degree or Level where one acquires values and aesthetic discrimination of one's own and interests which are genuinely cultural and intellectual. In this degree the development of the 'finer senses' is cultivated and one aspires to a more natural, artistic way of life and it is on this level that serious involvement in 'self-realization' begins and relationships become spiritual and deep.

In the 3rd Degree or Level life is exciting and adventurous, one has found one's own style and is searching for new ideas. Here one is constantly working on oneself, making changes and discoveries, experiencing for oneself what a great many things mean; what it 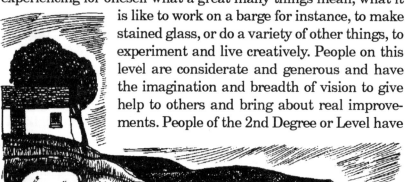 is like to work on a barge for instance, to make stained glass, or do a variety of other things, to experiment and live creatively. People on this level are considerate and generous and have the imagination and breadth of vision to give help to others and bring about real improvements. People of the 2nd Degree or Level have a vocation to give their lives to serve the community. They are responsible, conscientious and aware of themselves without having lost their sense of humour. Here real objectivity, which does not sacrifice the emotions, starts. People on this level are truly compassionate and are no longer afraid of the prejudices of inferior people. Thus superiority is associated with moral courage and humility, because it requires this to remain honest. The 7 degrees are degrees of purity and of goodness, but not the sickening holiness which unfortunately creeps into a great many spiritual movements. They are not static either, but flowing; fluid like every other institution of a Waterconscious society, they merge into each other and anyone can rise, or fall according to their inner condition, their 'goodness' or 'badness', to use two highly emotive and misapplied concepts.

In a Fireconscious world it is not generally understood that it is possible to change inwardly to become another, a different kind of person. Yet this is what will and must happen. Rebirth, which is nowadays an almost unknown concept, in a few decades will be the norm and as familiar as 'becoming redundant' is now. Rebirth means a move to a different, a higher degree on the scale. The Hindus and Buddhists believe that one has to die to be born again, but it is a widely ignored part of Christianity that one can be born again in this life: "The wind bloweth where it listeth and thou hearest the sound thereof but canst not tell whence it cometh and wither it goeth: so is every one that is born of the spirit." Rebirth is like walking out of a door onto a landscape the existence of which one never suspected, a world one did not know of. This is to be set inwardly free, to eventually arrive in a realm with brighter colours, clearer sounds and sharper shapes, to be liberated from un-necessary worry and concern, from having to consider things which do not really exist, like the 'feelings' many people are supposed to have.

Liberation, purification, healing and mediation are the four functions of the new religion or the Mentate, apart from giving knowledge, confidence, method and motivation. The 'Mediator' is in the 'Salubriat' at certain times, to help people settle their differences, listen to complaints and proffer advice.

Purification may, in a future society, be as important to everyone as economics is today, because it will be generally appreciated that we have a soul as well as a body and even the most loutish brute will have to recognise this fact. One's soul is the same as one's psyche, it is the region where our deeper, or Inner, feelings come from. As long as we are coldly indifferent, or react aggressively to what happens around us, compete and force ourselves to be constantly active, it is not possible to be aware of these feelings. When we cease to react and are still, this awareness will come. It is the means by which we reach a higher, an expanded consciousness. This is purification, for just as our body gets rid of waste material, so our soul will know naturally and instinctively how to become free from bad influences and effects. By emptying our mind, becoming still and surrendering to the 'Life Force'- we also become free from imaginary guilt. It is quite un-necessary to see ourselves as 'miserable sinners'- or to morbidly dwell on our past mistakes. As long as we are motivated by goodwill and wish to love and improve we can not be bad in any way. We must accept ourselves as we naturally are, it is unhealthy to feel guilty about things we do by accident, thoughts we involuntarily have, or our physical inclinations. Sexual fantasies are to be understood, not repressed, and we must learn to accept each other as we are. It is the pretence, the repression, the falsehood which causes the impurity; not the instinctive urge which has been with us from birth onwards. Re-Orientation means a different social order, a scale of values based on the quality of the human psyche. It means aspiring towards becoming better human beings: A step upwards on the evolutionary ladder.

This way of seeing people is absolutely *new*. So, if the reader feels negative about this part, it is quite understandable. Until now the only classifications in common usage have been: a) hereditary = the so-called class-system; b) financial = how much is he/she worth?; c) racial = what colour is he/she, where does he/she come from?; d) religious = is he/she a Jew, Roman Catholic or Protestant?

RE-ORIENTATION

The reference to wishing to be 'programmed' on Degree or Level 6 will make many idealistic readers go pale with righteous horror. But, think about it. Would you, for example, invite a blind-drunk, boorish ruffian to come into your dining-room, or kitchen for a meal, particularly if you have lovely crockery? The answer must be *no*, no sane person would do this, can you imagine the mess? Similarly, to elect someone on levels 6 or 7 to be the leader of your country is plainly mad, in fact, in recent history (Hitler and Stalin and even more recently Idi Amin, Emperor Bokassa and Saddam Hussein) when this *was done* they managed to murder between them, yes murder, about 16 *million* innocent people, if not more. Such is the dreadful result of putting people with a 'poor quality of being' in a position of high authority and esteem where their horrendous examples are imitated by many impressionable citizens.

Under the proposed 'System of Communication' (a dual system of public service, both spiritual and temporal, giving access to therapy, guidance and advice) 'Communicators', 'Mediators' and 'Nominators' have to qualify for their positions and there is complete democracy so that anyone, from any race or social background can, through dint of loyal work and acclaim and the manifestation of their determination, self sacrifice, sanctity, humility and lack of egoism or pride and ability to work with others rise to be the highest in the land. It not by chance that the majority of miracles (whatever you may personally think of Roman Catholicism) have happened to young people from peasant communities. In England we are now so far from this word 'humility', something everyone should have, that it has become a cover-up for the worst sort of arrogance and pride. Naturally one thinks of many people who have managed to get themselves elected to the House of Commons.

CHAPTER 3.

RETRACTION

EAR by year, as the atmosphere, the seas and waters are polluted and the piles of plastic rubbish grow, mankind, standing on the cusp of evolution, is prone to wonder how the planet's nature could survive...

Nothing can expand indefinitely and so it is with industrialization, the mechanised manufacture of consumer goods, which can not exist without having to create larger and larger concerns in a capitalist and uncontrolled situation. This began with establishing factories in which many craftsmen were set to work together. Later, after steam engines provided energy for mechanical looms, lathes and all the other machines, unskilled labour could be employed for very little money and large profits created more and bigger works. Later still, firms of manufactures amalgamated and acquired new machinery and up-to-date methods in order to grow bigger still, swallowing up other, smaller firms and updating their equipment, replacing men by automatons and producing more and more. This is called 'Productivity'.

A balloon which is inflated indefinitely will, sooner or later, burst and a fat man, if he continues to grow fatter will, at a certain weight, become so unhealthy that he will die because his organs cannot cope. Thus it is with the economy also: One can either by control on production seek to provide what is really necessary, or, as in this competitive world, produce a plethora of inferior consumer goods for the sake of money and so-called industrial 'growth'. This approach carries, like the man who grows ever fatter, its own death warrant. The inflationary state of affairs and the subsequent recession which has come about in recent times is indicative and this is why it is often called a malaise. Apart from patching-up the

86

old system there are two different remedies, the first is the central-ized state control of the Socialism or Communism we are familiar with, which has everyone employed by the government; the sec-ond is the one we are about to propose in this chapter. It is perhaps best seen in the analogy of the fat man who must reduce if he wishes to lose weight and become healthy, should his over-eating have made him ill. The cause of his greed, which is likely to be frustration and dissatisfaction, *must* be removed for this remedy to be effective.

When one looks at the average industrial area, with its plants for making motor cars and processed food, the impersonal, bleak and totally soulless atmosphere is what hits one first. The more modern, the more devoid of any character are such places. The reason for this is that they are motivated by what are basically dishonest and bad, grasping attitudes. The men who control, or controlled, such industry (and therefore initiated or prolong its mores) look upon deception and advantage-taking as justifiable means of assembling, promoting and selling their product. They think of sensitivity as weakness and effeminacy and are convinced that only ruthless attitudes will bring about success and 'growth'. This ruthlessness has bred the aggression of the unions, because in a soulless and impersonal atmosphere no-one cares for the job he is doing. Manufacturer and worker are pitted against each other and the workers who are meant to produce the stuff are by their own actions undermining the means of production. Whether a worker helps make one car or a hundred, he receives the same weekly wage and the money he earns is all he cares for, he does not give a damn for the company profits or losses.

So far in the history of industrialisation the aspect of soullessness has been hardly considered, not even by the Church. Religion was meant to be one thing and work another. It does not seem to have occurred to anyone in an influential position that anything of a prac-tical nature might possibly include feeling and be done in a sensitive way. The human element in planning and building, in shaping the environment was ignored. The idea that a happy person is healthy, that children should be loved, that animals should be given as much freedom as possible, that distressed people should be cared for was relegated to the nursery, charitable institutions and Utopia.

87

Despite warnings from the 1960's onwards, the factories, power stations and internal combustion engines of the world are continuing to contaminate the water, the earth and the air to such an extent that forests die and lakes become sterile. Increasingly people are growing aware of the dangers which this 'productivity' and the soulless, inhuman world created by technology and the convenience it serves, are causing. Two different worlds exist: A 'plastic', dangerous and mass-producing one and an organic, healthy, safe and sensitive one. The 'plastic' world is constantly presented on the television, with its high rise buildings and empty, garish, modern interiors. The organic world is centred around wholefood shops and places which have been conserved like Covent Garden and Camden Lock in London and is gaining support from an increasing number of discerning people. These people, all over the country, prefer food which has been grown without poisonous fertilizers and was not intensively reared or processed in a factory. If therefore, as one would hope, these factories (which includes farms) increasingly become redundant and close down, the things we need like soap, shirts, or shoes will have to come from the other, the 'alternative' source. This is already happening!

A certain new type of craftsman, who is resourceful without being selfish will start making soap or shirts or shoes in his own home, or in a shed and sell them on a stall in a market. One can envisage supermarkets closing down, because they rely on a dying industry. People will have to buy home-made goods which are wholesome, durable and attractive. This is the beginning of local manufacture for and by the local community. Meanwhile the ravaged landscape on the outskirts of the towns can be reclaimed and the empty factories demolished. In order to do this all that terrible country, that subtopia where these factories are, would have to be nationalised. It is a curious idea that this nationalization would be in order to bring inhuman industrial installations to an end and to distribute the assets among the workshops which replace them.

It must be clear why a massive re-orientation of the popular mind should proceed this kind of change. The majority of people, conditioned to be self-seeking and hardened by ugliness, should be given access to their inner resources to discover what kind of work they would wish to do and what the possibilities for this work are. They must form co-operatives, acquire the tools they need and find suitable workshops. All this, the designing and projecting which is necessary, requires imagination and the imaginative faculty needs to be awakened and developed. There must be a slowing down, co-operation instead of competition and a gentle, kind approach induced by reflection. This can only be learnt in groups led by trained, very human Communicators and on Community Holidays where 'Anelog Work' is practised. This work teaches self-awareness through Natural Psychology and an intuitive, spontaneous yet methodical way of performing a large variety of tasks. It includes 'Self Discovery Through Art' and 'The Awakening': a course of music, movement and drama. Programmes on the television about such work can show the way, once a breakthrough for another way of living has been achieved. This is bound to happen. In the 1970's Friends of the Earth and Greenpeace were given neither encouragement nor credibility; now, a couple of decades later, long television programmes are devoted to their concern for environmental problems. The human aspect has, so far, been ignored – but soon this will be different.

A future of unbridled industrial expansion is unthinkable; a completely ugly and spoilt, artificial environment alienates and brutalizes those who are forced to live in it. It will drive many millions of people mad and we will have nothing but violent crime and psychoses. A fair number of people have already lost touch with reality, but a growing number of others who have retained a healthy mind will continue to care and protest against this happening. The Green Movement will grow, just as socialism did

AD 1950 - 1991

89

in the first half of this century and a green government will certainly come about. Such a government will represent that section of the community which is motivated by a deep concern for all that gives life meaning, creates a healthy world and will be a positive influence for good, ordinary, decent people. It will put a retracting society into effect and de-centralise and devolve all power. This means the reversal of a trend towards competition and expansion which began in this country in the late 15th century, when commercial centres became powerful and trade all important. At that time descendants of bankers and wool merchants assumed positions which had so far been held by war lords. The *de Medicis* in Florence are the most prominent example and the significance of the woolsack in the House of Lords illustrates this point further. Modern history began with exploration and discovery of all kinds: printing, gunpowder, clocks, telescopes, America and anatomy. It was conducted almost exclusively by men, probing, analysing and experimenting. We have had 500 years of this and it has succeeded in doing all it can.

Space rockets and hydrogen bombs add nothing to human welfare. Science-fiction, which projects a future of concrete and press buttons, of unlimited speed and trickery sees everything in terms of one or two archetypes only, that of the analytical mind, 'the Logician' and that of the manipulator, 'the Trickster', a deluded scientist and a crazy inventor. This leaves out an undeniable and ineradicable fact: that we exist as sensitive organisms, as part of an organic, natural whole, together with weeds, wild animals, trees and insects. Most people nowadays do not experience themselves in this way, to them the Pine Martin, the Willow Warbler and the Celandine are irrelevant and unfamiliar and nothing they can relate to. Through pernicious propaganda and conditioning they do not see themselves against any other than a harsh and metallic background. Women are bamboozled and confused by the men they get involved with, who in turn, are persuaded by clever advertisers to install plastic coated kitchens and

90

every sort of labour saving gadget. It is commonly supposed that all kinds of machines and instruments are indispensable, things we cannot do without, forgetting that these are merely part of a superfluous mentality. It makes no difference at all to what is really unavoidable, that the bindweed and the nettles will come back and the dandelion will eventually break through the tarmac.

A separation also occurred between the spiritual and the commercial worlds, the Inner and the Outer, which in Medieval cathedral cities had been prevented by the way guilds were organised. All aspects of life then related to the cathedral church which dominated the small, exquisite city from its central position. Medieval painting, furniture and objects have religious connotations and no one, not even the dullest and most brutal of men was unable to reflect, or at least be confronted by the need for this ability. This no longer is the case: English Protestantism led the World from its destructive beginnings, initiated by the vandalism of Henry VIII, into the acceptance of dreary tastelessness, until now religious institutions everywhere are affected by it. Christianity went hopelessly wrong from the moment usury and big business were tolerated. One knows the tree by its fruit and the art, the artefacts of the whole period from the 10th until the 15th century are pure and perfectly lovely. Only after 1450 does the Gothic style show signs of decadence and – presumably for such reasons – the Catholic religion and its institutions precipitated protest and the demand for reform.

A retracting society is inevitable if mankind is to preserve its sanity and the Earth its resources. The population should decline, deserts be made fertile, the land made wholesome and the seas and oceans purified. This country, responsible as it is for the introduction of steam-engines and industrialization, should give the example for the return to an organic and human society, devoid of the injustices, poverty and exploitation which existed when the Industrial Revolution began in the 1780's. It should regain the idyllic beauty, the humility and sweetness which market and cathedral towns and their surrounding countryside had until the early 19th century.

The population of Britain could decline drastically if only those people had children and set up families who really, deeply, wished to do this. So many unfortunate babies are born unwanted; initially perhaps wanted by the mother, but soon rejected or badly cared for. It is a national disgrace that we read in the papers of British babies being battered, starved and neglected, of children treated with horrible, disgusting brutality. Sexual relationships usually leave much to be desired and are often disastrous. Attitudes towards sexuality, marriage and lifestyles should change. It is not inevitable that happiness can only result from heterosexual monogamy. It is, however, of the greatest importance that the ideas of self-development, inner growth and awareness become established and commonly accepted. It is possible, when certain types of men are able to surrender their egoism and obey their feelings, that true love can once more be experienced and admitted to. An extraordinary and quite unfamiliar spiritual/psychic energy may thus be released. This love is far more often *unconsciously* present between members of the same sex than is commonly supposed.

There is a true, emotional attraction between 'opposite' psychological, or soul types which in Natural Psychology are called *dard* and *voy*. A *voy* person (fulfilling him/her self in realising his/her feminine side) is *magnetically* attracted to his/her opposite *dard* friends and vice-versa. A *dard* person fulfils him/her self in realising his/her masculinity, however outwardly feminine their behaviour might be. Dard men and women are usually taller or bigger than their 'opposite' Voy types, who are prettier however much they may try to disguise this fact and adopt 'macho' attitudes. This understanding of soul types constitutes the most amazing discovery yet in the history of human psychology. Unfortunately because of fashions in behaviour, prejudice, ignorance and the over-riding fear of being condemned as a 'Queer' or a 'Poof', the anxiety about being ostracized, the denial of *real* love in favour of a socially-acceptable game is all too common. Boys will often make a great display of a superficial, physical attraction they feel towards girls to cover up their real, deeply felt, emotions. Once love is generally allowed and a serious interest is taken in psychology, young men and women will no longer need to be frightened of being themselves and nervous of revealing their true feelings. We will discuss this subject in greater detail in a later chapter (Sexuality, Chapter VI).

In Kentish Town, in north-west London, the authors have established the first Green Monastery. This community and its way

of life, may, now it is becoming
better known, appeal to many
young men and women. The
monastery, although demand-
ing a seemingly strict discipline
and harsh conditions for entry,
affords the ultimate 'Inner
Freedom'. Visitors are invariably moved and enchanted by
the very unusual atmosphere
brought about by the creativ-
ity and dedication of the
monks; it is as different from
that of a Christian monastery as that is of a Buddhist monastery –
and different from that again. Christian monasteries have always
been grey and cold; Buddhist, saffron, red and gaudy, but this new
kind of monastery is *green* and as rich in colour and life as a summer's garden. The habit of the monks is of green, russet and, sometimes, off-white striped cotton.

For the first time in the whole history of mankind religion *unites*
with nature; this religion is about the reconciliation of six pairs of
opposites and includes all that is relevant and best from every
culture that has ever been. In the chapel, temple, shrine or medi-
tation-room called the *Salubriat*, the floor is carpeted in a soft,
natural green strewn with large cushions of beautiful, often Oriental, materials. An ancient kelim covers a divan, the altar is a low
and narrow table with ritual objects: the Sword, the Wand, the
Chalice and the Plate of the Tarot; each of which has been made by
an artist-craftsman and was collected by the founders of the monastery with natural understanding, love and true appreciation.
On the walls are meaningful paintings, mostly by the monks, of an
exceptional quality; quite different from only too usually superficial, slick, contemporary art. The light in this magical room filters
through the leaves of a rambling rose and a buddleia and an ancient lace curtain. Behind it is the Hallowhall where meetings are
held around a wood-fire. It is furnished entirely with things which
were found, left behind or handed on and which opens out into the
walled, woodland garden. Against the back-wall of the garden a

93

pottery studio has been built from recycled, old materials which looks as if it has been there for several hundred years. Every room in the four-storey, mid-Victorian house is equally imaginative, cosy and amazing. Here are workshops for a variety of crafts and the spiritual, esoteric, artistic and political worlds which so far always were totally separate are brought together in this, the harbinger of 'Another Way of Living'. This is a suggested title of a film about life in the Graigian Monastery and was taken up and produced as the documentary called *The Original Green Men* (made by 'Taliesyn' in 1989), which was broadcast in Wales in 1990 and again in 1991 on H.T.V.

The extraordinary and miraculous life a mutation in consciousness causes becomes possible when the 'voy' novice surrenders to his love for the 'dard' Abbot, his 'Guru' and submits to the rule of the monastery. The total liberation of the Inner Self; or unconscious, which the new Green, or Graigian religion represents will seem very strange and perhaps improbable to the average person today, just as the restless rootlessness of the modern world would have seemed strange to a farmer in the 1930's. The Green Graigian Monastery serves as a model which will inspire and give hope. Every day at 10 am 'Matins' is held in the Salubriat. This is an hour of meditation and a dedication to the archetype(s) associated with that day. For example: 'water and earth' stand for water on the earth; rivers, lakes, seas and oceans and these represent depth, the unconscious and deep feeling. This archetype is a miraculous lady, 'Deeplake' who is associated with Moon or Monday. Please look at the archetypes, their meanings, the days of the week and the trees they relate to on page 179. Although the reference to the four esoteric elements and the notion of 12 Archetypes and 24 Soultypes may seem far-fetched and idiosyncratic, they are nevertheless a true and highly relevant means of understanding human relationships and a basis of an altogether different, and more organic, spiritual life than that of Christianity, or any other of the world religions for that matter. These are all permeated by artificiality, tastelessness, sentimentality and morbid dogma. Even Witchcraft is conducted in a rather crude way in often vulgar surroundings which are the result of impurity, onesidedness and lack of discrimination.

The stuff that all life is made from is threatened, the air is~

poisoned, the water is polluted and the earth contaminated. The fire is out of control.

The redeemer, the purified human being, bearing the symbols of the 4

elements, emerges and with love and right judgement will put the world in order ♃

The androgynous figure bears the signs of the four elements, the star for air (light), the seed for earth, the cup for water and the arrow for fire, signifying that she/he is a total human being, whereas those who are destroying the planet have lost their humanity.

Retraction brings purification and a reinstatement of the spiritual aspect of life. The water, air and earth will have to be purified but also the souls, minds and bodies of people. The modern world is full of badness: bad feelings, art, music, writing and architecture, bad ideas, theories, plans and food. Many people will have to wake up to the painful realization that most of what they have, say and believe in is sheer rubbish. How can we say this? Isn't that an arrogant assertion? Who are we to lay down the law about what is rubbish and what isn't?..... Galileo after having been forced to renounce his correct understanding of the solar system, after his interview with the Pope, was reputed to have said of the planet earth: "Still she turns!". Even if the ethos of our era makes no distinction between what is wholesome or unwholesome, beautiful or ugly, pure or impure, the knowledge of such an evaluation is yet with a few of us; those who are sensitive to the impressions they receive and have assimilated some cultural and historical insight. Rare and precious substances, things, or places do sometimes survive.

The idea of a 'New Age' unfortunately has come to mean a rather wishy-washy and unrealistic view of the future. Yet it need not be despised, just because it has been employed to project fanciful and improbable phantasies. 'The New Age', a culture in which the very opposite is the rule from the one we are accustomed to in 1994, may well come about. Competition, self indulgence, dishonesty and egotism are now the rule. This need not go on indefinitely. Certain trends will die out, there may be an end to glossy, highly-coloured advertising, speed, consumerism and the hardheadedness that go with automation. Nasty tabloids, videos and other thrills; the excrescences of that whole insensitive conglomerate which we refer to as 'incon world' (the industrial, con, conservative, convenience, consumer and contaminating world) may yet become extinct. In the 1970's it seemed as if the farming-industry had turned its back on 'culture' (agriculture) for good and there would be no end to the destruction of the countryside, to treating animals as if they were cabbages and plants as if they were things. In the late 1980's this was already different; organic farming began to be taken seriously, farmers are now advised to change their methods, consider wildlife and plant trees, for they have produced more (inferior) grain and milk than anyone can use. This trend – because of an increase in pressure from conservationists and because of a change in attitude amongst people generally, through education in magazines, on radio and television programmes – will continue until farmers and farming everywhere have become human and humane. The same applies to 'Ban the Bomb': CND started in the mid 1950's what seemed an impossible objective, after 40 years it looks as if the super-powers may indeed decide to do away with nuclear missiles altogether.

Inspiring examples may move all kinds of people to follow these, to support a new spiritual movement, to adopt new and enlightening values, to join groups through which their way of life will change, to grow inwardly, to become different and see the World with new eyes. Like yeast, like something which divides and multiplies, a wave of 'Inner Freedom' could be as catching as the Common Cold and consequently cause many people everywhere, perhaps millions of them, to discover what it is to deeply love once more. To love, not a Patriarchal God whom they do not understand and is worshipped in a bleak, unfriendly church, but a *spiritual* focal-point which is really warm and lovely and from which they can learn sensible, good, useful and helpful ways of organising their thoughts and lives. Why should this be a God *somewhere else*, above 'in Heaven'? Heaven could well be amongst us HERE ON EARTH!

Only a model, a most beautiful example, something which by its grace and simplicity will quite naturally be loved by those who are receptive to it, will cause the change necessary for a 'New Age' to come about. Retraction is the opposite of expansion, which is masculine, thrusting and hard. An expansive person fills his plate with beef and does not reflect on the fate of cows and calves. He smokes immoderately and has no regard or feeling for his lungs.

97

Amongst thoughtful people meat-eating and smoking are becoming rare. These people, who are the *avant garde*, the harbin-
gers of what is to come, eat wholefoods which they buy in shops
with old-fashioned counters, sacks of beans and grain and the
mellow atmosphere of 50 years ago. The signs are there to see; we
may thus increasingly revive and resurrect the character and
beauty that was sacrificed, all that it is possible to love. We may
also have a more feminine, retracting and smaller population in
the future.

Because people will be emotionally and inwardly *free*, they will
be much more spontaneous and happy than they are now. They
will have much to interest and delight them, a pall of boredom will
have lifted and where there are now grey walls there will be climb-
ing plants, Virginia creeper, roses and honeysuckle. Boredom, which
comes from superficiality, leads to seeking increasingly extreme
diversions, which with mindless Yobbos becomes vandalism and
may develop into very serious crime, accentuated by aggressive
and narrow-minded attitudes. These are very often bred on council estates. The militant male chauvinism of working class men is
based on a lack of inner freedom; the less enlightened, the more
rigidly conditioned people tend to be, the more they will adopt the
most negative of social tendencies. Because of their identification
with the proletariat, Communist regimes, so far, have put on an
aggressive, masculine face, are stridently militant and perpetuate
tight, restrictive, puritanical attitudes towards sex. Communist
propaganda posters are invariably brash and vulgar; as if life con-

sists exclusively of brandishing pick-axes and guns! Softness is seen as an impossible dream, or a dangerous weakness.

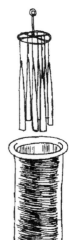

Here in the western part of Europe, in Britain, the Green, the environmental movement must profess a new and spiritual form of socialism if it wishes to restrain the egoism, the greedy force, the brutish masculine desire for senseless power which dominates the world today. By this we mean an overriding emphasis on how to live, as well as on social concern and individual welfare, health and state of mind. It means community and social work. Work which will uncover the true feelings and inner needs, the actual psychic purpose of each individual who has thus a greater chance to find fulfilment. Our understanding of the 24 psychological types (12 'Dard' and 12 'Voy') will bring a totally new dimension to this work. By spiritual socialism we mean a quite *different* approach to social problems from that of the Labour Party in the 1960's and the 1970's. Then, a hideously materialistic, streamlined world of high-rise council flats and motorways was planned. The empty 'modern' world of housing units, shopping centres and all the tawdry, 'futuristic' furnishings, flimsy plastic articles and gimmicks that are part of these, all the horrors of Birmingham, the devastation of the countryside, were then created. The men who were involved in this creation; anyone who made, and makes decisions which affect our way of life, our environment and economy are usually one of 6 types who repress their feelings, do not reflect and are unreceptive.

A glut of inferior, plastic products feeds a rapacious, wasteful world in which an ugly and bourgeois lifestyle is constantly proclaimed and pandered to by advertisements and television programmes. If it were possible to make more and more publicity for the reverse, to constantly advertise 'Another Way of Living' on television, then many of the more intelligent viewers would surely understand that by means of conservation, recycling and a careful life, a third, or less, material and production would be needed to sustain our daily needs. Everyone who wishes to, should be able to work for, or in their community: growing fruit or vegetables, baking bread, mending roofs, building and repairing furniture, or making wine, candles or clothes. This would need the advantage of 'Anelog work' which teaches how to make the simplest task enjoyable. With a community we mean an area, no bigger than a village, which people can emotionally relate to. Such an area has been, or is, often represented by a tenants' or a residents' association and should have its own voice at meetings of the local council. Boroughs and districts should be even smaller than these were before the present borough councils were created. The 'Communicator' would be chosen by a meeting of the community out of a number of candidates, recommended by the 'Mentate' where she, or he, has graduated.

The Communicator's Office, in every neighbourhood, should be a centre, a meeting place where people can sit outside when it is sunny on a wooden bench, or meet inside to discuss their plans and problems. It takes the place of council offices, or the Town Hall, and also of the Department of Social Security and the Police station. Inter-Communicators (the Communicator's assistants) would be capable of dealing with every kind of emergency or complaint as any one of them would be a graduate in law, architecture, medicine or economics. An entirely new system should operate to govern benefits, particularly of social security. The Communicator would know, in a very intimate way, what everybody's circumstances are in his/her community and thus *no-one* would be deprived, or be given scope to waste the money, get drunk, create a sordid atmosphere, be a nuisance, or a source of criminal activity. 'Signing-on' should be at this very local Communicator's Office too and the flats, houses and other buildings which are owned by the borough council in his/her area would come under the management of the Communicator and should be governed by the community. All problems and complaints could be dealt with in a personal and simple way. The Communicator's Office would be around the corner; the man or woman who does the repairs, a few doors away.

RETRACTION

Conventionality and fashion, bourgeois prejudices and customs are the pillars of a materialistic, insensitive society. The 'World' does *not* have to be competitive and hard, the 'spirit of the age', the Zeitgeist, *can* change and when the majority of people have become tolerant of an *un*-bourgeois way of life and are open and receptive by following an inspired teaching, the artificiality which they now espouse will be discarded. Together with their nylon clothes, net-curtains and their regimented gardens, their consumption of unhealthy and expensive, manufactured matter will no longer please them. A different kind of industry will naturally come about because of new tastes and inclinations. If nylon is no longer in demand, the factories which make this stuff will close and workshops where cotton, wool and linen will be woven in a wholesome way will thrive. These workshops must be places where people *love* to work and visit. Not large, impersonal, robotic, industrial buildings by a motorway, but small, local, friendly places - preferably old and revived, or newly built with feeling, should provide an inspiring environment for work which is enjoyable. The industrial syndrome of this mechanistic age will disappear when other than material values have replaced a boring, bourgeois set of habits.

Horrendous, sprawling, dead industrial estates are only fit to be demolished; to allow *natural* growth, to resurrect the countryside: there would be flowering chestnut trees in time again, cornfields bearing wheatsheaves, fields in which cornflowers and poppies grow again. There would be wagons drawn by horses lumbering along the flowered lanes, which were there until this *soulless* century. This is not unpractical romanticism, devoid of all reality, poetic nonsense, but that which is as necessary as fresh air for our survival, if we wish mankind to have a sane and healthy future. We do not need acid rain, a poisoned atmosphere produced by motor-cars, machinery and industry, but that which feeds our souls, the psyche, the Inner Self of human beings. Should we continue to deny this part mankind shall perish! It must be generally understood and accepted as a matter of course that human beings need love and loveliness to be whole, that they must be 'opened' to their Inner Feelings. This opening is the next step in our evolution, without it a happy future is unthinkable. A spiritual life style must become part of our daily existence, this will lead to a future which excludes all exploitation, horror, war and crime. Then a time will come in which humanity has conquered the diseases which tormented, killed and maimed a population with a divided consciousness. Spiritual life, as part of everyday existence, is requisite to a sensitive society. Such a life is totally different from that which most of our readers are familiar with. Not from the head: a superficial, dull acknowledgement of a bourgeois God who threatens you with 'Hell' if you don't obey his rules; but from the heart, from deep, miraculous feelings will devotion be to Lady Deeplake.

Although practically everyone prefers to own their house, their garden and their land, if any, these should not be used in a wasteful, wanton way and ownership should therefore be conditional. In other words, if the rights of ownership should be abused by, for instance, building a stinking factory, or altering an historic house or spoiling an old one, the landscape around, a feature, then controls should be enforced. At present, one must have permission from the local borough council to build or alter houses, change the use of buildings and build certain types of factories or warehouses in certain places. This does not apply to farming and unsightly modern sheds, silos and the like deface the countryside. Not only should restrictions be placed upon the building of these breezeblock and metal warts, farmers should be made wholly conscious of the damage they have done (and are doing) to the landscape. Examples of how to farm in a Water-Conscious way should be widely publicized; a series should be shown on television demonstrating how traditional agriculture is sacred, noble, part of spiritual awareness: bringing men and women back to the farm-work which is made enjoyable.

By treating labourers in a despicable way our ancestors brought discredit to themselves and to cultivation. Ploughing with horses or a team of oxen is for psychic, aesthetic and emotional reasons marvellous; so are reaping with a sickle and making haystacks, doing farm work in the way it has been done for centuries and

102

... AND NOW LETS HAVE A QUICK LOOK AT THE ECONOMIC FRONT...

LOOK, Mr. Free Market Economy it's the green shoots of Recovery!

CRASH!

GROAN – They weren't the green shoots of recovery they were the fruiting bodies of DRY ROT!

HURRAH! Mr. Industrial Growth we're on the upward spiral!

£ $ £

BOING!

LEAP!

JUMP!

AHHHRGH!

should be well rewarded. How different it would be to see a wheatfield reaped by rows of men once more, and other people, children, women, older men binding sheaves and stacking them; from one bored youth slumped inside the cabin of a massive combine-harvester listening to his Walkman box through earphones. This while dozens of his mates are out of work and take to drink, or drugs, or crime from aimlessness!

The term 'labour intensive', which is used in an almost abusive way, implies a misguided attitude to certain tasks. Working together, co-operating with a group of people, is extremely rewarding. This is understood in teamwork like in games and sport, but it applies just as much, for instance, to bringing in the harvest. Labour intensitivity is replaced by mechanical means which deprive their users of valuable experience of a natural kind and cause nothing but emptiness and boredom, with the resulting alienation and other social ills. Harvesting a cornfield, picking berries or collecting seeds as a positive community effort becomes festive and joyful, ending in a great celebration, a true, traditional harvest feast, like in paintings by Brueghel, reviving all manner of meaningful old customs. Whatever is done by hand in a 'labour intensive' way brings a satisfaction which working selfishly with machines just can't have. 'Labour intensivity' has social benefits which we negate at our peril. Products of such work are wholesome, are well made and have a natural quality.

THE FUTURE WILL BE GREEN

The countryside and coastline have really been perverted in the last 40 years, before that farms were not yet factories, fields, agri-deserts and fishing villages were still inhabited by fishermen. Because farmers had to compete – or thought they had to – with the most ruthless of them (and farmers usually belong to types who identify with being earthy at the expense of any vision or conscience) we have the 'farming industry'. Since everything in this system tends to increase, except the demand for the intensively grown produce piling up in 'butter mountains', or other heaps of surplus foodstuffs, farmers have to consider a different kind of cultivation if they don't wish to go bankrupt. The authors are not able to surmise to what extent farmers are kept going by means of subsidies. The solutions proffered by the government, the 'set-asides' and using farmland for diversions of some kind or another (so-called 'diversifications') are as unimaginative and ugly as you'd expect from men in nylon suits. It is quite likely that the kind of men and women who ought to work on farms, be farmers or be fishermen are now living in cities and those who have turned agriculture and fishing into 'industries' would be safer and better employed by demolition contractors, providing they demolish the developments of this century! There may be a number of farmers and fishermen who are dedicated to their culture and these we ask for their indulgence. Millions of idle, unhappy, aimless, unemployed young people could be introduced to the deeper meaning and the old-fashioned ways of agriculture to work on farms and with the benefit of Anelog Work and Natural Psychology, lead interesting and fulfilling lives.

Communities of smallholdings around common land and of fishers with small wooden boats can not come about without a bloodless crusade against mechanicality. By this we do not just mean machines, but a hard, materialistic, grasping, loveless attitude to work. If this was done away with the country will still yield the amount of produce needed and moreover organically grown food, which will be in demand because everyone will know in ten years' time that the other stuff can cause cancer and, anyway, is inferior in taste and texture. When mechanicality ceases the landscape will be softer, the elms will grow again, the thickets will be undisturbed, the butterflies will lay their eggs on uncontaminated 'weeds' and cornflowers once more will flourish in the rye. Poultry shall freely roam the farmyard and calves shall see both daylight and their mothers.

How is it all possible?

1) It is abundantly clear that factory-farming is generally disliked. The Graigian Society will do a survey on what people everywhere think of the farming industry. This will cause a change in the general outlook on this subject.

2) The slump which has hit farming will continue. The Graigian Society has started a fund to buy up farms and farmland to establish communities. These will act as examples and become well known.

3) With tough measures the Graigian Society will make sure that these communities are run in a disciplined way and that no bad influences take over. This is possible because of *Anelog work* and our knowledge of soul types (Natural Psychology).

4) A trend towards a different approach, which is organic, imaginative and traditional, will be set.

5) Because of a general appreciation and interest in this revival of agri*culture* there will be subsidies for organically and sensitively cultivating wholesome crops.

Movements for reform are not often taken seriously, either they are hopelessly idealistic and go off the rails, they are taken over by a swollen-headed egoist, there is some kind of fraud or corruption, or the leaders are not sufficiently practical and hardworking to see the scheme through. That is why a Graigian community consists of monks who are dedicated, single-minded and many-sided. Through their discipline and training they can give themselves to different kinds of work; dig as well as write poetry, mend a leaking roof as well as throw a pot or paint a picture. A new kind of abbey may *dominate* (how this word will press a multitude of 'buttons'!) the land in which the Graigian monks will be concerned with spreading the Graigian religion, which worships the purified, illumined Inner Self, the totality of the 12 Archetypes. They will show that all the lovely (so called romantic) things the 'modern age', the 20th century, rejected and despised (nostalgia indeed!) are vital to this Soul, which is the collective psyche of humanity. It matters very much indeed for our psychic well-being that we have chickens of

105

all different breeds together with a cock in shimmering feathers wandering free in every farmyard, that farmers work with horses, use farm carts and handmade ploughs and that there are flowers in the hayfields. It matters that all this is as important as sunlight, as salt, as uncontaminated water, air and food for our survival. The alternative is hell on earth, a loveless desert.

The monks can be of both sexes but will live in separate monasteries and abbeys, because the male monks will love their abbot and, through him, each other. It is for miraculous and mysterious reasons vital that men should love each other. The result of virile, voy males surrendering to this love and submitting to the will of Divine Inner Truth, is truly remarkable. The female monks will have to love their abbess for similar reasons. The abbots and abbesses, because of this, are always dard, which means that they possess a benign and a paternal quality which is motherly yet comforting. This 'God-Realized' aspect may be somewhat like that of the Indian Guru and the monastery or abbey could also be compared to an Indian Ashram. These monasteries and abbeys of the future would have outward features which resemble those of the Middle Ages, there may be a magnificent Salubriat, an amazing Hallowhall, a splendid Mentate, but they shall *never* be *oppressive* as such Christian institutions sometimes were – and perhaps still are. The most refreshing and amazing part will be that, exactly as with the medieval abbey, a cultural centre, a place of learning, literature and art will also be a farm. This 'green' farming of the future shall be a source of inspiration and vitality, it shall have the atmosphere of a fairy-tale and nevertheless be down to earth and grow a large variety of crops. In a largely vegetarian country this will become necessary. It will be everything a 'realist', limited by present concepts of what is possible, deems madness, just as flying to the moon or remote control would have seemed impossible to most 'realists' a century ago. The Graigian Society intends to start a pilot scheme as soon as this is possible. Young people who seriously wish to join a monastery and do farm work will be able to, without having to acquire a holding.

Flats and maisonettes or houses which are owned by the borough council are very often cared for in a remote and haphazard way and therefore stay vacant for some time, or are under-occupied.

Amelog 1952-1994 rt

This is why a neighbourhood committee, convened by the communicator, a pleasant, warm friendly meeting, should manage buildings which are under public ownership. The allocation of vacant
flats and houses would be dealt with by the Communicator who
would know the flat, the house, the street and everyone who lived,
or lives, there. A noisy family, or a boy who practices his drums

would not be put in the same house and above a quiet lady with her daughter or an old man on the top floor with many stairs to climb! Hopefully, and with Anelog Work, more than likely, communities would form in which a friendly, helpful atmosphere makes refuse collection with horse and cart – collecting different kinds of refuse on different days, so that these can be recycled – a delight. They would gladly take on planting trees and shrubs and repair the pavements. A new spirit would come about born of goodwill. Private ownership of several houses with flats or rooms for letting should be controlled. Indifferent landlords, directors of large companies owning property in various places, should be obliged to sell these usually unpleasantly converted houses to people (perhaps the tenants) who wish to lovingly restore them. The authors bought their Mid-Victorian house from such a property company and have changed it back to its original character.

Two different kinds of neighbourhood exist: Areas with a village atmosphere like Highgate, Hampstead, Kentish Town and Richmond in London and less friendly and attractive places where the inhabitants live isolated lives. These are bedsitter-districts and certain kinds of suburb, some with a quite terrifying atmosphere brought about by loneliness and despair. Such areas would have to be transformed and a retracting, sensitive society would work towards the end of lonely, tedious and sad existences in dreary, unloved parts of our enormous cities. Our own area in Kentish Town has changed dramatically since we first moved here in 1960. Because we cared and made a fuss when old, cast-iron lamp posts were replaced by concrete 'hockey sticks' a civic society was founded at Anelog's initiative. The streets are now lined with trees, there are pretty window-boxes and front gardens, once pruned to smithereens, are full of plants and shrubs. A friendly, caring spirit has been allowed to grow and neighbours now know each other, greet us when we have our midday break in the sunshine on the doorstep – squatting on a blanket in the doorway – and meeting in the cheerful grocer's shop which is like a village store: The kind of Greek grocery shop which exists in this part of London. The owner, who grew up here and his Armenian wife are actually *interested* in their customers and, being genuine and natural, create *goodwill* and concern for those in need.

RETRACTION

When a generous, free and loving lifestyle becomes known, it will be followed and there will be many places which give people's lives a secure and settled, happy background. Most built-up areas since late Victorian, large developments came about, have a cheerlessness and drabness which comes from the spirit in which they were conceived: Lack of generosity, taste, repressive so-called morals and demonic undercurrents, in which speculators thrived at the end of the last century and the beginning of this one, caused terrible districts to be built. This is the spirit which has ruled society and it is devilish. Modern mass-developments are often dreadful in a different way. Instead there must be places which are built in a new and wholesome spirit: 'villages' within the urbanized environment on a 'Human Scale', containing all that is required for most people's lives, their interests, their education, their needs, their work, their leisure and their entertainment.

Caring for one's town, neighbourhood, or village becomes possible when one feels *part* of it, when there is goodwill, which will come about when exploitation, which breeds indifference, ceases to be tolerated. It is only by making exploitation as popularly unacceptable as nudity, or sexual intercourse in public, is at present, that new and better values will become established. It can easily be seen that if a society wishes to banish certain behaviour this can be done and always has been done. In the contemporary world this is the case with love, which is restricted to only a very limited display, often without any feeling, whereby it is a *show* of love, without the actual emotion. It is, of course, just as much human nature to touch and stroke another person as it is for one child to pull another child's toy away; the latter is the beginning of advantage-taking. Exploitation in present-day society is a pest like blackfly which has been encouraged and allowed. Once this pest has been

controlled, the things it has been feeding on can flourish. When the parasite is removed that which seemed impossible because of it, becomes possible. When the examples everyone follows are good, integrity returns, together with the old cast-iron lamp posts, shedding a

109

pleasant, soft, yellow light. The York stone pavements will be cared for and preserved and along the verges of the road, devoid of motor-cars, the Buddleia, Hollyhock and Rosebay Willowherb will grow.

There are two totally opposing points of view: The point of view of those who wish to perpetuate the money system, extol the virtue of mindless work and regard hippies living on Social Security as parasites (the right-wing point of view) and the point of view we have already stated. It all depends whether one argues for a love of one's work, or not! Conventional life is based on the notion of putting up with tasks and a routine one dislikes, which one is compelled to continue in for the sake of security. We would like to put forward a case for going *with the grain* and this means that everyone is able to derive pleasure from their work, becomes absorbed in it and does it well.

It is appropriate to make sandals or shoes in one's own house, picture-frames, or clothes; and pottery in a garden shed. To smelt steel, however, one needs a blast-furnace and steelworks only exist in particular places where there are coal-mines. Such places have been associated with hardship and deprivation, with industry which turned them black with smoke and caused grim conditions for a soured and hardened people. Because this dismal world was so

dour and desolate it fathered unions which had to be as hard as nails with attitudes which matched the furnaces in fierceness: 'Flames lashing amber bright against the pit black soot'. By means of strikes and bargaining, material circumstances gradually improved, the work, however, remained as, if not more, impersonal and joyless. Spiritually there was very little gain; the men are still as hard and even brutal, their tastes as vulgar and destructive as they were, made worse by lurid artificial fashions and diversions of our present age. If such industry, where it is called for, could be broken down into smaller works and these managed individually and co-operatively by representatives of all the various groups who work there, or are in some other way involved; if every gripe or grouse could thus be ironed out, surely there would be no need for all that hardness!

Some of the representatives, sometimes, could be local residents who might have some interest or grievance in, or about the way a factory or business is run or conducted. A deputation of these, convened by the Communicator, might attend the meetings of this board. Should there be disagreements or dissension, then a Mediator would have to hear the case and help to find a solution. If everyone who works in a firm is equally concerned about its welfare and there are no gross discrepancies in earnings, it is unlikely that there will be conflict over wages. Men have to learn to work together, to be fair and as sensitive as possible to each other's needs. If they are unfeeling, brutal, indifferent or malicious, they will have to be made to feel and be taught. With a complete change in the mental climate, which a 'Water-Conscious', spiritual society will cause, the commercial world of today becomes like a bad dream. Thus co-operatively run companies may again belong to guilds which would be associated with the 'High Salubriat', the 'Church' of the Graigian Green Religion; as the guilds were in the Middle Ages part of the Cathedral church. Then there will again be moving dedications, services and processions and the people, once more living from their deeper feelings, would naturally be able to respond. That which was hidden in the human soul would be expressed, rather than the notions of a fixed and sterile intellect, prevalent today, with all its dreadful jargon.

Modern industry and administration are operated by computers. The programmers manipulating these gaze into flickering screens all day long. This, in all certainty, will have a bad effect on them and cause headaches, eye-strain and other sick conditions. The products made in this impersonal and robotic manner lack all life and are expected to be thrown away when they no longer satisfy - which is often very soon! The streets are littered with this plastic refuse. Automation is an important cause of massive unemployment. Unemployment and Social Security benefits exist to give millions of people a *basic income*, without which many of them would starve. But it is vital that the money goes where it is really needed *most*. Until recently the Department of Social Security in north-west London operated from an ugly tower-block at Archway where frustrated, angry or apathetic people waited all day long in dirty, soulless rooms, for all we know they are still obliged to go there with enquiries or complaints: (The administration is now done in Glasgow aided by computers). Because of the way this system operates, indifferently, without compassion, insight or understanding, holes were thumped in the badly made partitions in between the cubicles, where officers at long intervals show up to interview anyone whose name is called after hours of waiting. This senseless, centralised structure makes it possible for a dissolute drunkard to claim £100 for heating, blankets, sheets, a cooker etc. and spend this money in the pub, while a poor person, who is doing some useful work, may be persecuted for earning a little extra money on top of their dole. How much better would it be if every village, community or neighbourhood had its *own* small office where the Communicator knows both the drunkard and the poor person, whose work beside the dole would be understood and valued and is a personal friend! Thus the needy will receive the compassionate treatment and the benefits they truly deserve.

All work should be shared and with the coming of a 'basic wage' (which can be seen as a new name for Social Security payments) received by anyone in need of it, many people who get this might also do part-time work. This would often be in one of the small studios, offices, shops, workshops or factories which will have become the norm, employ no more than 100 people and like all industry should be subject to controls which ensure standards in quality and design. Every high street, for instance, should have its own bakery, where in the early morning the smell of baking, preferably from stone ovens, suffuses the air. Other, less vital, commodities would be made in those parts of the country where these have been traditionally manufactured. Sheffield, for instance, has for several centuries been the centre for cutlery. It would be marvellous to see once more many different and colourful, but this time non-polluting, factories in every district, producing a wide choice of brands, type, makes and varieties. Many workshops could

WOOD FIRING KILN

be housed in restored old barns or in sheds, often behind a row of terraced houses.

A change in attitude is what matters most. It is fruitless to try and force people to conform to a new approach, to bring in rules, penalties and fines, if there is no enthusiasm for it. Everyone must genuinely wish to co-operate, because they are helped with their personal difficulties and problems and are made to feel wanted and appreciated for what they are able to contribute. It is so very necessary and important to fight prejudice and intolerance through education and to show that nastiness just does not pay. If a bully or an extortionist is allowed to victimise, his victims, who will be initially shocked or astonished and seek redress, will react by being vindictive in their turn (the cause of vendettas or war), will become apathetic or live in fear, if justice is not forthcoming. This sets off a chain reaction of fear, bad feeling and mistrust. More criminals have been made this way by society than are born into it. We, even now, still are suffering from the after-effects of enclosures and clearances which continued until the 19th century, when villagers were dispossessed in bloody-minded and terrible ways by autocratic landlords and there was no help from anyone. There are still many respectable, bourgeois people with extraordinary double-standards. When pretentiousness, which is fortunately on the way out, has disappeared altogether, a lot of dishonesty will go too. When it has become the fashion to take oneself seriously and when simplicity is the rule, a greater regard for other people's rights will come about naturally.

In every aspect of life there is controversy and this requires sensible and just mediation. At present Civil Law is both cumbersome and expensive. The law is an ass which people are frightened of using! In the future, which we trust will tally with this prophecy, a small court will be held as often as necessary in every neighbourhood or district to deal with problems or issues which the local community can not solve. This court is presided over by a Mediator who is the equivalent of a present-day Magistrate, but who *also* has a spiritual role. The defending counsel will consist of Communicators and Inter-Communicators, who are serving their community and receive their livelihood from their 'parish', their community. Legal advice will be regarded as a *free* social service and the legal profession will become part of the system of 'Communication', that is to say lawyers will be fully trained Communicators and Inter-Communicators and have spiritual as well as secular status. Communicators dress in long blue or green robes and wear green cloaks. The court-room of the future will be light and white, pure and peaceful as a snowscape with green and pale-blue figures. In an atmosphere of receptivity and objectivity, in this amazing stillness, the horrid person's lies will run dry on his lips - and the truthfulness of the honest man will shine like a star. The case will be conducted in a spirit of fairness and no-one shall gain from being dishonest. No black Bible need be sworn on and no horrible gloomy bench, witness box or dock will be required. In this light and airy court which also serves as council chamber, an octagon or round hall, the 'Hallow Hall', the Mediator squats on a dais, covered by a kelim and those who face her/him squat on *dhurees* or cushions on the sanded floor. The accused or contesting party are in the centre, behind them the defending Communicators and at the back witnesses and spectators. The hallow hall is used in the evenings for 'hallowing', the spiritual exercise by which the Inner Self is purified and liberated, mentioned earlier. It is built over a kind of crypt, which is the ground floor where the lavatories, kitchen and refreshment room are.

Someone who starts a business and employs other people must regard them as partners who are asked to become interested in the way it is run and share in solving problems. This is an emotional investment which involves someone's labour. Standards for production, the quality and appearance of goods should be approved by experienced artists, craftsmen and designers. If anyone disagrees with their opinion he/she can put this complaint on the agenda of the next mediation: the meeting at which the Mediator holds his/her Court. It is good to encourage patience with such matters. Controls and rules are only necessary when and where there is no

The Archangel Gabriel, holding the chalice, reappears again in the border now with Michael, his companion, holding the sword. They serve as supporters of the heart, a pendant hanging from the Graigian chanter, a string of beads worn by the monks who count them in a particular chant. The leaves are of the 12 trees associated with the archetypes.

natural sense or discrimination. If no-one wants rubbish, no rubbish will be produced. If no-one tolerates a deceiver, deception becomes very difficult. One only has to reflect on the history of sexual morals to see this: Homosexuality – which is in fact a tendency as potent as any other – was rigorously condemned and associated with witchcraft, heresy and pantheism, so no-one would openly admit to homosexual emotions and fewer still would dare to be homosexual. But, because in those days commercial sharpshooting, trading in slaves and forced labour by children was regarded as 'normal' and the rich merchant who did these things was honoured with a title, we are now suffering from a terrible backlash of criminal and dishonest behaviour. Effeminacy in men was regarded with horror by the Edwardians who glorified war and produced the most terrifying, soulless environment that has ever been. In future days people will find it hard to believe that love between men was condemned and that death and destruction were preferred to it in a previous age.

The point we wish to make again is that fashion, that is to say what is customary, is extremely powerful. Few people wish to be social outcasts and therefore when it will become the custom to co-operate and to behave in a considerate and friendly way, most people will do this. Everything that is constructed needs a plan, or blueprint, and so it is with social structures. There must be models: An archetypal, or example place inhabited by a group of people who are admired, written about in newspapers and photographed. It will then not be necessary to maintain a boring and cumbersome bureaucracy implementing complicated legislation. People will relate to their community, find work there and interests. They will develop habits which reflect their better feelings and these, being voiced in their religion (Graigianity), will govern all their lives. The lamp-posts, the paving stones, the telephone and post boxes will again be part of one's *personal* life, one will know them intimately and love them and be *involved* with their care and repair. This wholehearted involvement in one's own environment could make the future very different from this present apathetic and discordant age. The point of view of young, cultured people will prevail, *not* that of old-fashioned, tree-lopping, machine-minded reactionaries who at present are still making practically all decisions which affect us. One must understand that what may seem far-fetched today is tomorrow's norm and thus it will be with participation and consultation in and with local government. Within a few decades it will be *unthinkable* for any official to make a decision affecting a locality, without consulting the people who live and work there first.

We have compared the huge, industrial complexes and commercial monopolies of today with the last, gigantic, prehistoric monsters which succumbed because they had become over-ponderous. An entirely new species, that of small mammals, took over and flourished. We must look to places where a new type of young person congregates to see the nature and quality of our future society. Such people are already making things which they sell in open-air markets like the one at Camden Lock in north-west London. The atmosphere here and the wares for sale have a certain quality, a wholesomeness and feeling which indicate the direction the future will take - for this magical atmosphere, this *Water-Consciousness* will, indeed, spread!

How can one see the West End and City of London in this context? What will happen to all those skyscrapers?..... Perhaps some of them could be adapted to an imaginative use, other tall buildings which are felt to be uncompromisingly useless and ugly are likely to be demolished. In their place new communities built around courtyards, with gardens on different levels, will bring people again to the centre of the capital and the same also applies to other cities.

THE FUTURE WILL BE GREEN

The City of London in the last 30 years has been made sterile and even old buildings look dead and 'dolled up', whereas the West End still has some genuine life, although it is populated on summer nights mainly by busloads of tourists. A great deal of what is for sale in the shops is rubbish made for this tourist industry and does not relate to Londoners. The West End, like the Zoo, is a curiosity and provides a perhaps rather sad entertainment. It is interesting and will always be a show-case, yet Londoners should live again in the centre of their city. Mayfair, Soho, Charing Cross and Ludgate should once more be neighbourhoods with all the lively intercourse of an ordinary locality. This would in turn promote the formation of neighbourhood associations which can monitor traffic, encourage tree-planting, the establishment of real shops, like greengrocers with a display of vegetables outside.

When the market moved out of Covent Garden and the local community organised itself and protested against demolition and redevelopment, we had a foretaste of what may happen all over the West End and in any other town, once the money making forces are defeated. Gardens sprang up in unexpected places, there was street theatre, all manner of interesting shops and workshops opened and there was a spirit of adventurous excitement, a fresh, lively and engaging atmosphere. Naturally all sorts of things went wrong, there was confrontation between idealism and vandalism. Negative and selfish motives sabotaged good intentions, people were fickle, gave up, were unreliable and felt wronged. This is in-evitable where there are no clear, common objectives or generally recognized guiding principles. Even with these, people are likely to quarrel and disagree! This is why communication, self-develop-ment, mediation and the understanding of the 6 basic conflicts (defined in NATURAL PSYCHOLOGY) are of such vital importance if and when people wish to relate to each other properly. This is why there should be experienced and wise Communicators and Mediators.

When each area is more self-sufficient and cut-throat competi-tion no longer threatens small business, when no one is harassed or exploited a sigh of relief will go up and everyone will relax into a slower pace. This will be the end of the rush hour, of people having to travel long distances to work. The once bowler hatted commuter will be as much part of history as the muffin man and the frantic

van driver will no longer curse the traffic. Delivery in fact won't be such a problem because the roads will be less congested. With less haste more leisurely ways of moving about will come again into their own. Canals and goods trains will once more be able to take all that needs transporting from place to place. Gaily painted barges, pulled by horses or powered by steam engines, will go slowly up and down the canals worked by people who do this for enjoyment. How much better than moping all day in front of a television set on the 9th story of a block of flats situated in a sea of concrete, with bleary eyes, feeling bored, disconsolate and hopeless! Why such an archaic, slow and cumbersome form of transport? Because it is fun, interesting, cheap, environmentally friendly and beautiful and why should life *not* be a delight? Without all that mad, demonic need to get there first, to win some pointless race, to pressurise and make it all go faster, work becomes a relaxation and one's livelihood, one's leisure. What is the point of producing more than is required?* It is a terrible, a horrific scandal that we should have

*This sentence was first written by us in 1975. A decade later 50% of EEC money was spent on destroying excess food. Goodness knows what goes on now in 1994!

had this hideous farming industry inflicted on the countryside, merely to churn out unwanted butter, grain and other foodstuff which was, or still is, dumped. Once 'industrial growth' is off the official agenda we can begin to dispense with stinking lorries and turn transport into a joyful pastime.

There is a modern myth that we live in an efficient world, that our transport-system of 'juggernauts', Jumbo-jets and freightliners is quick. What tends to be forgotten is that such depersonalized work is done by men who are careless and indifferent. We actually live in a remarkably inefficient, wasteful age. It takes months for an order to be delivered and even longer to have something quite ordinary made. All kinds of materials, skiploads of them, are left to rot instead of being recycled. Half the lorries on a motorway are returning empty from their destination. The monstrous airports of the 1960's should revert to farmland, or heath, (which one of them obviously once was) and air-travel reduced to sensible proportions. Smaller planes could be used and the whole enterprise might become exciting, adventurous and dramatic as it was in the early days of aviation. In many ways something died in 1914 which is now being revived. There is a curious reconnecting with the art and fashions of the period before the First World War with Tiffany lamps, Art Nouveau lettering and the decorative art of Leon Bakst, Gustav Klimt, Egon Schiele, Fabergé and Kay Nielsen. In the same way the design of aeroplanes, motor-cars, buses and trams could revert to the style of that period when even lorries had character, railway trains were at their best and carriages had an elegance which has entirely vanished.

Why should life *not* be enjoyable? We mean a joy for *human* beings, with what they really love and thus public transport too could be delightful. We could bring back old fashioned trams and buses with stairs outside, all painted in the good old London Transport red once more, so that we would feel a happy glow from their familiarity. The trams and buses could be made and run by people who would enjoy this work, like those who run old steam-trains as a hobby. It has become almost impossible to find parking spaces during weekdays in most city centres; plentiful and cheap public transport would cut down the need for cars. The manufacture of these could be restricted to different types of small cars only, the same size as the 'Mini Metro', with a hatch back and a folding back-seat, using only entirely harmless fuel. This type of car should be perfected and made to last, so that a reliable service for (inexpensive) spare-parts could come about. If this really happens we might have an obliging, friendly, helpful and reasonable service for repairs and renewal as well, even in London. Thus in time perhaps, one hopes, only a limited number of new cars need be made. All expensive status cars would have to be banned and a kind of charabanc brought into use instead, which holds a dozen people and picks up passengers for a certain destination and delivers them back home. Also a certain standard size of lorry, like those of the 20's and 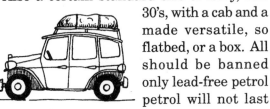 30's, with a cab and a chassis could be made versatile, so that it could hold a flatbed, or a box. All other lorries really should be banned and furthermore, only lead-free petrol sold. The supply of petrol will not last forever and for this reason also - apart from congested roads - cars with only the driver in them should be discouraged.

A law could be passed prohibiting cars with only one occupant, in towns and cities, which do not display a notice of exemption to this rule (e.g. a doctor; a particular delivery, a taxi, a driver collecting something or someone). Instead of the roads being blocked by traffic during the rush-hours, people could share their cars with 3 passengers, or the equivalent of a school bus could go round collecting employees and directors alike of a particular firm or firms; for each part of a conurbation a bus. People will thus get to know each other and a more friendly spirit could easily develop.

When class-consciousness and prejudice have made way for goodwill, a quite different society can come about. In this the need for transport and for travel diminishes, most things would be at hand, the place one lives in would be magically beautiful and almost self-sufficient and life would be enthralling in one's own home: This will happen, because it is happening already, it just has not reached the great majority of people yet. This is so, it has been admitted by people who have come to visit us, who have told us that they (and this includes even the daughter of an MP) had not suspected the existence of a house as 'magical' as ours and that they were amazed, astonished, that this wonderful alternative exists. Remember, the blockage against love and deeper feeling by the establishment has conditioned countless people to go against themselves and to behave like chained-up dogs, yapping at the sight, or approach of anything unusual. This is why the 'mentally mutilated multitude' will keep the repression of, the 'blockage' against real love going, which is reflected in the kind of people who are constantly elected to represent their interests. When liberating and enlightening publicity can penetrate a wall of blind resistance, a way of life will open out which to anyone unused to it will seem like Paradise.

It will then be possible for the marooned, suburban housewife, the lonely old-age pensioner and the school-leaver without a future, all of whom have lost hope, to be helped out of their predicament. With inspiring exhibitions, shows, programmes on radio and television, the advent of positive emotion and enthusiasm, with dedicated social services and with therapy and group-work, a new life will be available to all. Many people have assumed quite wrongly that evolution stopped at the dawn of history and that their hopeless values are the only ones and will carry on forever. In our father's youth the wonders of technology were hailed with bated breath and before that in the times of our grand or great grandfathers H. G. Wells and Jules Verne described a future world of exploration and scientific exploits. To them an age of high technology is all we can expect and a highly artificial future lies before us. This dream has turned into a nightmare; for instance there is a trend which speculates on the possible existence of life on other planets, or of colonising these. Such phantasies are highly unat-

tractive and devoid of any regard or reverence for the earth and its natural loveliness, or spiritual and human values. If their devotees are as soulless as these terrible projections, it might be better that they made a rocket big enough to take them all and shot off into outer space for good. The journey which really matters now is within ourselves.

RETRACTION

In the 1950's in a few isolated and pleasant places like the area around Well Walk in Hampstead* and Coombe Springs in Kingston-upon-Thames * a new, surprising consciousness welled up amongst a small fraternity. These were 'outsiders' who took an interest in Gurdjieff, Subud, Jung and Reich, the Tarot-cards and the I Ching. They were thought of by the cynics who ruled the press of that time as 'cranks' and their interests as 'mad' and inconsequential. Yet 40 years onwards the interest in such esoteric subjects has increased a hundredfold and there are most probably more people involved in these, or related subjects, than worship in the Church of England. With widespread involvement of this kind, with self-realisation and self-development, a new stage in man's consciousness will be reached. So far, in history, the man of action and the poet were irreconcilable, the intellectual and the peasant were like two different species. Now inner and outer, head and body can be reconciled. When there is greater objectivity and freedom from inhibitions the human psyche can finally unfold and flourish. Most social problems are created by a lack of understanding, by pride and egotism which cling to fixed ideas about oneself and other people. In Protestant countries, like England and the USA, with their awful work ethic, there is an inordinate emphasis on 'trying hard', or 'getting on' and proving oneself. Conventional social life decrees that people hide their feelings, their true nature under a front, a show, which is their 'personality', or 'persona'. This false performance, this artificial, sad display, contrived by mental trickery, is compulsively put on to demonstrate that one is a 'success', 'OK' and acceptable, one of the boys or girls or gang. Rebels who are emotionally free tend to live in a whimsical world all of their own. Meanwhile the visual arts, literature and music in recent times have become so meaningless and ephemeral that people are bamboozled and confused about them and no longer know if they can rely on their own sensibility and judgement. Utter trash is declared to be of the greatest value and something of real depth

*One of the authors was born here in 1950 shortly before the other was spontaneously drawn here, where they met in 1957.

*J.G.Bennett founded his Gurdjieff Institute here in the late 1940's. Subud arrived here in 1956. Note: 'Well Walk' and 'Coombe Springs', both sources of water.

and beauty is disregarded by the pundits. As a result of all this
official deception few of us are still able to trust ourselves. The
media, willy-nilly, were sucked into a void of cultural despair and
by this tendency many young and cultured people gave up hope.

Just as a thunderstorm will break the sultry drought and sweeping rain will drive the dust cloud from the air, a mighty upsurge of
release and joy shall surely come, a wave of Water-Consciousness
will wash away the debris. This debris is all shoddiness and ugly
rubbish, the scarred and desecrated land, the last remains of a
conscienceless and a polluted world. It seemed, in the late 1960's,
as if this was at long last happening, but 'Flower Power' had no
staying power and no solid basis for survival. In spite of this lack of
real solidity the late 1960's period had an enduring, enlivening
and healthy effect: young people discovered, in junk shops and
attics, characterful clothes and beads; exciting and exotic Kaftans
coats and shawls were imported from places like Afghanistan, both
boys and girls grew long hair and walking barefoot became common. Sadly, no strong, integrated movement ever grew out of this;
everyone simply wanted to do their own thing. Because of this,
and because there was no rallying-point, nothing which could possibly bring the various and diverse forms of Water-Consciousness
together, there was *no* unity of purpose. Just as a firework ex-
plodes into separate flowers which divide and sub-divide, the 'Esoteric' or New Age movement now exists in countless small groups,
lodges and societies: each with their own therapy, method, way of
life or guru. A number of these rather faddish movements were
derived from Yoga, became a cult in California and
reached England via the American enthusiasts.
They seem rootless and usually only last for a decade, after which the guru, who is out of touch with
reality, the external world, does something quite
ridiculous and vanishes into limbo. Their atmosphere is artificial, a surrogate for actual life and
feeling; plastic and North American, lacking in integrity and character. When the forerunner of the
Graigian Society, the Positive Movement, organized a carnival in Finsbury Park in 1969, a large
papier-mâché bird with outstretched wings pushed

on a handcart symbolized happiness and Inner Freedom. In 1971 an elephant of the same material, with a golden crown between its enormous ears, pushed on the same handcart, expressed a wish for solidarity, enthusiasm and support.

The Positive Movement distributed the very first green leaflets at that time, called 'Solution and Pollution', (printed in green ink) when it organized the second carnival, this time on Parliament Hill Fields. Thousands of people came to this fantastic event and its distinctive spirit survives in the street festivals which have since been held in various parts of Camden. The third symbol will be a phoenix rising, not from the ashes of a war, a holocaust, but from the demise of a society which gave evil honour. The evil forces which have to be overcome are those of a particular kind of egoism, self-interest and cynicism by which established and successful businessmen, millionaires, journalists, executives and directors are possessed. Since certain types who, because they have denied their deeper feelings, are already in a position of authority, only similar types who have streamlined themselves get promoted. In the Tarot cards the 'Devil' holds up one hand in a denying gesture, sticks-out his tongue and has two small demons captive who could easily remove the nooses which lie loosely around their necks. They represent the many people, only concerned with their security and status, who 'tow the line' and follow mindlessly silly, money spinning fashions. Because honesty, integrity and most of all innocent sincerity are a source of embarrassment and would seem threatening to the usual trendy types, they would rather be kept in bondage to their fashionable pretentiousness, the false performance and hollow showing-off, the rôles they play, than be free. Money making cynicism is putting our lives in danger. In 1987 two frightful disasters occurred as a result of carelessness and the cynicism which has made men who work for large impersonal companies, as well as men who carry out repairs etc, selfish and unconcerned to an extraordinary degree: several hundred passengers on the 'Herald of Free Enterprise' drowned outside the harbour of Zeebrugge and 30 people burnt to death in Kings Cross underground station. Because of this appalling mentality, which has crystallised and become habitual, set rock hard and part of 'life', such disasters may continue to happen until we are taken seriously and selfish men are shocked, shaken and made to feel. Had the Green Movement, from the day of our carnival in 1971 onwards, not grown to oppose the exploitation of natural resources, all the earth would end up as one big tip, an uninhabitable hell.

Retraction means withdrawing, pulling back, and this is what has to happen to bring back to their senses all who have no conscience. A new teaching and awareness can defeat the demons which are in control. With this we don't mean that somebody is a 'demon' and nothing else beside, anyone is capable of change and people have many different sides, both good and bad. It very much depends which side wins the conflict between arrogance or pride and giving way to goodness. In the Revelation of St. John it is depicted as the victory of St Michael over the demonic forces. Because of this the Monastic Graigian Community in Kentish Town, although not Christian, has chosen the image of this Archangel as its hope and inspiration and is named after it.

CHAPTER 4.

DEVOLUTION

 NE thousand, or more, years ago the British Isles consisted of a number of small, warring, tribal countries whose size and contours varied from season to season according to their strength or weakness and the chance of inter-marriage or inheritance. Across the centuries these fragmented Kingdoms were united under a central government which not only ruled over remote Scottish, or Irish islands, but also eventually controlled a vast empire. This centralized government has, in the course of time, taken on more and more responsibility for more and more departments which govern the various aspects of our daily life and has indeed become a power-trap which, in many ways, alienates the governed from the governors. Thus the reverse process was set in motion. The various parts of the Empire gained independence until very little remained and in these islands first the Irish, and later the Scottish and Welsh nations, clamoured to regain their identity and make their own decisions.

Nationhood is a sacred and special state of affairs in which, like a closely knit family, everyone participates and makes their contribution. It implies an identity, a fervour and unity of purpose which unfortunately is broken up by class consciousness, cultural differences, politics and religion. An overriding cause has to exist to keep all this together. In history a common enemy has been such a cause, in peace time those who fought together and buried their arguments, again form their own party or club to oppose other factions. Unless you are a patriot, you have a very vague idea indeed of what your nationality means and now we have come to such a low cultural ebb, enthusiasm for any inspiring idea at all has made way for apathy. Many people in our sprawling cities (and those who have retired to bungalows in the countryside) have no real affinity with the place where they live, there is a loss of local pride and tradition. In order to make England, Scotland and Wales into *one* nation they had, in a sense, their guts torn out. The people, once living a simple rural life, became bourgeois, respectable and afraid to show feelings which were considered vulgar and primitive. The Welsh language and Gaelic in Scotland were sacrificed to English respectability. That is why nationalism in Scotland and Wales took such a long time to take root and is still comparatively weak. The English masters suppressed not only the language - but *also* the culture of their hapless subordinates and, because of their dominant position lost their natural humility and thus became arrogant, condescending and hypocritical. The present generation in England is embarrassed by this past and many of its reactions are an attempt to efface the effects of a stiff upper lip and rigid opinions. Forty years ago one could still say what an Englishman was, but this idea now, fortunately, no longer holds. There is *no* standard English national character left, thank goodness!

There are however – although badly in need of a revival – regional accents, customs, food, and architectural traditions. It seems only logical that when Wales secedes (which it will do eventually) England and Scotland are divided into parts of a similar size. This island naturally separates into 12 countries (see map):

1) The Home Counties; with the counties of Bedford, Hertford, Essex, London, Surrey, Kent and Sussex.

(For reasons of history and character we have used the old boundaries and names).

2) Wessex; with the counties of Berkshire, Wiltshire, Hampshire, Dorset and Somerset.

3) The West Country; with the counties of Devon and Cornwall, the Channel Islands.

4) Mercia; with the counties of Buckingham, Oxford, Gloucester, Worcester, Hereford, and Shropshire.

5) Anglia; with the counties of Suffolk, Cambridge, Huntingdon, Norfolk and Lincoln.

6) The Midlands; with the counties of Northampton, Warwick, Leicester, Rutland, Nottingham, Derby and Stafford.

7) Lancaster; with the counties of Lancashire, Westmorland, Cumberland, Cheshire and the Isle of Man.

The map of Britain shows the division into 12 proposed nation states. Their names are open to revision; for instance, 'The Islands', the Gaelic speaking part of Scotland incorportes some of the mainland. Another name might also be found for 'Midland', although for psychological reasons it matters greatly that the map and the names have a fairytale quality.

8) York; with the counties of Yorkshire, Durham and Northumberland.

Scotland

9) The Lowlands; 13 counties.

10) The Highlands; Fife, Kinross, Clackmannan, Stirling, Dumbarton, Argyll, Perth, Angus, Kincardine, Aberdeen, Banff, Moray, Nairn.

11) The Islands; Inverness, Ross and Cromarty, Sutherland, Caithness, the Inner and the Outer Hebrides, the Orkney Islands and the Shetland Islands.

Wales

12) Wales; 13 counties.

The Isle of Man and the Channel Islands already have their own parliaments, but also have an allegiance to Britain. This historical allegiance could, eventually, shift to one of these proposed, newly independent countries on which they would depend for transport, supplies of food and goods etc. It is by no means suggested that anything should change in the way these islands are governed. If this devolution of government came to pass, the 12 new countries would form a federation of mutually-supportive states, each with its own characteristic railways, army, post office and all the other mechanisms of a modern infra-structure. The 'dream' we are advocating, the ethos behind this book is that every country *within* the protective boundary known as Britain will be *self-governing*, thus rediscovering its own character and traditions and marvel at them. The relative independence of the Isle of Man and the Channel Islands could serve as an example to the rest of Britain.

When the parliament at Whitehall came into being it represented no more than 6 million people, it now governs a nation of 60 million, ten times more people's interests have to be considered. The people of North Wales who have elected members of Plaid Cymru to represent them, wish for a Welsh-speaking parliament in an independent Wales, thus their government would speak their language and be appreciative of their problems. Instead of being alien, remote and even hostile, their government would become familiar to them, personal and therefore easier to comprehend, approach and trust. The same applies to the Gaelic-speaking North of Scotland, hence the 'Islands' as a separate country. There have been proposals from the major political parties for divisions of this kind, but these have been devoid of any real significance. They invariably ignore the central problem; the crying need to break down the huge, impersonal bureaucratic structures which dominate our society. When we say that national administration should be de-centralised we actually mean de-centralised and made local, not the kind of de-centralization which puts the tax-office for Kentish Town in Newcastle! Because we have a small-holding in North Wales, we recently received a government notice, warning us 'not to go into confined places' (e.g. in a silo, or silage-tank where there is a lack of oxygen). This notice, idiotically was sent from Epsom, Surrey; presumably farmers in Surrey receive their circulars from Bangor!

Creating ineffective assemblies in Scotland and Wales, simply to allay nationalism is mere tinkering. Who is to say that these assemblies will be any more representative of people's real wishes than the voice of their present MP at Westminster? If we are to create new nations, or to be more accurate, liberate very old ones, then these must mean something to the nationals, who must feel enthusiasm for their country and derive inspiration from the love of it and their respective languages, customs, history, folklore, architecture, legends and traditions: their nationhood. All this will have to be taught and propagated so that each country will be able to express its individuality and develop in the way which is appropriate. Certain cultures (how objectionable that word 'industry' has become) are peculiar to certain regions; with sheep farming goes making wool and weaving and in different places a different type of tweed, woollen cloth, or fabric has been, and would be, made. Each region has its own cheese, or beer, or special dish, its own way of making furniture or tools. This is what makes for character, something which has been gradually destroyed in the 'modern world'; the superficial, slick, industrial society of this century.

Without character a human being is unreal and hopeless - and a town, a landscape and a country likewise.

Politics in Britain, a 'ding-dong' between the Labour and Tory parties ("I'm the king of the castle and you're a dirty rascal"), used to be uninteresting to say the least, until the emergence of the Green Party and the SDP. With the Alliance turning into the Social and Liberal Democrats (now, Lib Dems) as a 'third force' the jaded political arena has become somewhat more animated. The Labour Party - weakened by the loss of its more right-wing leaders and their following - moved further to the left, espousing such radical causes as unilateral disarmament and the phasing out of nuclear power and then because of losing votes, back to the right. All the same, whether you deplore, or applaud this, the bitter truth remains that the majority of people feel quite alienated from the decision-making processes. The British are most habitual and it has become a matter of routine for many people where they place their cross once in a while, except the 30 odd active members of the local majority party. Yet a true alternative to conventional party politics, a strong Graigian Green Movement which is able to reach the hearts of ordinary people has enormous potential. It stands for the kind of representation put forward in this book, re-orientation, devolution, conservation and nature. It would have to gain support from the more enlightened people in the Labour Party; for it also stands for nuclear disarmament and the abolition of nuclear power. Because the Tories could and would not support policies which are human, radical and far-sighted, the Conservative Party may well decline and may - with an accumulation of disasters - lose its conscienceless support, and disappear forever.

The signs of the decline of modern capitalism (greed and 'growth') based on a free-for-all are already with us in the Stockmarket Crash and the weakening of the US dollar. This process will grow, for it is a natural one, until integrity is re-discovered. Natural values, a natural way of living based on sense and kindness, the ability to work with others, rather than against them, will then be taught everywhere and be expected from everyone to attain this desirable state. All industry and commercial or administrative structures must be divided up into their component parts, broken down so that each part becomes more personal and human.

In this context it seems reasonable that in a United Europe the member states should be of a similar size to the Netherlands, or Belgium, the home of the European Community. For instance, Welsh MEPs are now at a disadvantage because they are working through a British system geared to the English language and English attitudes. The same applies to Brittany in its dependence on France. At present we are burdened with a top-heavy, unapproachable, Victorian style administration: A large house is difficult to keep in order by just one person, one room is likely to gain supremacy and while others are neglected. This applies to nations also, as it does in the UK. With the formation of new, small countries this will change, each region has its own specific problems and a new parliament in any one of the 12 new capitals would consist of members who represent opinions about issues which are of true local significance.

There are two different ways of creating such a representation. One is that the Communes or Commons where the members represent community interests and the other is proportional representation of national, political parties. Britain, at present, has a mixture of both in which political parties nominate the candidates for a constituency, which is usually a substitute for a community. If the 'communes' were actually represented, each neighbourhood would nominate a number of candidates, in the way in which a committee of a residents association is formed at a public meeting. Members of these committees would choose a local organiser or convener: the Communicator whom we have mentioned in previous chapters. He/she employs and trains Inter-Communicators to help him/her at a Communicator's office. It is their job to involve the neighbourhood in common activities of which the residents' or tenants' association is the governing body. Communicators belonging to the various communities which make up a borough (which has been reduced to a sixth of its present size) confer and consult with representatives of all the different residents' and tenants' associations and this will be the new Borough Council.

At the moment pressure groups consisting of representatives of a number of residents' associations are usually formed to oppose decisions made by the existing Borough Council. They are thus 'anti-councils' which actually express what the majority of local people feel about a motorway extension, a housing development, a wash-house closing down, or a traffic scheme. If these anti-councils became the real councils they could propose one of their number as representative of their borough or constituency, that is to say to represent the actual feelings of the majority of people. It has become very clear in the last few decades that no-one wants an airfield behind their back garden or a motorway crossing the street. Such feelings should be respected, but it has usually meant a long, drawn-out fight for the pressure groups to finally have a decision reversed. The 'Motorway-Box' planned in the 1970's for London is an example. Such a procedure is also very expensive, it involves a very lengthy public enquiry, the employment of solicitors and barristers, tons and tons of printed material and a fortune in postage stamps because all the objectors have to be kept informed. The Motorway-Box* in London was conceived by planners appointed by the GLC who wasted much time, money and energy on this misguided effort, an example of many schemes which should not have been dreamt up in the first place and which would not have been, if the councillors on the planning committees, or on highways' committees had been aware of local feeling.

Supposing this impersonal, ugly and unhappy machinery of County Councils and Town Halls breaks down because of some financial crisis and they go bankrupt. The whole, bungling, wasteful, stupid local administration we have now will have to be replaced and it seems to us that the system we are proposing could naturally come about. People in an emergency would have to organize themselves to cope with common needs: refuse collection, the maintenance of pavements and public places. They would have to do this via local associations sending representatives to 'working parties', which send representatives to the 'Commons' which then becomes true to its name.

*Also known as the Greater London Development Plan.

DEVOLUTION

To give an example: Kentish Town, where we live in North London, is part of the Borough of Camden. This borough was concocted in 1965 out of Holborn, St. Pancras and Hampstead, which had superseded the Parish Vestries of Victorian times. It is a meaningless entity and, like a robot, does not have a heart and any life it has is artificially induced. Its natural components are: Holborn, Bloomsbury, Camden Town, Kentish Town, a part of Highgate, Hampstead and Kilburn. All these have a real centre: a high street with a station, a library and public houses where people meet at cross-roads, as they have always done. These are the places people can emotionally identify with. The enlarged borough is cumbersome and unwieldy, it fails to function in a way which could meet the need for which it was created to provide efficient social, maintenance and welfare services. The education department in Camden, housed in the beautifully renovated Crowndale Centre, is an exception, because it deals with a limited number of schools: It has an accessible and friendly atmosphere. More often than not, however, the voice of the simple, sensitive and usually inarticulate person is drowned in a welter of bureaucratic anonymity at planning departments and housing offices. To ring up the council with a complaint means a lengthy business in which a kind of 'hunt the slipper' goes on for the only one person out of the staff of several hundred who deals with your particular area and issue. To go round to a Communicator's office, just around the corner, would be far simpler. The Communicator (or one of his/her assistants) would be able to deal with the problem in a direct and human way, it would all be neighbourly and personal, like going to a familiar shop.

135

If there were serious problems and should a really bad situation have developed, should the Communicator be unsuitable or the office not function properly, one would have recourse to the neighbourhood committee (residents' or tenants' association) or the local forum. This is an open meeting (like the 'moot' of the Anglo-Saxons) organized by the various local associations of, in our case, Kentish Town. Such a Forum was actually tried here and met regularly to discuss amongst other things Camden Council's proposed development of a large area of railway-land. The need for this was felt here in two ways: Firstly there were so many deputations at each monthly council meeting at the monolithic Town Hall in Euston Road that the meeting was held up for several hours and was often disrupted by demonstrations. Secondly the council's planning department wanted to initiate 'public participation' in introducing its new schemes. It was found however that the often unanimous opinion of the Forum was not in accordance with Council policy. The Forum produced its own plans and demonstrated with maps and colour slides how the scheme for the development of the railway land which the council's planning department had produced, ignored a number of human factors. It proposed to build warehouses near a residential area and the demolition of existing warehouses to make way for housing etc. The local authority, having already committed itself by the purchase of land and the handing out of contracts, ignored the Forum and thus the rift between people's feelings and dated political attitudes became wider. As a result the Forum – because it was impotent – lost its purpose and the interest of the community.

Added to the depersonalization of local government are the problems caused by mechanization. Traffic increases in the streets, houses deteriorate as a result of heavy lorries thundering past at all hours of the day and night while the quantity of rubbish thrown out by people grows. Refuse collection, in spite of cumbersome and expensive modern equipment becomes yearly more careless and inefficient. Another aspect of alienation between council and 'members of the public' is caused by the continual updating of procedure and equipment (again at vast expense) which in effect means that anything done in a personal way is taken over by a computer or a video-tape machine. How different all this will be if the kind of local government we are suggesting is to come about in the future! We will use Kentish Town again as our example: This 'village' is, like ancient Gaul, divided into 3 parts by the High Street which forks at its top end, above the station. The 3 parts are North, East and West Kentish Town, each with 6 or 7 residents and tenant associations, which vary according to whatever cause brings people together. Usually they represent 3 or 4 streets or a housing estate or even a single block of flats. A Kentish Town Council would con-  sist of representatives of every one of these, which, if they send only one member would consist of only 18 people, an ideal number for a 'working party'. Kentish Town would also have six Communicator's offices in corner shops, or in some other suitable and easily accessible buildings, rather like the Citizen's Advice Bureaux. The Communicators would be paid officials, but also would have a 'vocation' like social workers or priests. They would attend all the meetings of the new kind of council and would be assisted in their work by Inter-Communicators and 'Rangers', a *new* kind of police.

The reason for all this is that every age inherits problems caused by the actions of a previous age. The Victorian era inherited dirt and social degradation from the Industrial Revolution, this led to the Labour Movement of this century which, with its ideals of 'slum-clearance' and 'comprehensive redevelopment', 'hygiene and modernization' has caused the environmental and cultural disruptions we are now suffering from. The problems of the future are going to be spiritual ones: mental illness, violent and irresponsible behaviour and vandalism are going to need all our attention. The 'Ranger' will be a cross between a mental-nurse, a police man or woman and a social worker. She/he will dress in a way which we would now think of as unconventional, or 'hippy', with long hair and long flowing robes or narrow trousers, rather like the Mediaeval hose, made of wool and a cloak. The black uniform of the police, just as the black clothes of the priest, would be a thing of the past and

137

thought of as hopelessly 'straight' and depressing. Rangers would be in green, with a russet lining in their soft-green cloaks, colourful like the green woodpecker and because of their happy image attract many socially minded young people who would not *dream* of joining the police force at present. The Communicators will need to be trained psychologists to deal with the emotionally disturbed who will come crowding into their offices.

The new 'working-party' type of council would organize a monthly Forum, an *open* meeting held in a converted church, or a large hall. Here anyone would be able to voice her/his opinion or grievance and here also the council would show with the aid of slides, maps, and diagrams what it intended to do. The 3 parts of Kentish Town would each have its own refuse collection. This would consist of a horse and cart coming around on different days for different types of garbage, on one day for organic matter to be thrown on a communal compost heap, another day for plastic, paper, cans and bottles to be recycled. All this is joyful and interesting; the horse becomes a source of pleasure, children can ride on it, people can save up food for it and anyone can smack its fat rump. Rangers or other volunteers enjoy taking it round and instead of dustbins being emptied in a hateful spirit by grumpy men, the thrice-weekly collection is joined in by everybody. The stable for the horses is open to the people of Kentish Town and anyone who likes to help look after them is able to do so. It is obvious from the interest shown at the cart-horse parade each year in Regents' Park that after decades of nothing but motor-cars horses have become an attraction. (The above paragraph was written in 1976).

In 1987 Camden Council set up the Kentish Town Area Committee at a public meeting in a church hall, where subsequent meetings were also held. There was indeed a show of slides, there were maps and diagrams. It was exactly as we envisaged it 11 years before. The Area Committee was one of a number set up by the borough council to give its several parts some independence and it was intended that the committee should have its own fi-

nance from the council's budget. But Camden Council has since suffered a financial crisis and the money for the Area Committee ran out. On it tenants' and residents' associations were represented, apart from various local groups and two environmental societies (one initiated by Anelog: The Camden Civic Society, in 1963, the other by both the authors of this book: The Graigian Society, in 1983). Camden Council has also made a recycling depot, which, however, serves for the entire borough. Gradually our suggestions and ideas are tried out or put into practice. Eventually, perhaps, it will all be as we predicted in 1976 in the paragraph below:

The three parts of Kentish Town each would have a depot for unwanted materials and goods, the sort of things people give to jumble sales, but also wood thrown out during a renovating job, an old cupboard, left-over cement or bricks, old doors and windows, things which are now often thrown into a skip. Anyone in need of any of these things would be able to look for it in the depot. Paper for recycling would be taken to this new depot and bottles or metal containers. Apart from these things, the new borough would deal with council housing (maintenance, letting, rents and rehabilitation), health (clinics and inspection), the library, the wash and bath-house with its swimming pool, the roads (repairs and sweeping), the street lighting and such things as fairs, traffic, seats, public gardens and social services. All this will be dealt with in a far simpler and more homely way than at present. The social services until recently had a local office and would not have changed very much, only that 6 Communicators and their helpers would have taken a great deal of the load off its shoulders. Just as with the Police and the new Rangers the old system would continue while the new one gathers strength*. There would have to be a works department to deal with the street lights and the drains... and also a library and arts department, but these would not have to employ more than half a dozen people,

*The dreaded Tory government exacerbates social problems by cutting Camden's rate-support grant (1994).

practically all else could be done by Communicators. The new council would thus employ perhaps 100 full time staff (including the Police).

Parliament Hill Fields and Hampstead Heath are at present looked after by The City of London Corporation, which replaced the GLC and has since erected rather threatening black notice boards with the City's coat of arms supported by gleaming silver dragons. It also rebuilt the cosy, very characterful men's sunbathing enclosure, dividing it into two compartments for the sake of some religious fanatics and their phobia about nudity. Anelog, who first went swimming there, in this Highgate Pond, in 1951, would have had it carefully renovated, retaining its familiar atmosphere. This galumphing City of London authority would have to relinquish open spaces like 'the Heath' and 'the Fields' to the new State: The Home Counties, one of the 12 new states into which Britain would be divided. These would have the autonomy of a country like Luxemburg, which is part of the Benelux affiliation and part of the European Common Market. Each state would have its own form of parliament, its anthem, flag, uniforms, its own style and holidays. The eleven new administrative centres or capitals might be: Winchester (Wessex), Exeter (West Country or Cornwall) Gloucester (Mercia), Cardiff (Wales), Norwich (Anglia), Leicester (the Midlands), Lancaster (Lancaster), York (Northumbria or 'York'), Edinburgh (the Lowlands), Aberdeen (the Highlands), and Inverness (the Islands). Each of these states would have its own postal service, its own coinage (which is interchangeable, in the way that a Jersey penny is different and in a way a Scottish pound note is legal tender in England), its own military regiments and public transport. The railways obviously would need to be run internationally and there need likewise to be agreements on defence, the detection of crime and the post office. Central offices would have to deal with such matters, which effect the island as a whole. It would, for instance, be madness to set up barriers between the different countries. A way would have to be found to replace the National Grid with alternative and attractive, local sources of power. Eventually the giant power stations may be demolished and the pylons thankfully be dismantled, clearing the countryside of these dreadful contraptions.

DEVOLUTION

The point of all this is that Wales, or Cornwall, or the Highlands will be able to revive their own specific culture and acquire confidence in their own national identity. A 'Senedd', or a 'Home Counties Parliament', a 'Diet', or whichever name each country would wish to give to its governing body, will be able to decide on its own national way of doing things, but will have to consult the other 11 when the matter concerns the safety and well-being of the 12. Internationally this is already happening, when Britain joined the Common Market, not only Ireland, but also Denmark did so too. When Britain changed its currency, Ireland did likewise and it is this relationship between Britain and Eire which shows the way. Naturally the relationships between the 12 new states would be closer and there would be a permanent co-ordinating office in one of the capitals to make sure that decisions were mutually beneficial. Damming a river may be good for one country but a disaster for its neighbour. There would have to be constant consultation and negotiation, but there would not be this terrible concentration of power in London: London would become merely one of the 12 capitals, that of the Home Counties. The House of Commons is a monument to Victorian heaviness, as buildings go it is good, but like the law-courts it has been the acme of the repression of true feeling and a veritable cesspool of unconsciousness. It allowed factory farming, over-population and our natural environment to be destroyed. A Water-Conscious government requires a meeting place which is light and lovely, a tall round building, a hall with many

tall windows and doors opening onto gardens. The Houses of Parliament belong to a hard and masculine, Fire-Conscious past, the atmosphere in them is stuffy and oppressive.

Perhaps the War Office, which is a really terrible building, full of terrifying passages, could be demolished to make way for the new Assembly Hall on top of a landscaped mound of rubble. We mean a wild, natural garden with our old favourite the Buddleia, with Elderbushes, London Pride and Cow Parsley, Wild Roses, Great Mullein and Rosebay or Fireweed. Here the representatives of the boroughs would meet in a new Lower House and also the Mediators and Nominators in a Second Chamber. Mediators would be magistrates, but in some ways they would resemble bishops and their female equivalent. Their diocese or area would be that of 6 boroughs (roughly the present area of 1 borough) and they would have graduated from the ranks of the Communicators, who in their turn would start as Inter-Communicators. Mediators would thus have a wide experience of community work and would be able to mediate in disputes, sort out difficult problems and preside over courts of law. A Nominator would have the right to nominate the Mediators, she/he would be appointed by the Principle Nominator, or Nominator Princeps, the head of the national government, and one of the Nominators. A Nominator would be associated with the county or shire and convene meetings of the Communicators and Mediators of the shire. There would be 7 Home Counties, which means 7 Nominators, one of whom, London, would be the Nominator Princeps. The 7 Nominators would be to the Nation of the Home Counties or 'Kent', what the 6 Communicators would be to the borough of Kentish Town. By dividing large counties, like Yorkshire into four parts (by creating a South Riding) and other big counties, like Cumberland in half (North and South) every new country would have 6 or 7 shires, except Wales, The Lowlands, and the Highlands which have 13.

By some strange circumstance, or chance, these are all magic numbers: 12, 13, 6 and 7 and add to the mystery and spiritual significance of this new arrangement. It is by means of conscious acknowledgement of our deeper and true feelings that the individual and the state, the free and the organized are reconciled. The order which comes from true feelings is magical and liberating. Government can thus, in a feminine state, be a confirmation of our inner selves and not an imposition we have to endure. This does not mean that masculine judgement and toughness are denied, they must be applied when a situation demands it.

There will always be thoughtless, criminal and dishonest attitudes which will seek to undermine the most liberal and fair-minded arrangements and they will have to be met with severity and force: Nazi Germany was an example. Kindness must never mean the denial of strength, or flexibility that of discipline. There will have to be an armed force, there will have to be prisons and battleships, but with a greater receptivity and understanding it will be possible to turn the youths who in present day society make the streets unsafe and go thieving, into soldiers. The prisons which we have inherited from the Victorians do not serve a useful purpose, but a highly disciplined regiment of soldiers does and can be used for tasks other than fighting. We suggest that there will be a Positive Force which will be the depository of all those 'yobbos' who now idly roam the estates and streets of our cities. In this Force, to which they are sent by the Mediator, they will receive the treatment they crave and can be drilled and trained to do useful work.

Essentially there would be 2 tiers of government: the borough councils and the state. It, of course, depends on local circumstances which offices and which departments should be where and whether particular departments of county councils, already recently created, should remain. We are personally familiar with the way Camden Borough Council functions and we are also acquainted with Cyngor Sir Gwynedd (Gwynedd County Council) and Cyngor Dosbarth Dwyfor (the Dwyfor District Council) in North Wales. It is easier for us to visualise a total change in London. The District Councils are too large and impersonal and should devolve, but *how* would be a matter of local concern. In Wales the national administration may well be divided, because there are, in effect, two capitals: Caernarfon and Caerdydd (Cardiff) and two ways of speaking Welsh. In South Wales more people have been Anglicized. Owain Glyndwr held the last Welsh parliament at Machynlleth in Mid-Wales and this is where a new National Parliament of Wales could well be.

A Nominator is the new head of the county civil administration of which the legal (Mediation), finance, education, planning and highways departments would remain. These departments would have to work in consultation with the borough (district) councils. A new road, school, or a proposal to close down, or otherwise change

A new road, school, or a proposal to close down, or otherwise change an institution, public building etc. would need the full approval of those who are affected by it, e.g. people who live nearby; there must be much more planning consultation than we have at present. Any new proposal by the county would be on the agenda of the local councils and those concerned should have the power to reverse an unpopular decision. The Nominators nominating the mediators are spiritual leaders, or guides, as well as temporal officers. They therefore would need special, very spiritual, but also human qualities. A quite new kind of person would emerge for this position, someone who is artistic, sensitive and graceful, yet objectively discriminating, as well as highly organized. He/she would be the final judge on the excellence or otherwise of any product and add the 'Nominator's seal' to it. This, an imprint or a label, would mean that a roll of cloth, a pot, or a piece of furniture, a loaf of bread or a jar of marmalade is good value and wholesome, or in good taste. Naturally the potter, baker, cotton mill or workshop would be allowed to add this seal to their product. Apart from possessing a profound aesthetic judgement, a Nominator should have a deep insight into the human psyche. It must be stressed that this is nothing to do with academic qualifications, but the result of an apprenticeship in Graigian community work.

When we use the term 'Spiritual' we are not referring to religious sects, a belief in God, an afterlife, or a moral code, but to something which unites all religion. We are thinking mostly in terms of the human psyche and the insight which the knowledge of the 12 Archetypes and 24 Types brings. In time this will not be seen as debatable, but as a proper and objective realization, a demonstrable fact; just as we now realize that there are microbes, or that we are part of an evolutionary process. There is not a single person who has learnt about the 24 Psychological Types – and there must be several hundred by now – who has subsequently disputed this understanding. It is having a very accurate key to the recognition of what lies below the surface of people's outward appearance, of how they are 'supposed' to be. Because it goes far beyond the usual way of looking at people: 'Men are like this, women like that' and all the conditioning that goes with this (boys don't cry), it requires some degree of self-development.

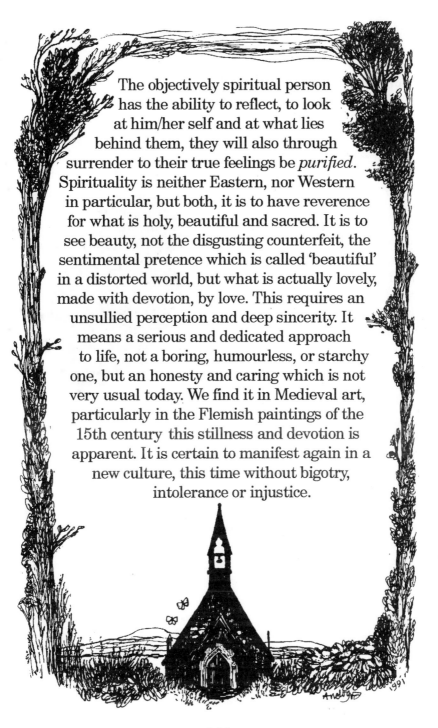

The objectively spiritual person
has the ability to reflect, to look
at him/her self and at what lies
behind them, they will also through
surrender to their true feelings be *purified*.
Spirituality is neither Eastern, nor Western
in particular, but both, it is to have reverence
for what is holy, beautiful and sacred. It is to
see beauty, not the disgusting counterfeit, the
sentimental pretence which is called 'beautiful'
in a distorted world, but what is actually lovely,
made with devotion, by love. This requires an
unsullied perception and deep sincerity. It
means a serious and dedicated approach
to life, not a boring, humourless, or starchy
one, but an honesty and caring which is not
very usual today. We find it in Medieval art,
particularly in the Flemish paintings of the
15th century this stillness and devotion is
apparent. It is certain to manifest again in a
new culture, this time without bigotry,
intolerance or injustice.

One of the many reasons for the general apathy and lack of expression, of life, is the contemporary insistence on being casual, or 'laid back' and putting everything in a 'low-key'. Everything that is publicly said and done has to be tailored for an inferior mass-consumption and be made to suit the common-denominator. 'In this day and age' it must be seen to be 'practical' and 'popular'. This means that an important and inspiring, a moving, aspect of life is neglected and negated. Without inspiring symbols, ceremonies and rituals life is pedestrian, flat and dull. The old religious and patriotic symbolism and forms of expression are associated with intolerance and 'jingoism', the rigidity and injustice of the past and no longer create an emotive impact. Church and state have therefore gone to the people and debased their already worn-out apparel to bring it 'up to date'. We need a new kind of unifying form which will excite religious fervour, a real enthusiasm and belief in life and the state which embodies it. These are not the denial of objectivity and relaxation, but their complement. People nowadays tend to be 'cool' at the expense of positive emotion and if they get excited at all it is in either a brawl or a row. Thus their enthusiasms tend to be ephemeral, connected with ideas and novelties and their beliefs disconnected from anything that might be deeply moving (because it is a universal truth), but in a multitude of suppositions.

When we do have national celebrations, the examples that are set, the visual aspects of the promotion, are worse than third rate. The enlarged colour-photographs of royal personages displayed in shops and people's windows, the souvenirs, the decorations and so on are in the taste of fifties Hollywood. The plastic flags and stickers must be most gratifying to the capitalizing manufacturers; the 'general public' doesn't love these things, they merely accept them and are meanwhile inwardly crying out for something which will really turn it on. The vast majority of people lost their roots, their culture, their 'folklore' twice: when they moved from their country background to the growing cities, from the 18th century onwards and the second time when the modern flats were built in between the 1960's and the 1980's, when 'modern', plastic, bourgeois tastelessness was copied everywhere. That time what was still left of their way of life, their honest heritage was abandoned: The simple wooden chairs and kitchen tables, the earthen crocks, all that was unpretentious and 'old fashioned', to find its way into the houses of professional and artistic people. Ever since then the vast majority of people has been deprived of any guidance, any standards, or criteria other than the prejudices of their daily papers and the advertisements, the soap operas and lives of pop-stars featured on the television and in highly-coloured magazines. People who possess discernment have no truck with all the plastic bunting, the artificial binge, the revels of a 'National Occasion'. Hypocritically they may pander to the idea of it, but no one is actually moved. When one reads in the newspaper that the most avid monarchist in the crowd watching a procession was covered in Union Jacks and even wore red, white and blue underpants, one realizes that a certain kind of popularism cannot sink any lower.

All through this book runs the theme of the example, we need excellence and nobility of 'being', not nobility associated with property and titles, but of character and presence to inspire and to heighten, elevate our consciousness. The single alternative to a monarch as the Head of State in a democracy is understood to be a president, one can either have a monarchy, or a republic in the world we have today. There is, however, another, a more wonderful alternative which we would want to be considered. This is a 'Principality' with a Prince(ss) Nominator, or 'Nominator Princeps' as Head of State. She/he is a Nominator chosen for life by the Mediators and the Nominators of a country, which choice the government is able to accept. Mediators (you may remember) would be nominated by the Nominators and appointed by the government as magistrates out of the most suitable Communicators. These are dedicated, spiritual social workers. Inter-Communicators are students, or helpers, who may be 'initiated' into the 'office' of Communicator. The Nominator Princeps is a 'Princess' or 'Prince' of the 'Salubriat', the spiritual body off this alternative. It is therefore a spiritual rank, like a Tibetan Lama or a Cardinal, a chosen ruler, who is acclaimed and celebrated with one voice by all the people. She/he, as we know, is an example of objective sensitivity and taste, of generosity and goodness, to reign and teach. This, like the life peer of our House of Lords today, is a 'Life' spiritual and constitutional Monarch.

THE FUTURE WILL BE GREEN

As we said before a quite new, almost unknown, kind of person will emerge for this position, like a butterfly from a chrysalis. He/She will be both feminine and masculine, a man or woman who is 'unconditioned', wise and will inspire love. In the 'modern' world such a 'Being' has no place and hides like a rare, wild creature in a remote and sympathetic spot, to develop courage, detachment and resilience. She/he will proceed with great dignity and presence, for he/she is an initiate, a saint, a complete and lovely human being. Nominators and in particular the Nominator Princeps would be worth listening to and watching. Perhaps we can compare her/him to an Indian Guru, in whose presence 'Darshan' is received, a blessing. Their elevation to this high position has been 'received' that is, arrived upon after searching, meditating and spiritual testing.

For many centuries, in our society, social eminence has been based on heredity, wealth and status. The idea that a person's 'being' should qualify her/him for office is quite revolutionary. 'Being' is not something which is generally understood, but most people would be affected by it. It is the quality of goodness, integrity and natural grace that emanates from a lovely, truly human person and bears no relation to their class, or race, or background, except perhaps to the sensitivity and 'goodness' of the family from which they come. It may be a family living on some wild common in which the children grow up with this quality. It exists in the most primitive of tribes as well as in old manor houses, and there should always be wild, untarnished nature and good feeling. The actual reverse is taught at schools and universities in our present day society, which aim at cultivating artificial attitudes.

At certain sacred places, an island in the Thames near Wargrave, a mount or hill near Aberdaron, at the far end of the Lleyn Peninsula in Wales, investitures and initiations in this very different, far off, sensitive society, take place. All the Nominators of the whole of Britain may come to an amazing, beautiful and holy tryst and make encampments there with banners, carved and painted caravans, mediaeval tents, dogs and horses to meet a new member of their 'college' and to celebrate their inauguration. The new Nominator is chosen from amongst the Mediators on the retirement or on the death of his/her predecessor and is given the Nominator's cloak of golden-yellow wool, hand-woven, with a fine light brown

This is a drawing of 'Lady Deeplake', the archetype of the soul or pyche
(℧Φ). There is a similar large painting in the 'Salubriat' at the Graigian
monastery, almost entirely in dark, mostly blue, colours. The cards are
the four aces for the four elements, the trees are poplars, associated
with this world.

linen lining. These colours signify brilliance tempered by restraint. All the Nominators wear blue robes or vestments on this occasion below their golden yellow cloaks and when the investiture takes place a hymn is sung in Gaelic, Welsh and English:

> *"Even so the sun shines in the mighty heavens*
> *Far, far beyond the swirling of the clouds*
> *So our chosen Nominator has a golden cloak,*
> *Falling brightly on her/his deep and gentle,*
> *soothing robe,*
> *Blue as water, blue as all that is mysterious.*
> *The glinting sunlight penetrates the water*
> *And reveals the truth".*

The sea is visible from several sides of the ancient, sacred mount, which has acquired an immense significance, where the Nominators are standing in a circle amongst the heather, gorse and bracken. The sun shines and a skylark rises singing in the gentle breeze. Then the Nominator who is here ordained and consecrated receives a staff of hazel-wood and also an embroidered purse to signify his/her worldly duties.

Ceremonies for the initiation of those who dedicate their lives to spiritual work, who may become novice monks, Inter-communicators and other kinds of acolytes, to install a new Communicator, or appoint a Mediator could be extraordinarily inspiring. Particularly the acclamation of a Nominator Princeps and their anointing would become a national occasion of great significance and be moving to a marvellous degree. This truly would have the splendour and mystery of the world of fairy-tales.

Once more the lovely, venerable cathedrals would come into their own. These were originally Roman Catholic and usually abbeys which Henry VIII appropriated and ransacked. They were built by master masons in a spirit which is said to have been inspired by esoteric understanding. Since the reformation their character was totally changed. Mediaeval Christianity was very different from the Church of England. There were many pagan elements and the statues of the saints embodied ancient deities. Its flavour is preserved for us in the Canterbury Tales and the carvings which survive in misericords and doorways. These are earthy and have an easy-going atmosphere which is like that of our own time; dress and behaviour were then, as now, casual and relaxed. In the Middle Ages people squatted on the floor of a church, suckled their babies and made a noise during mass (as the Irish, French and Belgians sometimes still do). It was altogether lacking in the self-conscious stiffness and restraint which has bound the English nation increasingly since then. Yet a natural, spontaneous and lively spirit will return! It may happen that the national religion will be once more reformed to serve a sweet and loving Mother, or a deeply wonderful and beautiful Goddess, rather than a stiff, old Patriarch and a colonizing Warrior. Its ancient churches and cathedrals may be graced by being given to a use which will revive the true and inner feelings of the people and set them free! Instead of smelling cold and musty they would then be warm and smell of incense and of beeswax. Everyone, should this happen, will flock to them for they will be dedicated to 12 Archetypes instead of only two. This must be the meaning of what the Book of Revelation prophesies and which has, until now, not been understood.

The National Government of the Home Counties at Westminster will in this future scheme be run by a Cabinet of Ministers, just as it is now and each Minister will be the Head of a Department. The Home Office will be concerned with the affairs of the Home Counties only and the Department of the Environment likewise, the Treasury will tax only the inhabitants of this new country and the other ministers, including the Foreign Office will be those of this national government. All the 12 National Governments in the 12 new countries will have their own entire system which is run in their own way. This means that there will be 12 Home Offices in Britain instead of one and 12 Foreign Offices and Ministries of Defence also and that the work of these offices is greatly simplified, but also the Diplomatic Service is totally changed. It would be common sense to have but one Embassy in China for the whole of Britain. This Embassy could have amongst its staff attachés from each of the 12 countries who report back to their own Foreign Office. Thus Welsh or Highland interests could be represented abroad. It may be time that the whole 'fuddy-duddy', hide-bound rattletrap was overhauled anyway. These institutions date back to the days of Queen Victoria as do their offices and are likely to have become very much patched up. We have not been inside the Foreign Office and cannot therefore suggest exactly how it could be made different, renewed or purified.

Taxation could be simplified greatly and with new governments, new methods could be tried. Each country would have its own legal system and code. The boroughs and the rural districts would become the new constituencies, sending a local council member as representative to Parliament with the consent of the majority of voters. He/she would be concerned with local interests and local people. The political divisions of today are likely to become meaningless in a Green Society, in which the vast majority of people is opened to the Inner Self. Centralised commerce, monolithic industry and huge bureaucratic structures have been ecologically disastrous and would not survive. Probably, should new political divisions arise, proportional representation of these would be married to the system of representing 'communes', or localities. MPs, however would have to live in the place they represent. The House of Lords becomes the House of Mediators and Nominators. The Lord

Chancellor will be one of the Nominators, but not the Nominator Princeps, who as Head of State can attend sessions of the Upper House, but only presides on state occasions like the opening of Parliament when she/he addresses both Houses, much as happens now. The 18th century image of such occasions will probably decline, the ceremony will become more spiritual than it is now, it will have a lyrical and dreamlike quality. It will be Water-Conscious and full of moving imagery and symbolism which may be quite unpremeditated. The stiffness and contrivance, which these occasions now have, will go.

The Prime Minister and her/his cabinet advise the Nominator Princeps who endorses all final decisions. He/she has no spiritual authority, which the Nominator Princeps possesses. The latter can withhold assent and has the right to intervene, whether it is over the colour of new bricks for a building or major educational reform. The Head of State also has an aura of sanctity which is at present not associated with that kind of position and can be compared to that of the Dalai Lama of Tibet. Like him, it would be quite out of the question for a Nominator Princeps to have a family, because she/he would need to give out so much emotional and creative energy to her/his country. He/she will represent a quite new and wholesome spirit. The House of Commons will have a new building – on the site of the War Office – and so will the House of Mediators and Nominators for their day-to-day business, but will still use the old Houses of Parliament on some occasions, in the winter, or for some special vote where the old procedure may be re-enacted. This developed over many centuries and is meaningful: the speaker on such occasions may still wear a wig and Black Rod will still knock at the door of the Chamber.

The Heads of State in our proposed system started as social workers, became magistrates and finally high officials, because this is what Communicators, Mediators and Nominators would be. This system also would bind the 12 countries together because the College of 100 Nominators, which would approve the election of any one of their number, would meet in convocation, or in conclave when it would have to choose one of the 12 Nominators Princeps as their 'chair'. This is the Nominator Princeps Prior who, should the need arise, can call together a general synod of all Nominators and all Mediators. English policy would be decided upon by a council elected from eight regional Parliaments and would bring its decisions to Scotland and Wales. In case of a threat to this island, an Emergency Council like a war-time cabinet would have to be set up.

With real de-centralization of government much of the civil service will become superfluous and local government officers will become truly local. They would be local people, who may even do some of their work voluntarily, as they now do on their local amenity, tenants' and residents' committees, preparing surveys and alternative schemes. Policing will be combined with social work and the policeman or woman becomes a member of the local community. The present troubles with criminals and terrorists might have been 'nipped in the bud', if a caring, but active local community had been interested in the potential hoodlum. Bureaucracy need not be one-sided, boring, remote and ugly. One office, with an enlightened staff, concerned with the community to which it belongs, can deal much more effectively with housing, health and other problems, than a dozen impersonal and bleak council or government departments.

CHAPTER 5.

SPIRITUALITY

T THE very best for the majority of people in the English-speaking world the idea of spirituality will probably still mean the practice of the Christian religion, a rather cold and bleak, unaesthetic but ascetic life in which love is preached but seldom visibly* present: in a sense an unbeautiful life. Those who lead it tend to regard themselves as holier, or on a higher level, than those who do not (and this in some cases may be quite true), whereas those who lead a 'normal' materialistic life, concerned with job, family, possessions, ambitions and sexual fantasies think of religious practices as a waste of time and shudder at the thought of entering a gloomy church. On the whole, in our society, spiritual people are sectarian and dogmatic, precious and even hypocritical. They do not have any positive effect on the rest of 'normal', run-of-the-mill, non-religious people who are concerned with 'having a good time', that is to say are 'hell-bent' on self-indulgence. There have never been so many people with nothing but money and sex to believe in as there are today and at the same time no society has ever had the same degree of social justice as Britain has now**. But although well-fed and adequately clothed, all these people are deprived of the kind of guidance and the kind of emotional climate, the environment in which human, rather than economic growth could flourish. The Christian religion fails to bring this about, and as a result we live in an extremely loveless, but broad and fair-minded country in which very few achieve any real fulfilment or happiness. Our modern culture is ugly; its forms are profane, its conventional costumes and customs dreary and its architecture and art a bad example to everyone. A spiritual revival is long overdue.

*Christian institutions seldom have a lovely atmosphere.

**This was written in 1976.

To be spiritual is to be devoted to the life of one's inner feelings, to self-perfection and ultimately the rejection of worldly and material pursuits. One can, however, be involved with everyday earthly business and *still* lead a spiritual life by remaining receptive and sensitive to the feelings of other people and aware of the pitfalls of egoism and self-deception. Spirituality does not necessarily mean the practice of a particular religion. One does not have to worship a god or goddess to lead a spiritual life; Buddhists, for instance, regard *only* man's Inner Self as potentially divine. A spiritual person is – by definition – very careful, considerate and devout, by devoting him or herself to the things, the places, the person, the images, the gods he or she worships. For many people in the world this has been or is a so-called guru and his teachings, the way of life he prescribes. Guru is an Indian word meaning a master; in this sense Jesus Christ was a guru and so was Socrates. The guru is surrounded by disciples, and they are wanderers, or live in an 'ashram', an encampment. Here the believers can gain 'darshan', for in India any man who has attained a certain state becomes a divinity, just as Jesus did for the Christians. Darshan is a silent blessing, obtained by sitting in the presence of a 'God-realised' person.

In England today many young people are turning towards a spiritual life which Christianity can no longer offer them. Hinduism has an extraordinary tolerance of differing opinions, in fact to the Hindu opinions do not matter frightfully; it is *beyond* opinion and *beyond* thought that eternal bliss is to be found; not in an

156

after-life either, but here, now. Hinduism is also exotic and colourful. In the last few decades there has been a growing fashion for Indian things. The Hare Krishna devotees became a familiar sight in the West End of London as they shuffled up and down the shopping streets with their drums and cymbals and their strange dress, chanting hypnotically. Then we had the 'orange brigade', the followers of Bhagwan Shree Rajneesh who dressed entirely in orange clothes. When someone becomes a follower of such a sect he or she in fact falls in love with the guru. They may have a sexual relationship with their boy or girl friend, but their real love, which they have in common with the other devotees, their deep, spiritual love is for their spiritual guide. To be able to give oneself totally to the guru, all one's love, physical, emotional and spiritual would not mean just a 'sacrifice' but also an act of laying oneself open to change, to becoming reborn, to shedding an old identity and growing into a new person. This is why spiritual teachers, 'gurus', will always lay great stress on surrender and submission to their love and their teaching or discipline. Their followers change their names, adopt certain mannerisms, ways of dressing and behaving, they will develop their own jargon, prayers and rituals and this gives them a sense of being different from other people and separate from the rest of the world, which they can thus convert or influence from their stronghold.

The image of Jesus and his 12 disciples is a prototype of this kind of devotion, where the guru or teacher demands total surrender, submission and undivided love. It is therefore only logical that the followers or devotees should have no spiritual or emotional attachment to anyone else. The relationship between guru and *chela*, or disciple, of whichever sex – because some gurus have been masculine-type (dard) women* and the disciple is more often than not a girl – is really a love affair. Usually the spiritual love felt for the deified master is separated from physical love, which creates a division between higher and lower emotions. The teaching is as a result full of admonitions, because it is easy to stray from the fold. Sexual feelings between master and disciples, although these are present and sometimes very strongly, are in most cases repressed for the sake of the group. The master must show no pre-

*'Dard' will be fully explained later in this chapter.

ference to avoid jealousy and therefore will be careful to emphasize his detachment from desire and possessive passions.

Many spiritual leaders and original thinkers have been the same psychological type; this is characterised by a heavy face, large, expressive eyes, a powerful, dominating personality and a tendency towards corpulence. Rabindranath Tagore, Leo Tolstoy and Karl Marx all looked like old Testament prophets, G. I. Gurdjieff had a large, dome-like head with heavy features and a strange intensity in his eyes. They naturally attract, like a stag his herd of hinds, their sexual opposites: psychological types who need to relate to a father-figure, who yearn for security, because they are naturally frail and weak* and wish for guidance and support. Christ's disciples are quite wrongly depicted as fatherly and masculine types.

After the demise of the Master his most devoted disciples will carry on The Work. This consists of all the vestments, relics, rules, exercises, myths, legends, prayers, books, rituals and buildings which have grown up around the Master so that the teaching is perpetuated and his name is kept alive as the focal point of a religion. Christ, Buddha and Marx all started off wishing to disseminate ideas about the improvement of mankind. None of them saw themselves as potential icons or idols or hugely enlarged photographs to which future generations would bring offerings, light candles and pray, or sing ecstatic hymns of praise. They were all three concerned with imparting to their followers basic precepts about behaviour and relationships. In the case of Christ it was that we should love each other, in the case of Buddha that we should give up our desires and in the case of Marx that we should co-operate. All three doctrines have led to a terrible onesidedness; Christian love becomes sentimental for lack of objectivity and helpless through lack of strength, Buddhist detachment becomes remote because it denies the emotions, and Marxist equality becomes faceless because it lacks character and refinement. In terms of colour, the Christians are too wishy-washy turquoise, the Marxists too

**With this we mean naturally reflective or thinking-types who will try and make themselves strong, not the conventional stereo-typed idea of weak-willed individuals who succumb to some hypnotic influence.

militantly red and the Buddhists too dry and neutral (off white or pale grey, although their monasteries and temples are most gaudily decorated). A religion which combines these three elements and manages to incorporate a hedonistic, pink and purple element as well would be ideal!

For the seekers of today there are a number of 'alternative' bookshops in places like Camden Town and Brighton where an extensive literature on every kind of occult society and esoteric teaching is for sale. There are equally alternative spiritual centres in Gloucestershire and in Scotland where mostly young (and often American) men and women congregate on their quest. One of the most prominent schools at the moment is that of Gurdjieff. His teaching was first promoted by Ouspensky in England and later by J. G. Bennett in his Institute at Coombe Springs in Kingston-on-Thames and in an academy at Sherborne in Gloucestershire, after Coombe Springs was given away to the Sufis, whom Mr Bennett considered to be Gurdjieff's spiritual 'ancestors'. Unfortunately Idries Shah, who was the recipient, shamefully sold this old house and grounds to

developers. Sherborne too, since Bennett's death in 1974 has been taken over by the Sufis who have a farm and centre, called Beshara, nearby. Sufism is an Islamic spiritual movement which originated in the Near-East, where Gurdjieff is said to have travelled extensively in his youth, encountering many remarkable teachings and remarkable men.

Gurdjieff's own teaching is based on the assumption that man is normally mechanical and asleep. When this state of sleep can be broken, some other, greater life becomes possible, when we are awake. This implies breaking down barriers in ourselves and between people; most politeness and conventional helpfulness is designed to stop people having a real effect on each other. Gurdjieff distinguishes between inner and outer considering; in the first case you are only considering your image, your identity and how you appear to others, in the second you are genuinely aware of how other people are and what they really need. Crucial in the Gurdjieff work is 'self-remembering', the awareness of one's physical presence in a situation. Once you are aware of yourself walking or talking in a habitual or mechanical way, 'being asleep', or living in a 'dream', you can do something about it. Similarly, when you observe that someone needs help or that an accident might occur you can take steps to intervene. Through being emotion-  ally alive and yet observant you find yourself and become real. Many of our readers who may not have had anything to do with self-development may find this particular approach to life very strange and yet it can bring about a radical change in one's consciousness. During the late fifties, Mr Bennett introduced a new element into his institute, a new guru. This was Pak Subuh, an Indonesian who had been teaching in Java since 1935 when, as happened at different times to gurus before and after him, he had a mystical experience. This led to a ritual which is performed by him and his helpers known as 'opening', when through an act of submission and surrender the participant becomes a channel for the 'life-force'.

At Coombe Springs an imaginative hall for Gurdjieff's exercises had been built. It was called the 'Jami' and is the prototype of what we, earlier in this book, have called a 'Hallowhall'. The exercises or movements were designed by Gurdjieff to liberate various energies in the body which are never normally felt because of our Western conditioning. To these was now added the 'Latihan' of 'Subud', an abbreviation of Susila Budhi Dharma, or the Law of Great Virtue Derived from Truth. The 'Latihan' (an Indonesian word for exercise) does not follow a pattern; Pak Subuh (his surname is coincidental with the name of his organisation), did not believe in any particular method. He asked only that his followers surrender to the life-force, but they are in theory encouraged to practise their own religion, for the Latihan of Subud is meant to be an addition, a kind of stimulant, a re-inforcement. However, the kind of people who are attracted towards Subud tend to have no specific beliefs and many Subud members became converted to Islam, the religion of their spiritual guide, or began to practise a kind of Subud religion of which Bapak (as Pak Subuh is called) became the god.

The Latihan is meant to be totally spontaneous, a movement from within which is allowed to express itself. Someone who is opened and enters into the exercise with a group of people – the sexes are segregated – in a carpeted hall, dimly lit, is surprised by what happens to him/her and may sing, or dance, or move about, squat or lie down in an unpremeditated way as the 'spirit' takes her or him. It is very personal and many of the Subud followers felt themselves transformed and their lifestyles altered, not because they were taught anything, but because their outlook on life was changed from within.

Mr Bennett, who was the St. Paul of the Gurdjieff movement, found it impossible to serve two masters and when Pak Subuh demanded that his helpers should practise no other exercise he gave up promoting Subud which became a separate organisation. Similarly, Rudolf Steiner's Anthroposophy and the Krishnamurti Foundation Trust are break-away organisations from the Theosophical Society, whose founder, Madame Blavatsky, like Gurdjieff, was Russian, spent her youth in the near East and travelled extensively. She was also embarrassingly eccentric and not above very dubious behaviour, but she did open up avenues which in the fuddy-duddy Victorian world would otherwise have remained closed. She bridged the gap between East and West; between Christian tradition and an objective interest in not only psychic phenomena, but also mystical psychology. She made Europeans aware of Hinduism and is therefore one of the first exponents of the marvellous compendium of alternative religions and spiritual practices we now have. Just as Darwin broke the ground for biology, so Madame Blavatsky pioneered a territory which was later made respectable by Carl Gustav Jung. Together with books on Gurdjieff and on the

Tarot, Jung's writings, or books about him, feature prominently on the shelves of alternative bookshops. Both Gurdjieff and Jung wanted people generally to become conscious of their nature and behave in an unaffected, unneurotic way; they wished to liberate the West-Europeans from their artificial conditioning. In this they were pioneers; Indian gurus like Bhagwan Shree Rajneesh, who attract a following in the West are trading on the mystique of their Indianness and are otherwise treading in the footsteps of these two European Masters, or Prophets.

Jung called the process of becoming conscious of one's true, but often deeply buried feelings, 'individuation'. His outlook was totally different from that of Gurdjieff whose work is about the reconciliation of the Emotional with the Detached self or sides of the personality (the Actress or Lover and the Observer) through the Body and the Outer, whereas Jung's work is about the reconciliation of the Carefree with the Careful Self (the Fool and the Wise Old Woman) through the Head and the Inner [What this means will explained later in this chapter]. Jung is concerned with the 'Unconscious', the inner world of dreams and visions and the interpretation of its symbolism. Although Jung and Gurdjieff were active at the same time (the former in Switzerland and the latter mainly in Russia and France) during the first half of this century, because their approach to self-development was so different, they never met and could never have seen the relevance of each other's work. Yet both have an equally important and potent message for mankind. Jung says: "Look inside yourself and you will discover a wealth of symbolism, which when objectively understood can give your life meaning, depth and fullness. The psyche is a treasure chest which contains not only the jumble of your own experiences and reactions, but also the mythology of mankind". Gurdjieff says:

"Look at yourself and observe and remember what is going on, wake up out of your 'sleep' and you will develop extraordinary powers, you will become efficient and effective and you will feel fully alive, you will acquire 'Being'". Their lifestyles reflected these two opposing ways, Jung sedately and reflectively in a tower built by himself beside a lake, peering into ancient treatises on Alchemy, and Gurdjieff living haphazardly from day to day on money scraped together by all sorts of strange means at his school for the 'Harmonious Development of Man' in the Prieuré, a château near Fontainebleu which he had leased.

Gurdjieff's work is practical and concerned with skill and being able 'To Do', being capable and adaptable, not becoming totally lost in involvement, (being 'identified') or remaining conventionally apathetic ("pouring the emptiness into the void")*. Gurdjieff wanted people to be alive to the situation in which they found themselves and not to escape into habitual behaviour. The emotions must be outward-going, not suppressed but put into physical action and the awareness should be in the body. That is to say you must become aware of your movements. He was forever inventing schemes to put his pupils to the test, building that extraordinary study-house at the Prieuré for instance, or making a Turkish bath. He loved to shock and surprise, to tell outrageous stories and make preposterous claims. He fooled his pupils and called them idiots, he confused them with unpronounceable, invented words like 'Hanbledzoin', 'Kundabuffer', 'Being-partkdolg-duty' and 'Harnel-Miatznel'. Everything and anything to wake them up. He was funny and unpredictable, taking his pupils on perilous journeys and confronting them with unfamiliar problems: arriving at a hotel after midnight and making impossible demands – a meal for 30 people – embarrassing everyone and yet creating out of a potentially dreadful situation a memorable and joyous occasion.

Jung's Psychotherapy is derived from Freudian analysis in which the 'patient' relaxes on a couch and is encouraged to talk about his feelings, to associate ideas with images from his dreams, or memories which re-occur, or with words which seem significant to the analyst. The subconscious or unconscious mind, the inner feelings of the 'patient' become liberated, 'The Fool' (the liberated self) is spilling out secrets from the psyche while 'The Old Woman' (the methodical and experienced self) is making sense of it, and carefully sorting it all out and storing it away. Jung had noticed in his practice as a psychiatrist that various symbolic expressions kept cropping up amongst his patients and that these were similar to

*This is a Gurdjieff phrase.

certain myths from ancient religions and distant tribes. He thus formulated his concept of the 'Collective Unconscious', the 'feeling-mind', unconsciously expressed - where there is no interference from the censorship of conditioned consciousness - in what people throw away, or drop, or spill, or reveal when they forget themselves. There is a symbolic language common to all ages and all peoples: fire always glows and is always hot and to the primitive mind a most extraordinary, dangerous and magical thing; water is always soft and flowing, transparent and wet, these are the first experiences of any child. Fire is therefore to everyone who thinks about it symbolic of all that is fierce and energetic; a fiery person is lively, whereas someone who is watery drifts along. Jung distinguished two general types of behaviour which follow from this basic difference, which he calls extroverted and introverted, outward-going and inward-looking.

Although it is possible to divide people between those who are concerned mostly with the external world, their environment and politics; and those who are mostly preoccupied with their own state, their own feelings, this is more a question of outlook than of type. Jung also observed that people generally have a natural disposition towards one of four 'functions'. He defines these as 'thinking, feeling, sensation and intuition'. These definitions are explained in a book by him called 'Psychological Types', in which he divides each of his four 'functions' into an introverted and an extroverted form, thus ending up with 8 psychological types. Although Jung's descriptions of these types may in some cases seem apt, they are nevertheless not generally successful.

In 1960 it was found by a number of people working together, using Jung's theory, that it is more accurate to speak of earthy and instinctive as opposed to airy and intellectual, watery and sensitive as opposed to fiery and resilient, rather than using Jung's confusing terminology. It was then discovered that human nature corresponds to 12 'Archetypes'. This concept of an 'Archetype' also derives from Jung, who however did not make any comprehensive definitions, and one ends up by being rather confused about the exact meaning of this mysterious entity. For instance, he mentions the 'Trickster' but not in relation to its opposite, the 'Anima', the Dreaming Lady of the Deep.

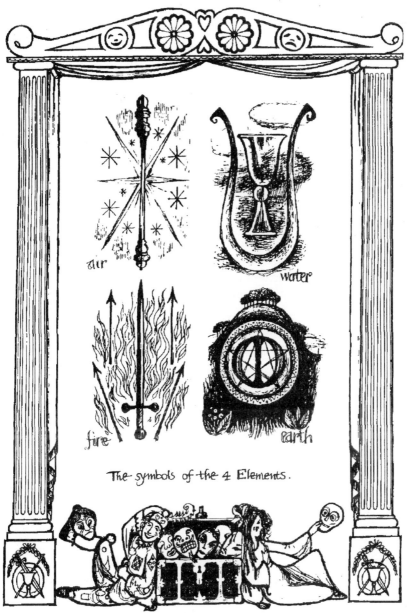

The symbols of the 4 Elements.

The symbols of the elements as described overleaf. The masks in the chest are of 5 archetypes, while the boy and the girl hold 2 others. They are from left to right: Old Mother Careful (Φ✴), Maresbun (Φ↑), Roth (↑Φ), Deeplake (℧Φ), Frostbeard (✴℧), Goldlight (✴↑) *and* Twilight (✴Φ). *The boy represents* Carenought (↑℧) *and the girl* Rainbow (℧↑).

165

By associating Archetypes with colours and with the four elements a much clearer picture emerged of each distinct figure. These figures are not to be compared with astrological signs and neither are they human beings, but aspects of human nature deeply embedded in the 'Collective Unconscious' and therefore meaningful to anyone who is at all in touch with him/herself.

Archetypes appear in myths and fairy tales, as gods, goddesses, heroes and heroines. The 'Patriarch' archetype, for instance, figures as God the Father as well as Father Christmas (Saint Nicholas, or Santa Claus). In fairy tales he is represented as 'the King', in Greek mythology, by Zeus; the Romans had Jupiter and the Teutons, Wotan.

Everyone is naturally one of 12 things: someone is essentially critical or accepting, curious or instinctive, rebellious or sweet, spontaneous or careful, playful or dreamy and emotional or detached. We are all inwardly and unconsciously compelled to compensate for these natures by developing their opposite characteristics. The naturally critical person needs to be accepting and will therefore react against his own intolerance, the naturally rebellious person does not like his own harshness and tries to efface himself and be kind. These conflicts within the psyche can either be reconciled or avoided. Psychological types were now defined by placing the four elements or ingredients into 24 different orders: A person who is essentially critical, that is to say has the Patriarch (Father or King) Archetype as his essence; is *air* (✳) first, *water* (℧) second, and then can be either *fire* (↑) third and *earth* (Φ) last, or vice versa. The Patriarch has the elements air and water ✳ ℧ which is frozen water, snow and frost. Air without fire is cold, water without earth is crystal clear. This gives us the symbolic imagery for the world of the Patriarch, a cold, clear, crystalline world of forms, pictures, writing, definitions and knowledge, judgements and theories.

Each of the 12 combinations of 2 elements gives us similar imagery; ℧ ✳ is mist or dew, clouds (water in the air), ℧ Φ is the sea, a river or a lake (water on the earth), ℧ ↑ is boiling water and steam (water in fire), ↑ ℧ is a discharge, thunder and lightning (fire in water), ↑ ✳ is hot air, heat (fire in air), ↑ Φ is a volcanic outburst (fire in earth), Φ ↑ is a brick, earthenware or rock (fired earth or earth in fire), Φ ✳ is dust (earth in air), ✳ Φ is the globe or the horizon (air on earth), ✳ ↑ is light, a flame (air in fire). Anyone who is able to associate ideas logically can connect symbols with imagery: Φ ∪ is mud and this is fertile soil, compost, a mixture, integration, roots, growth, settlement, vegetation, vegetables, fruits, baskets, crafts, weaving, wood, etc. To the imaginative reader this presents a 'world', a frame of mind or an atmosphere, a mood, a rhythm one gets into when one is gardening or making things out of natural materials, the world of 'Mother' nature, organic growth, forests and fertile soil.

AIRY ✳ WORLDS

	HERMIT ✳① DISTANCE	MAGICIAN ✳↑ LIGHT	KING ✳∪ HEIGHT	
WINTER	Air surrounds the earth or objects and creates the feeling of space, detachment, objectivity.	Air makes fire burn brightly creating light by which we can see, inquire, ask questions and analyse.	Air turns water into ice, preserving forms, making patterns and shapes, letters, books rules, knowledge.	**HEAD**

WATERY ∪ WORLDS

	PRINCESS ∪✳ SMALLNESS	ORACLE ∪① DEPTH	LOVER ∪↑ CLOSENESS	
SPRING	Water makes the air moist, forming mist and dew creating a tranquil atmosphere. The surface of the water reflects images.	Water on the earth creates lakes and seas where all life begins. In the depths of the water mysterious creatures swim and treasures are lost.	Hot water boils and creates steam causing movement, emotion, expression, theatre and drama.	**INNER**

FIERY ↑ WORLDS

	FOOL ↑∪ SPEED	TRICKSTER ↑✳ EMPTINESS	HERO ↑① BIGNESS	
SUMMER	Fire makes the water explode causing thunder and lightning, a discharge of energy a release, letting go.	Heat makes the air rise creating wind, is resilient and playful, play leads to skill and invention.	Fire in the earth is a volcano, an eruption, creation, strength, a mighty warrior.	**OUTER**

EARTHY ① WORLDS

	MOTHER ①↑ LOWNESS	WITCH ①∪ DARKNESS	GRAND MOTHER ①✳ SLOWNESS	
AUTUMN	Earth mulls the fire creating warmth, cosiness, conviviality, friends, family, the herd.	Earth turns water into mud, compost, creating fertile soil, growth, woods, continuity, settling.	Earth in the air creates dust which covers, collects, keeps, retains, boxes, security.	**BODY**

We are thus defining psychological types in terms of an arrangement of the four elements. The world of the first and second elements denotes someone's essential nature; that of the third and last elements the personality they are likely to develop. The third element in this arrangement of four elements becomes the pivot of this personality and will unconsciously affect every aspect of one's life. This usually is at the expense of the opposite 'worlds'. A boy who is of the following type: ✳ ℧ ↑ Φ who is essentially an airy, critical, thinking type, has fire third and earth last. He will therefore tend to 'live' in the three fiery 'worlds':

↑ ℧ spontaneity, abandon, freedom and negatively impulsive and extravagant behaviour. A flash of lightning travels from the thunderclouds to the earth, just as ↑ ℧ denotes an energy which goes from the head to the body and releases tension. The archetype is a Fool, who is generous and open-hearted, 'Carenaught', a wild, unreliable and rampant spirit.

↑ ✳ inventiveness, play, skill, cleverness, resilience and negatively cynical, malicious behaviour. Hot air and sparks rise from a fire and ↑ ✳ denotes an energy which stimulates and teases, experiments, seeks diversions and provokes reactions. The archetype is an Inventor, a Trickster, who is ingenious and manipulating, 'Sparklewheel', a playful, superficial and resourceful spirit.

↑ Φ action, force, energy, power and negatively aggressive, destructive behaviour. A volcanic outburst, or a forest fire is voracious and expansive, ↑ Φ denotes an energy which possesses all one's blood and body and gives one confidence. It is relentless, pushes on and fights. The archetype is a Worker, a Warrior, who is courageous, overpowering, 'Roth', a fierce, determined and an explosive spirit.

168

He may identify with these three 'worlds' at the expense of their opposites:

Φ ✳ method, restraint, commitment, security and negatively mean and repressive behaviour. Dust collects, chokes and covers all things with a monotonous and drab grey. The ash contains the fire which needs to be held in to serve us, dust or sand prevent the fire from spreading and deaden any fallen spark. The archetype is a Wise Old Woman, who is careful and considerate, 'Old Mother Careful', a slow; reliable and thoughtful spirit.

℧ Φ receptivity, appreciation, depth, sensitivity, intuition, grace and negatively morbid, credulous and pathetic behaviour. An expanse of water, the oceans, mountain lakes, or lochs have great depth into which the wrecks of many centuries have sunk, all that has fallen to this dark and mysterious world is like the 'unconscious' of mankind where it meets with what has evolved there since primeval times, the strangest forms of life. The archetype is a Dreamer or a Miraculous Madonna who is sincere and   truthful, 'Lady Deeplake', a graceful, soulful and a serious spirit.

℧ ✳ reflection, imagination, surrender, charity, softness and negatively weak, precious, spineless and helpless behaviour. The surface of the water mirrors all that is around it, dew is associated with what is beautiful, small and fragile, a spider's web, a blade of grass, a flower, mist softens and creates a dreamy atmosphere and clouds take on fantastic forms and are associated with imagination. The archetype is an Angel, a Fairy, who is peaceful, pure and kind, 'Dawndew', a sweet, gentle and a soothing spirit.

Unless he is able to reconcile the three masculine, fiery spirits

169

with their feminine opposites, he is likely to be wild and careless (for lack of restraint, Φ ∗), dishonest and cynical (for lack of grace, ℧ Φ) and cruel and destructive (for lack of charity, ℧ ∗). These are the characteristics of '*fire third*' and until he is made to reflect on his actions, brought back to himself, experiences his inner feelings and slows down, such a boy will be impure, 'smelly', unappreciative and rash. When he says he loves a woman, he means that he needs comfort and mothering, for of real love he knows absolutely nothing, no matter how much he makes a show of it. This denial of feeling and emotion is called in *Natural Psychology* 'water in the box', for when Kenneth Carter first saw this amazing phenomenon he drew a box around the second element: ∗ ℧̄ ↑ Φ. He said: "There are two conflicts within each type; one between the 'personality', or 'ideal self' and its opposite the 'essential' or 'real self' (someone's nature)", in *this* case ↑ Φ, Φ ↑ and ∗ ℧, ℧ ∗. "The other conflict is between what we will call the 'usual self' and its opposite, what we will call the 'shadow self'", in this case ∗ ↑, ↑ ∗ and Φ ℧, ℧ Φ.

↑ Φ is action and Φ ↑ is acceptance, combined they are the physical world. ∗ ℧ is judgement and ℧ ∗ is reflection, combined they are the literary, poetic world. It is the conflict between the worldly and the unworldly; awareness and unawareness, the 'higher' and the 'lower'.

∗ ↑ is analysis and ↑ ∗ play, combined they are the world of computers. Φ ℧ is nature and ℧ Φ deep feeling, combined they are the 'collective unconscious', the totally feminine aspect of instinct and intuition, an old, mysterious world. It is the conflict between the conscious 'bright', modern, streamlined, metallic mentality and the 'unconscious', organic dream-like and fairy-tale forest, the undercurrent, mysterious and dark, 'shadowstained', textured and magical.

Kenneth Carter, a graduate in history of Lincoln College, Oxford, had met Anelog there in 1956. That summer Anelog experienced a rebirth in the Thames at Wargrave on the way from Oxford to London. He had already understood that the vowels A and I expressed and symbolised masculinity and the vowels O and U, femininity: Dynamic words like hard, fast, hall and army, or angry are 'A words'; ice, identity, intellect, spire and think are 'I words'. Round words like hole, hollow, post, roll and pot, or whole are 'O words'; cup, vulva, under, undulate, humour and human are 'U words'. He saw the upsilon, or water sign, in the sky at night and knew it was a cup, or a receptacle, the sign from which our letter 'U' derives and means receptivity. A number of such synchronistic happenings led to heightened consciousness, a total and enlightening change which made him grow into quite a different person within the next few years. He went to live in Hampstead, where he had lived before, and in 1960 Kenneth Carter came to live in the same house on Christ Church Hill. Here in a little attic room from which one could still see St. Paul's cathedral in the distance in those days – this view is now, no doubt, obscured by tower-blocks – after reading Jung's 'Psychological Types' and reflecting on the notes Anelog had made during that period of his life, Carter realised the truth about the types. There are in fact 24, instead of Jung's 8 types, 12 types are 'dard' and 12 'voy'. These words were invented by the authors of this book to avoid the confusion, consternation and even shock the terms 'masculine' and 'feminine' types arouse. A voy man may behave in an aggressive, 'macho', heterosexual way and many male 'voy' types do this, to say that they are 'feminine' would cause misunderstanding, but those with 'eyes to see' can understand that such a man is voy because he would *fulfill* himself if he could *relax* and 'be himself', i.e. surrender to his feelings and the life-force.

In December 1960 Anelog moved to Kentish Town, on the other side of Hampstead Heath, to the house which is now the Graigian Monastery. He was joined there by Carter and a group of friends of whom some were painters and three graduates of St. John's College, Cambridge which, strangely, had owned the land on which this house in Lady Somerset Road is built. Here the understanding of the types and archetypes developed. Anelog was the first to see how the four elements combine to create 12 images which have given countless similes to the English language: stick in the mud, head in the clouds, airy-fairy, hot-air, bright-spark, letting off steam, bubbly, a flow, a torrent, tempestuous, down to earth etc. Unconsciously common sense had, from time immemorial, seen the analogy between natural phenomena and human traits. The 'analogues' are quite astounding (the name Anelog, though, comes from the Welsh verb 'anelu' which means to aim; pronounce the "e" as it is in sent, or scent and stress it; to be aimed, or guided, is anèlog) but not everyone, only people who are awakened to the Inner Self can appreciate the full extent of the amazing revelation which combining the four elements affords.

This work has continued ever since and is now entering its 34th year. The house in which all four floors, converted into flats, were rented was bought by the two authors of this book in 1974, together with a friend, who sold his part to them in 1979. Until the monastery was founded in 1983 a great deal of their time was spent in building work, pulling down partitions and putting in recycled Victorian doors and new windows. They also built a pottery in the garden entirely of recycled materials and repeatedly experienced periods of magical and heightened consciousness during which they came to understand exactly what the six polarities, or conflicts within the psyche of mankind consist of and how these dualities are reconciled. They saw that these correspond to 6 dimensions, 3

environmentally conscious worm ——>

of which we are familiar with: length, height, breadth, (or, if you prefer, distance, degree and circumference) and 3 which are unfamiliar: content, speed, weight (or capacity, time, density).

Everything within our solar system can be measured with these 6 dimensions by using various devices, like a clock or a ruler, showing how basic, true and applicable the 12 'worlds' are, which also give an explanation of the symbolism in the 'Book of Revelation' which describes the 'Holy City' as having three gates on each of its four sides and the 'tree of life' which 'bare twelve manner of fruits'. C. G. Jung recalls a dream, described fully in the Introduction to this book, but so significant that it is worth repeating, in which he found himself on a gold Renaissance chair in a magnificent Italian loggia where a white bird descended and changed into a little girl who played with his children. When she changed into the bird again she said: "Only in the first hours of the night can I transform myself into a human being, while the male dove is busy with the 12 dead". Jung was unable to find a solution to this enigma and writes: "All I knew with any certainty was that the dream indicated an unusual activation of the unconscious. But I knew no technique whereby I might get to the bottom of my inner processes and so there remained nothing for me do but wait, go on with my life and pay close attention to my fantasies". What has been discovered about these '12 dead', like all world-shattering discoveries; that of the solar system, of microbes and of evolution, causes, because of rigidly held assumptions, misunderstanding, disbelief and negative reactions.

The last element in the alignment which defines a type of person, for anyone of any type, denotes the key to their fulfilment. It is what he or she grows into, that which he or she must be, or needs to be to reach maturity, be whole, confident, at ease and natural. In a society in which *fulfilment* is not the aim of life, the idea of it is hard to grasp. For the boy (or girl, or man, or woman for that matter) of our example type: ✳ ☊ ↑ Φ, it is:

Φ↑ submission, acceptance, relaxation, tolerance, warmth and negatively slavish, ignorant and lax behaviour. A fire warms the earth and bakes it solid; around the hearth a tribe, or group of people, congregates with their cats and dogs. The archetype is a Mother, someone who cooks food and feeds the baby, is basic, 'down to earth' and practical, 'Maresbun', a cosy, comforting and friendly spirit.

Becoming at one with this spirit means submission, which is to be humble and agree with, obey, or follow someone else. To be earthy in this way means having *no* authority, to be under, or below one's master/mistress, like a horse below its rider. This has sexual implications, for one partner derives pleasure from being in control, the one who is *Dard* and the other from being dominated, who is *Voy*, each fulfil themselves that way. Very often, though, because of conditioned rôle-playing the voy man acts the leading part in his *fire* or *air third* and the dard woman subjects herself to this in her *water* or *earth third*.

This creates a neurotic situation which is gone into in Chapter VI, 'Sexuality'. The boy who is ✳ ℧ ↑ Φ usually wants to be 'earthy', combines this with being 'fiery' and will show this by his dirty clothes, his job on a building site, on a farm, as a mechanic, or he will want to go about as a Gypsy with a horse and a van and be a 'hippy'. Until he can really, truly surrender to his feelings and submit to sensible guidance he will be inwardly unhappy and unfulfilled.

'Dard' and 'Voy' are NOTHING to do with the two sexes, superficial, 'normal', masculine, or feminine rôle-playing, conditioning, or behaviour and with being 'gay' or 'lesbian'. Large, solid-looking men and women on the whole are dard; small, slender men and women are usually voy. Some voy persons may be tall and even fat, but they will have narrow shoulders and small, usually pretty faces. Dard persons often have larger, rougher faces (the Duchess in 'Alice') and broad shoulders even when they are small. To know whether someone is 'dard' or 'voy' is a question of feeling. Voy people (including women) may 'put on' a masculine, assertive/aggressive performance and 'dard' people (which includes 'camp' men), a feminine one. Dard persons have *air*, or *fire* as their last element, voy persons *earth* or *water*. We are all attracted to the types who have the elements of our 'essential self' as their last two elements. Someone who is ✳ ℧ ↑ Φ has two voy 'opposites' with *air* third (Φ ↑ ✳ ℧ and ↑ Φ ✳ ℧). There is a vicarious, sensual attraction between 'opposite' voy types and, because of this, marriages and sexual relationships occur between them, usually because *neither* of them have experienced true love, or want to be sexually involved with someone who is going to be serious about the relationship. In what 'Natural Psychology' calls 'the Outer', 'the Incon World' or 'the mechanical society' people are NOT expected to fulfil themselves, they merely follow fashions and play up to each other, they don't become whole, in all four elements, live in 12 worlds and discover their real feelings. Our teaching hasn't reached the majority of the people yet because the leaders of politics, unions and industry, the journalists and editors who run the world are usually types who deny feeling and have their 'water in the box'. A psychological type, as we saw, with water second ('in the box') tends to be unreceptive, goes against his own feelings and represses his emotions. This phenomenon is not confined to water second types only, because of the 'conditioning' most children receive in a world without true feeling. Many men, particularly, are not in touch with themselves and find it difficult to express their emotions. It will, however, be seen that the most destructive, cynical and indifferent of men and women have *water second*, or 'in the box'.

The type we used as our example: ✳ ℧ ↑ Φ, has ✳ ℧ as his/her nature. This makes him/her rather critical and didactic as we shall see when we look at their other 'opposites'. These have *water third* (℧ 3rd) and *air last* which means that they are Dard. Their first two elements are either earth (Φ) or fire (↑), thus: Φ ↑ ℧ ✳ or ↑ Φ ℧ ✳. These types are fulfilled by having authority and being fully aware and conscious in:

✳ ℧   judgement, knowledge, discrimination, discipline, perfection and negatively dogmatic, opinionated, stiff and intolerant behaviour. Air (without fire) is freezing cold and crystallizes water into ice, this is severe, strict and rigid, preserves all that has been gripped by it and makes patterns on the windows or snowflakes which are crystals with wonderful six sided forms. These are like signs or symbols, the shapes we use for writing. Snow covers all the landscape with a brilliant white, revealing by their imprint who or whatever went there. Anything stands out against it and, on the highest mountains it is always present. The archetype is God, the supreme Father Figure with hoary, snow white beard, the Patriarch, or King sitting on his throne in judgement infallible and just 'Frostbeard', an all-wise and commanding spirit.

Here we have the bearded patriarch type, that of religious leaders, Greek and Russian monks and priests. Many writers, painters, sculptors, architects and actors are amongst it too, Albrecht Dürer, Augustus John, Tolstoy, Renoir, Rodin and Peter Ustinov, for instance. In fact there are two types who are thus fulfilled, one with Earth, the other with Fire first: William Morris, Dante Gabriel Rosetti (both in love with the same woman) and other Pre-Raphaelites *always* painted portraits of their 'opposites'. We see the faces of youths and maidens who have ✳ ℧ ↑ Φ and ℧ ✳ ↑ Φ in their pictures. Boticelli is another painter who painted the lovely faces of these types and so did Leonardo and Michael Angelo who used their voy apprentices as models.

The Patriarch/Matriarch types have either ↑ or Φ first, that is to say their nature is either that of ↑ Φ or Φ ↑, the Warrior, or the Mother archetypes. Someone who has ↑ Φ ℧ ✳ is essentially, or naturally, a blustering, breezy type, noisy and explosive with a hearty appetite and laughter, but is *water third*, self-indulgent, soft and credulous, taken in and victimised by his/her opposite should he/she fall in love. He/she has to learn to be independent in:

✳ Φ   detachment, objectivity, attention, stillness and with types which have this negatively, indifferent, callous, unresponsive and pedestrian behaviour. The air surrounds the globe in space and air, sky and earth meet at the horizon; this we associate with distance. The archetype is an Observer, some one who is distant and impassive, 'Twilight', a calm, cool and 'collected' spirit.

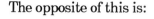

The opposite of this is:

℧ ↑   emotion, involvement, attachment, expression and negatively subjective, self-indulgent, clinging, self dramatising and dependent behaviour. The fire makes the water boil, causing

movement, bubbles, a stir and steam. The archetype is a passionate Lover, some one who is romantic and responsive, 'Rainbow', an excited and a colourful spirit.

The *earth first* patriarch/matriarch (Φ ↑ Ʊ ✳) is essentially or naturally a friendly, practical and easy going type. He/she also has the faults of Ʊ 3rd accentuated by the *fire second*, or fire 'in the box' [↑]. This means a lack of energy, giving this type a tendency towards being rather passive. Being slow and quite methodical he/she has an aptitude for crafts, upholstery, woodcarving, making furniture and weaving, unlike the other type with ✳ last, the ebullient, foody 'character' who 'lives in the Fool' (↑ 1st and Ʊ 3rd) and has *earth second*, or Earth 'in the box' [Φ] which means that the virtues of 'Old Mother Careful' in particular are absent:

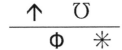

↑	Ʊ	: Usual self
Φ	✳	: Shadow self

which makes this type unorganised, rash, hasty, careless and unmethodical.

The other aspects of [Φ] 'in the box' are a lack of tolerance, which leads to snobbery, tension and high-handedness and a lack of:

Φ Ʊ integrity, simplicity, artlessness, naturalness, instinctiveness and with types which have this negatively sloppy, sleepy, 'stick in the mud', habitual and unconscious behaviour. Water turns the earth into mud and with fallen leaves and refuse this turns into fertile compost in which plants and trees

can grow. This is the organic world of roots; insects, birds and animals in which humans settle to cultivate the soil. The archetype is a gnarled, old peasant woman or Old Witch, or someone who is close to nature and full of character, 'Fertility', an unchanging and a drowsy, heavy spirit.

177

The opposite of this is:

✳ ↑ Analysis, precision, clarity, change, discovery, speculation and negatively artificial, restless, interfering and complicating behaviour. Flames feed on air which increases the brightness of the light they give. The sun is a ball of burning gas. Light gives us sight and by this we can distinguish everything around us, a child asks: 'What is this and that?' We find out and by pulling things to pieces we discover more, examine, prod the myriad substances and matters and penetrate the mysteries. The archetype is an Alchemist or Wizard, or someone who is brilliant and forever searching: 'Goldlight', an inquisitive and ever-changing spirit.

The 12 worlds and archetypes are given in the chart opposite. Briefly they can be described as:

Masculinity	**Femininity**	**Dimension**
Distant: the factual, dry world.	*Close:* the romantic, stirring world.	*Length*
Light: the scientific, bright world.	*Dense:* the natural, muted world.	*Density*
High: the academic, formal world.	*Low:* the ordinary, relaxed world.	*Height*
Fast: the erratic, shocking world.	*Slow:* the methodical, orderly world.	*Time*
Empty: the commercial, slick world.	*Full:* the psychic, mysterious world.	*Capacity*
Big: the competitive, hard world.	*Small:* the spiritual, gentle world.	*Breadth*

* Φ	∪ ↑	* ↑	Φ ∪	* ∪	Φ ↑
impassive	passionate	intellectual	organic	formal	informal
to be calm	to be stirred	to be conscious	to be settled	to be correct	to be relaxed
parchment	purple	brilliant yellow	dark brown	sharp yellow	warm brown
attention	emotion	interest	instinct	authority	submission
an observatory	a paradise	a study	a forest	a cathedral	a tribe
'Twilight'	'Rainbow'	'Goldlight'	'Fertility'	'Frostbeard'	'Maresbun'
OBSERVER	ACTRESS	SEEKER	SLEEPER	FATHER	MOTHER
HERMIT	LOVER	WIZARD (magician)	OLD WITCH (mother nature)	KING (patriarch)	SUBJECT (slave)
Saturday	Friday	Sunday	Tuesday	Wednesday	Thursday
space	waves boiling water steam	light	darkness	ice	ground the hearth
stillness	movement	sight	digestion	crystallization	warmth
detachment	attachment	change	continuity	discrimination	acceptance
objectivity	expression	analysis	integration	significance	necessity
independence	involvement	precision	growth	judgement	practicality
serenity	love	clarity	rest	perfection	comfort
birch tree	linden tree	beech tree	elder tree	ash tree	chestnut tree

↑ ∪	Φ *	↑ *	∪ Φ	↑ Φ	∪ *
spontaneous	methodical	inventive	receptive	expansive	reflective
to be free	to be committed	to be clever	to be sensitive	to be active	to be peaceful
pink	grey	orange	deep blue	bloodred	soft green
abandon	organisation	play	intuition	strength	beauty
a riot	an establishment	a game	a trance	a task	a shrine
'Carenought'	'Old Mother Careful'	'Sparklewheel'	'Deeplake'	'Roth'	'Dawndew'
FOOL	KEEPER	TRICKSTER	DREAMER	WORKER	VIRGIN
LIBERTINE	WISE WOMAN (old woman)	PLAYER (joker)	THE MIRACULOUS MADONNA (enchantress)	WARRIOR HERO	ANGEL (child)
Friday	Saturday	Tuesday	Monday	Thursday	Wednesday
lightning	dust	heat	water a lake	lava a fire	dew a cloud
speed	conservation	resilience	depth	force	tenderness
release	restraint	ingenuity	appreciation	conquest	surrender
life	care	technology	mystery	acquisition	sacrifice
vivacity	reliability	convenience	grace	confidence	sanctity
fun	security	skill	truth	power	purity
elm tree	hazel tree	pine tree	poplar tree	oak tree	willow tree

✳ ∪	*Height:*	The Father Archetype symbolises		*the highest* (most elevated: i.e. God)
Φ ↑	"	"	Mother	"	"	*the lowliest* (most humble: i.e. the Earth)
↑ Φ	*Breadth:*	"	Hero	"	"	*the largest* (most powerful, or strongest)
∪ ✳	"	"	Fairy	"	"	*the smallest* (most gentle, or weakest)
✳ Φ	*Length:*	"	Observer	"	"	*the furthest* (most detached, indifferent)
∪ ↑	"	"	Lover	"	"	*the closest* (most involved, dearest)
↑ ∪	*Time:*	"	Fool	"	"	*the quickest* (most liberated, freest)
Φ ✳	"	"	Spinster	"	"	*the slowest* (most bound, restrained)
∪ Φ	*Capacity:*	"	Dreamer	"	"	*the deepest* (most profound, sincere)
↑ ✳	"	"	Trickster	"	"	*the emptiest* (most superficial, clever)
Φ ∪	*Density:*	"	Sleeper	"	"	*the heaviest* (most weighty, substantial)
✳ ↑	"	"	Seeker	"	"	*the lightest* (most brilliant, awake)

We have attempted to explain how 12 dard types relate to 12 voy and how this relates to 12 worlds and their archetypes, using a particular polarity, that of ✳ ∪ and Φ ↑ and a particular type as our example. This shows that founders of religions and their acolytes, Buddha, Jesus Christ, Mohammed, one may assume, and certainly Gurdjieff, Bhagwan (Osho) and Maharishi were, and are, types who fulfil themselves in ✳ ∪, the Patriarch. Their chief acolytes are their voy opposites who submit themselves in Φ ↑ to find fulfilment and follow their admired Lord whom they worship and

adore. The same is true of the relationship between a great many
Abbots and their monks. In other spiritual communities, for instance the 'Whirling Dervishes', the acolytes revolve around the
Master. Karl Marx and Leo Tolstoy are two outstanding examples
of these patriarchal types and amongst kings Edward VII is typical of ↑ Φ ʊ ✳. What their opposite types call love, what they are
looking for is warmth and cosiness, they want a mother (Φ ↑) and,
strangely, will see their genial, benign and quite often pot-bellied
lover thus. What they love in him is the Mother archetype, but
with a woman of the same type this is more obvious. What the
dard person calls love is worship and he/she sees his opposites as
adoring angels. This is how the image of God, the Father 'in heaven,'
surrounded by his angels came to be embedded in the 'collective-
unconscious of mankind'.

There are two other dard types with *water third*, those who
have fire last: ✳ Φ ʊ ↑ and Φ ✳ ʊ ↑. These fulfil themselves in ↑
ʊ, abandon, in being carefree, 'the Fool' who is shocking, funny
and exuberant. Their opposites are *air third* and earth last and
are thus studious, in search of answers, Sphinx-like and rather
silent; they are looking for security in Φ ✳ and fulfil themselves in
becoming committed. Jung was ✳ Φ ʊ ↑ and one is struck by the
fact that nowhere in his autobiography does he talk about relationships with other people and that he is happy to loosen all ties
and bonds until he is on his own, in a room he made for this purpose, where he can be totally free, at Bollingen. Like all types with
ʊ 3rd he was attracted to the arts, the theatre, literature, the
spiritual and psychic worlds.

The teaching profession, the academic and the scientific worlds,
libraries, bookshops and the civil service are the domain of *air third*.
Farming, gardening, building (many young, casual labourers are
↑ third Φ last, the picture by Holman Hunt called 'Work' shows
several of these types) and ordinary businesses are run by men
with *earth third*. Advertising, snazzy and dynamic or cut-throat
business, horse and car racing, television, journalism, pop-music,
stardom and crime attract *fire third*.

There are four dard types with *earth third*: two with fire last
and two with air last:

✳ ʊ Φ ↑, is a usually a tall, thin, military type, like Sherlock

Holmes, often gawky and drawn to athletics, mountaineering and travel, or if not, languages. These people hide their feelings and can be quite perverse.

℧ ✳ Φ ↑, is an adventurous type, a daring businessman, a pioneer or a cowboy, but has also a strong psychic side. Air 'in the box' causes difficulty with factual, formal or intellectual matters. These people can be childish and subjective, Φ ℧ (in their usual self) causes them to become keen gardeners. Essentially they are poetic and imaginative and can be romantic.

℧ ↑ Φ ✳, is a quiet, careful type. When not in the usual Φ 3rd. occupations; farming, carpentry, commerce, the veterinary and dental professions, these people are often musical and famous musicians and conductors belong to it.

↑ ℧ Φ ✳; most modern politicians are this type and also factory-farmers, they fulfil themselves in ✳ Φ, the Observer. The conditions of the modern world are favourable to these dard men in

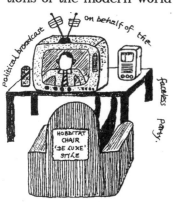

particular and their calm detachment furthers their ambition (↑ Φ, part of their usual self). Wilson, behind his pipe, Gorbachev, presidents Carter, Kennedy and Clinton, Churchill, Kruschev and Bevan all share the down-to-earthness which made, and makes, them popular. Their ↑ 1st gives them the resilience, energy, confidence and stamina they need to stand up to pressure. Because they are the followers of established doctrines, customs and conventions they go down well with the electorate who hate originality, thus they have done absolutely nothing to change the world, although they are its leaders, win wars, sign treaties and decide upon momentous policies. They are not visionaries and neither are they distinguished by their taste, their discrimination, or their style. In George Orwell's 'Animal Farm' the inspiration comes from an old boar called 'Major', but it is 'Pig Napoleon', true to his human namesake doubtlessly the type in question, who becomes the hero of the revolution. In Russia, Lenin, a sly man, was the *Voy* alternative: ↑ ℧ ✳ Φ, like Jeremy Thorpe, most probably Tony Blair and many women politicians, like the 'Iron Lady', Mrs. Thatcher. Stalin, the man of steel, was ↑ 3rd., like Hitler (dictators are usually Φ ℧ ↑ ✳). When the situation became more relaxed in Russia, Kruschev took over and in spite of blusterings and bangings calmed down the warlike situation.

These politicians' wives (also of the quiet, careful, sensible type ℧ ↑ Φ ✳, usually NOT in politics), are *fire third* and water last and see life in terms of ↑ ℧, ℧ ↑, energies, moods and movement. The natural self of one of these is ✳ Φ, objectivity and stillness, the Φ is second, 'in the box', which means that they dislike all practicality (Φ ↑), dirt (Φ ℧) and commitment (Φ ✳), whereas the other type (Φ ✳ ↑ ℧) is robust, earthy and unlike the former, not intellectual at all, in fact inclined to let others do their thinking for them (The Queen Mother is this type, so was Lady Churchill). There are two more voy types with *air third*, one of these (↑ Φ ✳ ℧) is quite imperious and superior, regal and refined and the other (Φ ↑ ✳ ℧) more sociable and homely (The Queen is this type); and two dard types, studious men who are either serious and sensitive (℧ Φ ✳ ↑), or heavy, ponderous types (Φ ℧ ✳ ↑), according to their natures. Edward Heath is an example of the latter. The *fire third* variants have these natures but are dynamic – the proverbial sergeant-major, earlier we mentioned dictators (Saddam Hussein) – or are exuberant and emotional with ℧ 1st. and Φ 2nd. Their opposites have *earth* or *water third* and have ✳ ↑ (analysis) or ↑ ✳ (play, skill) as their essential natures. These types are attracted to the arts and crafts, can be psychic and keen gardeners which their dard partners are not. The ones with ↑ first are like Puck and may be very funny. All these types are described more fully in Anelog's booklet 'Natural Psychology', soon to be published as *The Psychology of Fulfilment* in an extended form.

Anyone who is in touch with his/her feelings should know whether he/she is 'dard' or 'voy'. A dard type feels fulfilled by masculinity and has no truck in posturing, the display of toughness by a pretty boy, the 'wild' example we first used, because this is a denial and a suppression of their femininity rather than its complement. The 'male chauvinist' and the yobbo understand nothing about femininity and are frightened of it. The football hero might be only concerned with his own prowess, and a display of masculine strength which totally contradicts what is in his heart. He may very well indeed have a secret wish to be beaten on his bare buttocks and be subdued by a master, or parade in frilly pants before his mistress! We will develop this theme more thoroughly in our chapter on sexuality, but it must be emphasized that the man who needs to display his masculinity in order to feel that he is acceptable to others does this to hide his femininity; a dard man may do the reverse and be so much immersed in his feelings (particularly if he is 'gay'), that he is not conscious of his unrealised masculinity. Most people will – although with guilt and shame and in secret – be aware of their sexual fantasies and of the rôle which gives them the greatest pleasure. Even here, though, there may be self-deception at work; homosexuality has been taboo for so many centuries that it is surrounded by more hypocrisy, misunderstanding and prejudice than anything else, and the idea that a fully developed human being should be both masculine and feminine is quite new. Boys are made to feel that they should not be 'pansies', 'fairies' or 'poofs' and girls that they should not be 'butch': the greater the pressure to become a replica male or female example specimen, the more 'conditioned' someone is, and therefore unreal, unnatural and repressed, the more difficult it will be to know their type.

Typology, being able to tell which type someone belongs to, is the most dramatic and extraordinary part of the discovery made in 1960. Yet ironically it is the part which can least help people to develop inwardly. Understanding psychological types is only possible if one starts by taking a serious interest in the 12 'Worlds' and their Archetypes and what these really mean. Then one can observe their presence or absence in oneself and in others. This psychology is not primarily designed for clinical use. It is meant to give general insight into the human psyche so that people might be able to understand themselves and their relationships better. It is not a theory because it is based on observations; it is demonstrably true and anyone who cares to become involved in it will recognise its value as a profound and remarkable discovery. It cannot be used as a game, and any attempt to glibly answering the question: "What type am I?" will prove to be ineffectual. It is no use at all to be convinced that one is a type one is actually not, or even to get it right and not to be able to relate to this knowledge. Real self-discovery begins with a sincere wish to be honest and therefore devoid of all pretence. This will lead to the development of an independent mind, which in turn will bring about discernment and insight.

People with such an awareness often realise that certain colours have meaning to them and that certain combinations harmonise and others conflict. An obvious example is vermilion against a deep blue background which will seem to jump up and down, or oscillate if you look at it for more than a few seconds; blood red against emerald green has the same effect. Psychedelic pop posters in the 1960's used this device. Vermilion is a colour we associate with heat (↑✳) and blood red with anger; action, danger etc. (↑Φ), blue we associate with water and emerald green with freshness and Ireland, a watery, misty country (℧Φ and ℧✳). The colours of the 12 worlds are shown in the diagram on page 186 as well as the associations with the 4 seasons; those with the 4 directions are shown on page 187.

The colours of ↑✳ and ↑Φ, the 'Outer', fire, conflict with the colours of ℧Φ and ℧✳, the 'Inner', water. This is reconciled by the neutral colours of Φ✳ and ✳Φ the Wise Old Woman and the Observer, that is to say fear and awkwardness (negative ℧✳ and ℧Φ) are overcome by becoming calm and preparing oneself properly, by method and by being organised. The fire must be guarded and confined and the water detached and still, separate and on its own. The Outer has to be 'in the old woman' and the Inner 'in the observer'. To reach the inner from the outer we have to give it space, be still and meditate. To reach the outer from the inner we have to use restraint. The more we hold ourselves in, 'pull ourselves together', the more we will gain confidence and become resilient enough to cope. There are thus objective reasons why certain colours harmonise and are in 'good taste', for they show that aspects of ourselves are reconciled: Bright red and crimson look lovely against a background of greys and ochre and blue or green against ivory; or parchment. This reconciliation can be 'in the head' (Buddhism) or 'in the body' (Yoga).

The head (✳↑, ✳℧) and the body (Φ↑, Φ℧) are reconciled by ↑℧ and ℧↑. Pink and violet bring brilliant yellow/white and sombre dark brown/black together. The one (↑ Ʊ) abandons worry, undue consideration and tension, attitudes and prejudices, the other (Ʊ ↑) moves, inspires, stirs and motivates the sluggish, torpid, apathetic, dumb and downtrodden. Thoughts and discoveries must be moving, inspire and excite and our physical existence unbound from bad habits and compulsions, unrestricted in the way we should function naturally. The head must be in love, or 'in the lover' and the body 'in the fool'. We must express moving thoughts, questions and opinions and allow what happens in the body, thus a releasing energy (↑ Ʊ) will run down the spine, make us shake and feel relaxed, or a reviving energy (Ʊ ↑) will go up and make us tingle with excitement. Browns look wonderful against pink and golden or greenish yellow 'sing' against violet or purple. This reconciliation can be 'in the Inner' (Christianity at its best, which is about love and freedom and the master who is the servant), or 'in the Outer' (Socialism); both, with their original fervour.

The emotions (℧ ↑) and detachment (✳ Φ) are reconciled by ↑ ✳, ↑ Φ and Φ ↑, Φ ℧. Violet and parchment (or purple and cream) are a disgusting combination, violet or purple against red sings and parchment, grey or cream against brown is natural and good. The emotions must be in the 'Outer', to give play, or action motivating energy, like the steam in an engine; and the awareness must be in the body. In natural conditions it is not good to go about with one's attention on the rag-bag of ideas and thoughts that are passing through one's mind; to be 'in the head', as so many people in our urban culture are. To be 'in the body' means to be present, to experience where one is and what is happening around one. This is to be in possession of oneself, to be truly independent and aware of the emotions that are passing through one's body. A bad emotional condition is cured by relaxation (Φ ↑) and rest (Φ ℧), after which an objective state returns; negative detachment ends when activity and play take over, when a effort is made (↑ ℧) or excitement and stimulation (↑ ✳) shake someone out of it and bring about emotion.

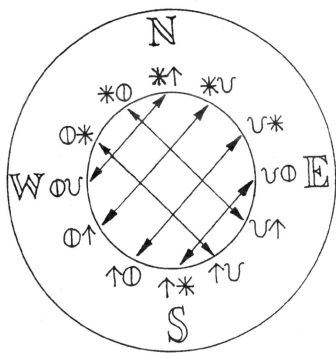

Restraint (Φ ✴) and freedom (↑ ʊ) are reconciled by ✴ ↑, ✴ ʊ and ʊ ✴, ʊ Φ. Light-brown or ochre against yellow is amazing, whereas against pink it 'swears'; pink against blue or green is magical. Negative restraint, a self-conscious, inhibited and hide-bound state, concern and cares, disappear when it is possible to surrender to liberating, stirring or moving feelings, to allow one-self to experience these feelings and give way to sounds and move-ments which come spontaneously from within oneself. Negative freedom: dispersal and chaos, must be disciplined and sorted out: ✴ ʊ, ✴ ↑ combined with ʊ ✴ and ʊ Φ are 'waterconsciousness', the making conscious of what is hidden in the inner depth, the un- or sub-conscious. This was mentioned earlier in this chapter, as was the reconciliation of emotion (ʊ ↑) and detachment (✴ Φ), which can be either fast in ↑ ʊ or slow in Φ ✴. Teutonic paganism with its Walhalla and warrior gods and witchcraft with its emphasis on the body are concerned with this reconciliation. Waterconsciousness, which reconciles restraint and freedom can be in the emotions (ʊ ↑) or in detachment (✴ Φ), the latter would be psycho-analysis or therapy, the former to do with art and magic, the occult.

All this is connected with the liberation of the True Self which is 'Inner Freedom'. Psychic liberation leads to the kind of experience which distinguishes spirituality from religious observance; it also makes possible the discovery of psychological truths. One such truth is about 'closed' and 'open' states. To be 'closed', or' identified' is to be 'in the head', this, as we saw earlier, has to be 'in the emotions' and these 'in the outer', play, inventiveness and action are fired by enthusiasm, love or a passionate desire and this needs to be tem-pered by restraint: 'the outer in the old woman'. For thoughts to be clear, correct and coherent we must think in a careful way which is to have 'the old woman in the head'. We therefore speak of six

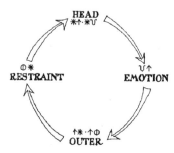

The 4 conflicts and their reconciliations

'closed worlds' which, as is shown in the diagram, relate to each other in a cycle which runs clockwise. To be 'open' one must be attentive, look and listen 'in the Observer', this must be relaxed and restful 'in the body' and that uninhibited and free 'in the fool' and that 'in the inner', bringing memories and unconscious feelings to life. These worlds relate to each other in a cycle which runs anti-clockwise and together form a selfless state, one of sainthood, or of the blissful and ecstatic experience of the mystic which entertains no dogmatically held notions, but whose utterances may lead to new religious beliefs. Mohammed had all manner of things revealed to him and so had St. John. Many Muslims and Christians, who have become believers of such revelations, just like the Pharisees, merely go through a number of ablutions, rites and ceremonies.

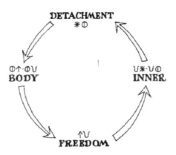

Orthodoxy, although it is a superficial approach once the form has become devoid of content, tends to have a modifying effect on the general behaviour of a religious community and lends it a certain character and style which our present-day society, having no unifying culture, lacks. When a particular religion becomes established and identified with the State, however, and when it is associated with repressive power, it becomes intolerant of deviations and revisions and religious wars or persecutions are the result. In this kind of emotional climate spiritual discovery tends to be driven underground. In our own age, with its laxity, unlike the gloomy, repressive 17th Century, for instance, there is an upsurge of spiritual experience which, because any formal way of preserving it is not present, tends to dissipate itself.

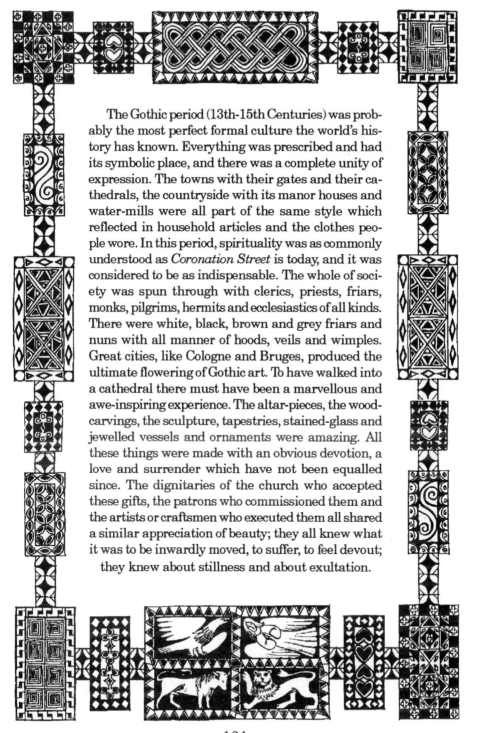

The Gothic period (13th-15th Centuries) was probably the most perfect formal culture the world's history has known. Everything was prescribed and had its symbolic place, and there was a complete unity of expression. The towns with their gates and their cathedrals, the countryside with its manor houses and water-mills were all part of the same style which reflected in household articles and the clothes people wore. In this period, spirituality was as commonly understood as *Coronation Street* is today, and it was considered to be as indispensable. The whole of society was spun through with clerics, priests, friars, monks, pilgrims, hermits and ecclesiastics of all kinds. There were white, black, brown and grey friars and nuns with all manner of hoods, veils and wimples. Great cities, like Cologne and Bruges, produced the ultimate flowering of Gothic art. To have walked into a cathedral there must have been a marvellous and awe-inspiring experience. The altar-pieces, the wood-carvings, the sculpture, tapestries, stained-glass and jewelled vessels and ornaments were amazing. All these things were made with an obvious devotion, a love and surrender which have not been equalled since. The dignitaries of the church who accepted these gifts, the patrons who commissioned them and the artists or craftsmen who executed them all shared a similar appreciation of beauty; they all knew what it was to be inwardly moved, to suffer, to feel devout; they knew about stillness and about exultation.

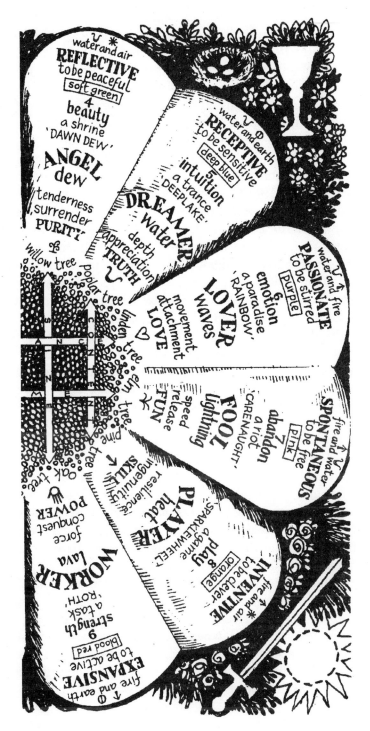

THE FUTURE WILL BE GREEN

With the decadence of this culture in Germany and the Netherlands came the Reformation and a new secular art inspired by the Italian Renaissance. The equivalent of the Gothic lifestyle, as a cultural phenomenon, in our own time is the 'progress' of technology which reached its zenith at the beginning of this century and has since lost its purpose. The more significant discoveries which have changed the world were made between 1700 and 1900 – (Leonardo da Vinci had already, before then, made drawings of helicopters and submarines). Electricity was discovered in the 18th Century and the 19th Century saw the internal combustion engine, telegraphy and sound-recording, as well as photography and the telephone. The 20th Century has merely perfected and popularised these things, which, just as relics, indulgences and all the other paraphernalia of religious life in the 16th Century, have become commonplace, shabby and distasteful. Therefore we can with good reason assume that there will be a momentous reaction to them and the culture which is based on their maintenance.

All through the Gothic period various reforming movements occurred without having the success Luther and Calvin achieved. William Morris who wanted a return with Socialism to an agricultural (and spiritual) society was before his time, just as Huss and Wycliffe were in the Middle Ages. Most people at the beginning of the 16th Century would still have assumed that the authority of the institutions of Roman Catholic Christendom would remain unchallenged and would endure forever as they knew them, just as people today believe that the progress of mechanicality and the development of technical wonders in the industrial society will continue *ad infinitum*. In social terms mass-production has played an important role in making consumer goods available to everybody. In cultural terms however it has brought about a dissemination of bad and dehumanising values, leading to a spiritual void, a deadening of the emotions and a numbing of sensual perception. The Fabians and other founders of the Socialist Movement imagined that once the working class had been emancipated and social justice had been established, when the soot and grime had been removed, people would naturally lead a good life. William Morris in *News From Nowhere* does not take human psychology into account and assumes that in a rosy future people would respond to their egalitarian conditions and their clean environment in a loving, sensitive and grateful way. He is a firm believer in procreative sex (and a bit of a male chauvinist), and yet nowhere does he foresee that with better living conditions and improved medical care, overpopulation, an urban sprawl, or at least congested 'housing' would be inevitable. The first advocates of birth control and of a serious approach to non-procreative sex will have statues as big as the Albert Memorial erected to their memory and the persecution they suffered in their fight against prejudice, stupidity, ignorance and the repressive attitudes of Church and State.

The impending reaction against mechanicality will endure and gain massive support because our society and all its works have become decadent. The products of our factories and farms are shoddy, flimsy, unhealthy, polluting and bad. Nylon, plastic, polythene, PVC, oil and expanded polystyrene are contaminating our open country and our beaches. Their use should be strictly limited, but they are the mainstay of British industry, an industry which is neither providing enough work, nor producing what is really necessary for a good life. Young people who realise this are beginning to buy second-hand clothes even, often made 40 or 50 years ago*, which are now becoming fashionable. Our own kitchen utensils and our furniture were found abandoned 20 years ago* or picked up in junk shops at that time. These were things made at the beginning of this century when quality still existed: now they have become valuable. The people who threw these things away to buy modern furniture instead, at great expense, to go with their 'tellys' and their new flats, are, now that they have worn out their second set of plastic, finding out that they were mistaken, just as those silly housing committees and planning officers of the late fifties and early sixties are now discovering that skyscraper council flats are a disaster. The 'long-haired aesthetic cranks' – a perhaps dated conventional name for people like ourselves – have turned out to be right at every turn, mostly because they were guided by intuitive feeling rather than by trendy egoism. This is why a reaction against the technological cult will meet with a genuine and general response when the generation born before, during, or soon after, the Second World War is no longer in control. No one with

*This was in 1976.

any real sense believes in this sort of 'progress' any more; those who do are either cynical or totally unimaginative.

The new, spiritual society which will come about in the next 30 years will be based on seriousness, this means that 'Another Way of Living' will have reached the hearts of another generation who will be sick of games and humbug * and wish to live by sharing and co-operation. Their style and fashions will hark back to simple, earthy peasant cultures: the extraordinary thing will be that the life of the poor cottager at the turn of the century, so despised by the conventional world today and painful to those old men and women who grew up in it, will become generally attractive to a younger generation. They will, out of their own choice, return to a form of poverty, wearing torn and patched clothes of hand-woven material, dyed with vegetable and natural dyes. This will be fashionable and they will love to think that the wool they wear has come from sheep they keep themselves or from a farm they know well, and that the flax for their linen was grown in a familiar field. They will walk barefoot as some girls already do, or wear simple leather sandals or clogs. The pavements of our city streets are often littered with broken glass because a swinish 'fire third' way of life still has the upper hand; this will not be so when sensitive people are able to have influence. Eventually, as sensitivity replaces crude materialism, the whole of our society will be vegetarian, although fish will still be eaten. A spiritual culture means that the majority of people has been given a conscience and that they have been made aware of the pain, suffering and fear that an imprisoned animal must endure, not just in the slaughterhouse, but also in knowing, for surely it must know, that the men and women who look after it will eventually betray it. This is a point which is not understood or appreciated generally yet, but it

*On the 30th of December 1987 the Church of England still condemmed homosexual practices; it did not condemm the effects of industry which destroy our natural environment.

196

will and when these things are shown on television many people will not want to eat meat any more and dairy farming will change drastically. We shall still keep cows and sheep and there will be oxen, but the atmosphere surrounding this will be oh, so very different! Agriculture will have become part of our spiritual life and it will fulfil another purpose, just as manufacture should. We will have to accept that foods, or materials, of excellent quality are not cheap and that it takes more trouble and time to produce them (Please see Appendix I). There will be poverty, if poverty means the absence of a glut of inferior and ugly stuff. Luxury is very much a question of what you value. For some it is luxury to sit on an outdoor, primitive and ramshackle lavatory with the door open to a deserted valley watching the sunrise, the dewy grass, the spiders and the soaring kestrel. This kind of poverty means relinquishing all bourgeois standards which, unfortunately, peasants and labourers have aspired to because they were made to feel, by the middle classes, that their own natural life-style was inferior. To those who are truly gentle and noble this sense of inferiority is alien and to them old and natural things are beautiful. When there are no longer any class-distinctions based on property and people are recognized for their inner, spiritual qualities, status-seeking and status symbols will be as dead as the Dodo. A new and very simple life-style will evolve, but one which is not at all puritanical and does not deny the body, colour and excitement. The reconciliation of the six conflicts will mean a magical ability to be both methodical and organised, yet free and eccentric, to work with one's hands, to dig and grow vegetables, and yet to do work involving the intellect also. Integrity and simplicity which are the ingredients of a solid, secure and homely en-

197

vironment and which have been mentioned all through this book, continued to exist where there had been no disruptive changes until the last war, but have since been modernised out of existence. This modernisation, which went into full swing in the 1960's (the swinging 60's, remember!) was really a kind of holocaust.

All that is valuable to a noble spirit was, like the proverbial baby, thrown out with the bath-water. The instigators of this destructive binge were (and are) 'qualified experts' who advise local authorities and industrial concerns. These people aim at efficiency at the expense of any human values, and they totally disregard the qualities of any existing situation. Often planners and architects working on redevelopment schemes know nothing about the history, the character or the nature of the area they are dealing with. As a result an entire estate of many houses and flats was built on sagging soil which had been dumped there over a century before and is now subsiding and breaking up these houses. Material considerations (so called 'feasibility') are put before common sense and feeling. It is all part of a stage in the evolution of our species, the change-over from a hard, structured, patriarchal society to one in which not only social security, but education was made available to everyone. Instead of being 'willy-nilly' obliged to submit to a grinding job at the age of 14, a great many more working class boys and girls were able to spend three or more years at art-schools, polytechnics and universities, trying out all sorts of materials, ideas and theories, reading books and talking intelligently to others in an easy-going atmosphere. This has not led, as one might think, to a heightening of culture, but to a cultural decline and decadence which has instead reached zero point, as we all know. One assumes, hopefully, that beneficial effects will show in time to come.

Education, and particularly higher education, will then be dramatically altered. The salutary influence of pioneers like A. S. Neil has already made itself felt in primary education, which has changed for the better and which has become more imaginative and orientated towards art and nature studies, with an informal, light and happy atmosphere, with more excursions out of school to places of interest. Children brought up under these circumstances will be more open, more sensible, more relaxed and carefree and because of this they are likely to have a positive attitude to life*. It makes no sense that this good primary education is still not followed by equally good secondary and higher education. This, however, is as yet abysmal, archaic and geared to examinations only. It does nothing to prepare children for adulthood or for life, to develop their spirit or refine their senses. Sensitive, artistic appreciation is nowhere taught, not even at art schools. One can only suppose that in obtaining a degree or a diploma, young people prepare themselves for a destructive, industrial mess in which it does not pay to be at all sensible of, or awake to, one's inner life. This means that the vast majority of people are only half there, or half alive in order to earn their living and have no means of enjoying the leisure they earn with their work. Education should be based on the experience of the subject, on learning to live with other people and changing one's self in the process. Natural Psychology, the nature of relationships, of love, of sex, of the relatedness of history, geography and biology, of languages, should be taught: there should be environmental studies, community work, comparative mythology and religion. Instead, higher education has become a degree factory; a processing plant for 'computer-fodder'.

Progressive education, the methods of Steiner, Fröbel and Montessori will influence the future of comprehensive schools far more than is commonly thought today. In a spiritual society education will be geared to self-development and will be a sacred initiation into life closely bound up with the Mentate (the self-development schools, where Natural Psychology is taught), the Hallow Hall (the Hall for 'Activation' or 'Hallowing' – a releasing exercise – 'Meditation' and Yoga) and the Salubriat (the name given to a place

*There is an tendency, nevertheless, amongst school-children, to reflect the adult world by behaving in a rude and licentious way, infected by the general cult of 'freedom'. This is part and parcel of the self-indulgence and gross materialism the consumerist society engenders and is not the fault of the schools, but of prevailing social trends promoted by advertising, the media etc.

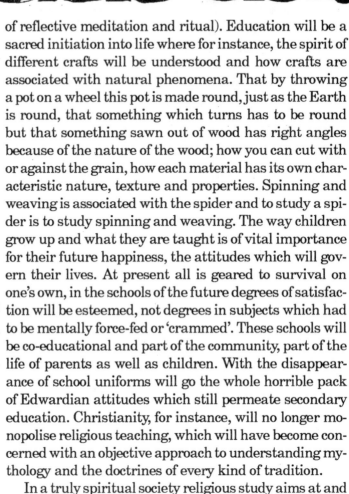

of reflective meditation and ritual). Education will be a sacred initiation into life where for instance, the spirit of different crafts will be understood and how crafts are associated with natural phenomena. That by throwing a pot on a wheel this pot is made round, just as the Earth is round, that something which turns has to be round but that something sawn out of wood has right angles because of the nature of the wood; how you can cut with or against the grain, how each material has its own characteristic nature, texture and properties. Spinning and weaving is associated with the spider and to study a spider is to study spinning and weaving. The way children grow up and what they are taught is of vital importance for their future happiness, the attitudes which will govern their lives. At present all is geared to survival on one's own, in the schools of the future degrees of satisfaction will be esteemed, not degrees in subjects which had to be mentally force-fed or 'crammed'. These schools will be co-educational and part of the community, part of the life of parents as well as children. With the disappearance of school uniforms will go the whole horrible pack of Edwardian attitudes which still permeate secondary education. Christianity, for instance, will no longer monopolise religious teaching, which will have become concerned with an objective approach to understanding mythology and the doctrines of every kind of tradition.

In a truly spiritual society religious study aims at and encourages understanding of religion rather than blind adherence to a particular dogma. There is no reason why patriarchal monotheism (an obsession with one archetype only) should be any more encouraged than a preoc-

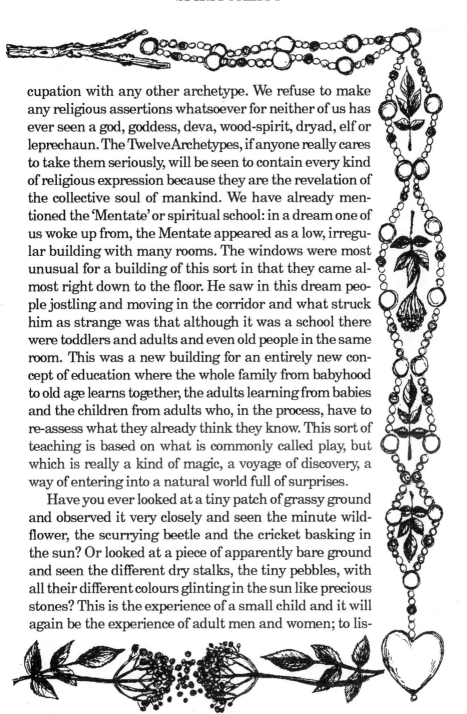

cupation with any other archetype. We refuse to make any religious assertions whatsoever for neither of us has ever seen a god, goddess, deva, wood-spirit, dryad, elf or leprechaun. The Twelve Archetypes, if anyone really cares to take them seriously, will be seen to contain every kind of religious expression because they are the revelation of the collective soul of mankind. We have already mentioned the 'Mentate' or spiritual school: in a dream one of us woke up from, the Mentate appeared as a low, irregular building with many rooms. The windows were most unusual for a building of this sort in that they came almost right down to the floor. He saw in this dream people jostling and moving in the corridor and what struck him as strange was that although it was a school there were toddlers and adults and even old people in the same room. This was a new building for an entirely new concept of education where the whole family from babyhood to old age learns together, the adults learning from babies and the children from adults who, in the process, have to re-assess what they already think they know. This sort of teaching is based on what is commonly called play, but which is really a kind of magic, a voyage of discovery, a way of entering into a natural world full of surprises.

Have you ever looked at a tiny patch of grassy ground and observed it very closely and seen the minute wildflower, the scurrying beetle and the cricket basking in the sun? Or looked at a piece of apparently bare ground and seen the different dry stalks, the tiny pebbles, with all their different colours glinting in the sun like precious stones? This is the experience of a small child and it will again be the experience of adult men and women; to listen for instance to the sound of things knocking against each other; how to make different sounds. This is the beginning of music. How liquid colour will run and mix, forming blobs and streaks. This is the beginning of art. To have such experience in a meaningful way means becoming still and receptive and this stillness and receptivity may lead to heightened consciousness; when there is love and the human soul rejoices. When all the nonsense and rubbish social conditioning, polite society and repressive education have foisted upon the individual, when all the extraneous worries and fears have dropped away, when there is perfect freedom it is possible for the mind to enter into a totally different awareness, to see and hear more acutely, to understand and comprehend more deeply. Heightened consciousness, the state of mind which the Indians call *God-realized*, the mentality of the prophet and the mystic, is the awareness of cosmic forces at work. Unfortunately egocentric or subjective people who were able to liberate their minds and become aware of their psychic power have not been able to cope with it and retain their sanity or common sense. A future generation will be able to take this kind of understanding for granted... and use it to purify the psyche, the villages, towns and cities, the land, rivers and lakes, the oceans, the heavens & the sea.

The signs of the 12 Archetypes

CHAPTER 6.

SEXUALITY

 NTO us a child is born! It is born with every kind of blessing including those of its sexual feelings and nature. But that sexuality, like everything else with a young child, is very fragile. Soon the baby discovers that it has been born into a world which is opposed to its sensitive and natural needs, a world geared to 'productivity' and 'progress', that is to say the furtherance of artificial conditions. During the subsequent 20 years he or she is forced to 'fit in' or 'adapt' and told all sorts of contradictory explanations of sexuality and is misled into thinking that sex is only for procreation and therefore can only be heterosexual and penetrative. If it has any other kind of desires it is made to feel that these are abnormal, shameful and ridiculous. Most learned books on sex call any sexuality which is not procreative a 'deviation' and give one to understand that such desires are in some way undesirable. Yet over-population has become one of the world's greatest problems and there are millions of unwanted children. To all intents and purposes nothing but the biological facts are known about our sexual motivation, the psychological reasons behind sexual attraction are generally ignored and what psychologists have written about these is mostly hypothesis. There is a tremendous emotional force behind everything surrounding sex and yet there is a cynical conspiracy to prevent people from becoming seriously interested in it.

With Natural Psychology we start from the premise that sexuality is not merely meant for procreation, and is therefore not just a biological function. It therefore follows that we are concerned with an exchange of sexual energy – whether this is consciously recognised by the partners in question or not – between human beings, whatever their sex, or age, or race, or history may be. If

two people can allow each other totally and be sensitive to each other's needs in sexual intercourse, without interference by ideas about themselves, or having to prove anything, they can have a remarkable effect on each other. Wonders happen where there is genuine love, expressed in a natural and spontaneous way as a true response. This presupposes receptivity, the ability to experience what is felt.

Everybody is one of 24 types: there are 12 'voy' and 12 'dard' types. As we explained in a previous chapter each type has one of 12 essential natures which are the opposite of what he/she WANTS to be, once he/she becomes conscious of it. Everyone needs their 'opposites', the types they feel drawn towards – 'opposite' from an inner, psychic point of view – the kind of person they need for their inner growth and fulfilment. This is entirely unconscious: consciously heterosexual men are sexually attracted to the idea of a woman, with such and such dimensions etc. (whatever happens to be fashionable, Venus de Milo or Marilyn Monroe). Sex derives consciously its impetus from difference; the man who desires a woman feels that he is in no respect a woman, whereas a homosexual identifies with being feminine, perhaps at the expense of his masculinity. This depends on what attitude one chooses to adopt, how one sees and experiences oneself, one's identity, which may be a projection and nothing to do with one's real self. A girlish looking boy with a baby face may think of himself as entirely masculine and heterosexual, yet in spite of himself he will feel the need for a relationship with perhaps an older man, a dard masculine type who may want to have sexual intercourse with him. Therefore a division occurs between the inner and unconscious self (the real self) and the outer and overtly conscious, acknowledged self (the ideal self): A 'Jekyll and Hyde' situation in which the one may be totally unaware that the other even exists, or if he does, will be likely to despise the helpless and feminine counterpart.

The 24 types divide into 3 groups according to the attraction of opposites: the "Nomadic", the "Agricultural" and the "Urban". These are only convenient names and do not necessarily relate to people's actual lifestyles. To the Nomadic group belong those types who have Φ ↑ (the Mother, Subject, Provider, Bearer or Slave) and ↑ Φ (the Warrior, Worker, Giant, Conqueror or Hero) as their essence or nature. This nature is what attracts their opposite types who have ✳ ☽ (the Patriarch, Father, King) and ☽ ✳ (the Fairy, Child, Angel) as their essence or nature, which is what complements the Warrior and the Mother, the fire and the earth which need to be given compassion by the Angel and form by the Patriarch, the water and the air. This group relates to the animal 'force', the vitality which can only be beneficial to us by being

controlled. We have here the image of the herd led by the Patriarch, the stag; like the Israelites by their Prophets, Kings and 'Ancient of Days', the Gypsies and the tribes of Central Asia and North America. The Nomadic group exists as the most basic of communities wandering across continents and deserts: warriors, mothers and children, cattle, sheep, goats, dogs and horses. People who belong to this group will unconsciously reflect in their sexual behaviour, their fantasies and dreams, characteristics of nomadic, tribal attitudes. They may, for instance, find monogamy difficult and the man or woman who has ☽ 3rd ✳ last, who has the Patriarch as his/her fulfilment, will want naturally to rule over a commune or group of boy and girl/friends, servants or wives, disciples or followers, and not to be bound by one relationship only. Their opposite types who have ↑ 3rd and Φ last will again accept their position in a group, harem or herd. This phenomenon was discussed in the previous chapter. To the Warrior (the man or woman

with Φ 3rd and ↑ last) being protective towards his/her opposite 'the Child' has the same significance as control over his subject (the Slave) has to the Patriarch.

The Agricultural group relates to the vegetable 'force', 'world' or 'kingdom' and a way of life which is not determined by a group but by pairing and coupling. It consists of those types who have Φ ℧ (the Peasant, the Wife, Cultivator, Settler and Native) and ℧ Φ (the Lady, the Enchanted, the Dreamer or the Madonna) as their essence or nature and attract the Wizard, Analyst or Scientist, the Magician and the Player, Trickster, Craftsman, or Inventor (✳ ↑ and ↑ ✳) who must have material to work on. Here cultivation, production and crafts, transformation, growth and change come into play. This is the life of settled communities, of traditional farmers with their implements, tools and the fabrication of them. Again men and women who belong to this group will display its characteristic unconsciously. They will tend to lead settled lives and relate to one person only, and the man (or woman) who has ↑ 3rd and ✳ last will want naturally to penetrate the darkness of his/her opposite Φ ℧, the black fertile earth, and thereby (in the case of man) produce offspring. Penetration is only one masculine sexual tendency of six. To someone with ✳ 3rd and ↑ last the tendency would be to tease, to excite, to stir the depth of his opposite Φ ℧, the bed of the lake. The third, the Urban group, relates to the mineral 'force' or 'kingdom' and the sexual habits of our own present-day, mineral society (totally dependent on oil and gas) which is that of masturbation on one's own in a private bed-sitter. The archetypes of this group are ✳ Φ, the 'Observer'; Φ ✳, the 'Wise Old Woman'; ℧ ↑, the 'Actress', 'Queen' or 'Lover', and ↑ ℧, the 'Fool'. The Observer is the Peeping Tom or Voyeur, the Fool is a Flasher or Shocker; the Exhibitionist, the Actress and the Old Woman are there to be watched and to be shocked.

We briefly mentioned these three groups to show a variety of different sexual attitudes and three ways of life, in a herd, as a couple or on one's own. Our present-day society, which is dominated by money derived from mining gold, silver, diamonds and coal etc. encourages privacy and independence, the self-sufficiency of the Wise Old Woman: Everybody in their own box, their flat or rented room, minding their own business, the way of mainly lonely people. Here there are few permanent relationships; either between two people or of a herd or group who relate to their leader or master. One must remember that we are talking about relationships in an emotional sense, a subtle energy which communicates itself on meeting: a vibration which like the correct note at the right time in a piece of music, can have a magical effect. When you look at water you can either look at the ripples and the reflections of the sun on the surface or you can look right down – if the water is clear – to the bottom, to the sand or stones, the pebbles and water weeds. It is the same with the human psyche – the deeper you look the more you discover. Many people can only see the surface, the reflections. From a psychic point of view therefore, sexual attraction exists between dard and voy types primarily and generally between types opposite to each other, irrespective of gender. The Greek myths, like those in all other mythology, are an expression of the 'Collective' unconscious (the kind of feelings we all unconsciously share) and give full recognition to a variety of sexual inclinations and without passing any moral judgement. The Christian tradition derives from Judaism with its emphasis on procreation and paternalism which forbids sexual practices outside marriage and causes a schism between spiritual love and animal passions which are condemned as evil.

For many centuries the connection between our psyche, or soul, and our sexual nature – which may include desires paradoxically considered to be 'unnatural' – was ignored and the majority of people today would still be frightened of and hostile towards, it. It was not until Sigmund Freud started probing into the neuroses of respectable Viennese citizens, that the subconscious venereal desires were at all taken seriously without embarrassment or fear. Thus the intelligentsia of Europe and America began to be more interested in and gradually became more broad-minded about sexuality. If people generally could become aware of the full potential of divine, receptive sexual intercourse they would be astounded at the power of the love and the magic that would be released. It would be like letting the wind and the sun into a musty cellar full of vermin, dust and rotting rubbish. By divine we mean a natural blessing, something which happens with great sincerity and spontaneity, something real and free from any impurities – it might be exhibitionism by a woman, or an older man gently touching a younger girl – without embarrassment, shame or guilt. Only when we can be innocent and receptive is it possible to experience a sexuality which is more than a feeble repetition of some boring idea. We will have to give up any possessiveness or jealousy, all ideas about respectability or normality and we will have to cultivate the objective receptivity which tells us when, and when not, to slow down, to be tender or fierce.

We will need to be naturally restrained which will stop us from going against what our inner feelings tell us and will prevent us from forcing and imposing ourselves on others. A new and just law will consider imposition to be offensive, not any particular kind of sex. Someone has a right to complain about being pestered. As

long as two people consider each other's feelings no act between them could be thought of as criminal. Popular newspapers thrive on sexual exposés, jeopardising the careers and private lives of their victims, whereas the parent who tortures his child with discipline is usually tolerated by the rest of conventional society.

Conditioning, so-called 'bringing-up', that is to say intimidating children to adapt themselves to a stereotyped pattern of sexual behaviour and rôle-playing has led to an inordinate amount of dishonesty. Particularly young voy males cease to live from their natural, inner selves and simulate feelings which, in fact, they do not possess. Instead of sexual intercourse originating from natural and live, spontaneous feelings it is misdirected to satisfy an egoistic pride. The head takes over where the heart should rule, and true love or honest passion becomes twisted and is repressed. A great many marriages are just for show, to keep up the old system of heterosexual monogamy. When people are not getting what they hoped for from a relationship they should be able to be quite honest about it, and not have to pretend that everything is as it ought to be. Within a marriage or a relationship both partners should allow each other the freedom to experience the kind of love, passion or treatment they need. A number of alarming circumstances present themselves:

Firstly, the amount of secrecy and dishonesty surrounding sexuality amongst adults. Secondly, the amount of real desire which should have been allowed, but was suppressed. Thirdly, the number of factors which prevent people from realizing what they actually feel.

Marriages between two voy types are very common. That is to say, a marriage in which the partners are deceiving themselves and each other that they have a love-relationship, when in fact it is only a domestic arrangement (or a friendship) with perhaps mutual interests and a superficial sexual attraction. That is to say a sexual attraction based on excitement or a thrill, not on any sincere and profound feelings which originate from an inner need. In a sense such an attraction is neurotic because it emphasises the negative aspects (the 3rd element) and prevents someone from reaching fulfilment. Voy types who are 'opposites' can be attracted to each other, for instance, someone with the following: $\Phi \uparrow * \mho$ has two voy types with Φ last in their group (the Nomadic) who will be attracted to the Φ and the $\uparrow$ but *really* need to have a dard type with $*$ last, a Patriarch or Matriarch to belong to.

There must be at least several million women in the British Isles who experience nothing but frustration and emptiness from their marriage, but who for the sake of their pride and self-esteem and for the sake of their children go along with the whole thing. Perhaps they long for some miraculous change in their husbands who, though, because of the situation, can never be challenged. As

long as a 'status quo' is maintained nothing can be done about it. Both partners meanwhile will be looking outside their marriage for dard types who can give guidance and emotional support. Paradoxically, sometimes the rejected homosexual, dard lover of the 'husband' may become the confidant or 'father-confessor' of the 'wife' and serve as a 'beacon' for both. Often the 'husband' will find his actual love-relationship in a vicarious way with a business partner or work-mate, whom he adores in secret and who usually doesn't suspect that he is more than just a good friend. Many voy men are forced by our sexual conventions to lead a double life, to be constantly on their guard and frightened of having their real feelings exposed. The wife, meanwhile, hopes that her husband will somehow, one day, start to express genuine feeling to her and that he will become really protective, understanding and paternal. By changing in a natural way, by relaxing and giving up all ideas about himself, by allowing himself to be free from inhibiting fears and letting his natural feelings come to the surface, however, he can only become more feminine. "All the king's horses and all the king's men" could not make him any different! This change has nothing to do with social or sexual behaviour. Most voy (or vey) — vey sounds better, the terms 'voy' and 'vey' mean the same — boys have sexual fantasies about women, quite separately from any deep love they may feel for a man. Growing relationships based on mutual respect and genuine feeling often are nothing to do with the sexual fantasies of either partner.

If people looked at Natural Psychology with as much interest as they do at their bank statements, their relationships would have a better chance of giving them the satisfaction they crave. Obedience to a number of socially accepted or fashionable rules may help one to 'get along' with other people, but this totally avoids any serious involvement; in most cases it is just playing a game. Games can be fun for a while, but unless deeply felt emotions are released, making love too becomes a bore. Life easily develops into a series of empty habits: kissing your girlfriend, or wife, and calling her '*darling*' and presenting her with a bouquet of flowers may be a deeply felt move, but it may just as easily be an empty gesture. No real reconciliation or understanding is possible between 'opposites' unless one is in touch with one's deeper feelings by reflecting on them, in order to distinguish that which is sincere and honest from that which is '*a load of old hooey*'. Love and sex should be taken seriously and there should and will be places, schools, institutes (mentates) devoted to Natural Psychology everywhere to relieve people of their guilt and shame and help them to understand their real sexual and emotional needs. Once people begin to operate from their inner selves it will become clear that guidance is absolutely necessary because 'normality' does not really exist. There are as many voy types, if not more, as dard types amongst males and this psychological fact in itself must prove that human beings are meant to be bisexual. On a community holiday devoted to Natural Psychology there were only 7 dard types, 3 of whom were girls amongst a group of over 50 members consisting mostly of young married couples. On this occasion where people relaxed, 'gave in' to their inner feelings and became more natural and receptive, couples of a dard and a voy type grew closer together, whereas voy relationships showed every sign of stress and neurotic disturbance.

Homosexuality in our society tends to be conducted behind an inordinate contrivance of mannerisms, silly gestures and superficial attitudes. It is associated with ideas of 'queerness', 'campness', 'gaiety' and other similar notions which originated in a theatrical atmosphere. Just as the suburban wedding, this generally has very little to do with what natural persons genuinely feel for each other. Love affairs in the artificial environment of our urban culture created by all kinds of pressures, tend to be 'cooked up' and this is particularly true of the 'gay world'. Because, like the leper in medieval cities, a boy had to declare himself to be a homosexual and was forced to identify with 'being queer' or 'gay' if he wished to be honest about his love for another boy or for a man, or

about his sexual desires (these need not be synonymous), homo-sexuality acquired its character, much as members of any nation, group or religion tend to do. Persecuted minorities usually develop freakish traits through fear and feelings of inferiority. Boys who decide to be queer or gay – a conscious decision, similar to that of deciding what one's career is to be, often made as a reaction to parents and the rest of conventional society – adopt all the para-phernalia of queerness or gaiety, become 'camp' or go to queer bars, eat gay food and wear queer clothes etc. whatever the gay fashion demands. This is usually a series of attitudes which emphasise subjective and effeminate behaviour and may well be just as much a shallow display as that of a skinhead or teddyboy or the affecta-tions of any other clique.

From a psychological point of view, a sexual relationship of any depth can only exist between a dard and a voy type of whichever sex and all else (two dard 'queers' or two voy 'normals') is of no account, doomed, and a source of frustration and neurosis. Only a dard and a voy type who are each other's 'opposites' can have the profound effect on each other which potentially lies hidden in the initial attraction between them. Because of external circumstances this potential may never be realized and the relationship may floun-der and come to an end. Sex refers to the sexes and is therefore not really the right word to denote an energy generated by the attrac-tion of one type for another, whether these are two men or two women, or a man and a woman. A man is only a member of his sex because he has the physical characteristics of masculinity – a pe-nis, a beard and so on; this however is not the criterion for his basic, natural experience of himself and the way he is psychically predisposed. His physical body can change, the nature of his soul cannot. Voy males have different facial characteristics from dard types: as young boys they are usually 'girlish' and pretty and this youthful beauty can remain into middle age. Shakespeare in one of his sonnets describes it as "A woman's face, with nature's own hand painted". Voy types look younger than they are, whereas dard types who have a heavy build and are more robust looking (with-out trying to) show their age. There is a facial resemblance within each type and with a great deal of practice it is possible to recog-nize the 24 types by looking at people.

It is a generally held belief that sexual intercourse between two men is unnatural and unsavoury, because of the physical implications. A male body is said to be made, or tailored, to fit into a female body like a key in a lock. This fittingness however is only very relative. Taken at face value it could mean something which is only mechanical and therefore insensitive (apart from physical sensation) and devoid of any psychic motivation. It is the latter which has real vitality and can bring about extraordinary, magical events when it is released from its conventional bondage. In the attraction of two opposite type males, or females, where the one is able naturally to affect the other and cause him or her to realize his/her masculine or feminine potential, fittingness of a *spiritual* kind can be achieved which is miraculous compared with the physical predisposition most people hold for all that is 'natural'. The magical possibilities which like 'Jack-in-the-Box' could be released from their subconscious prison are infinite and as yet unfamiliar to us; we know very little about love, just as people 100 years ago knew little about hygiene. We are, however, convinced that sexual energy when directed by the psyche, intuitively, will cause someone to act in a way entirely beneficial to their partner. Such acts are not practices, but spontaneous gestures, in the form of some kind of touching, massage, manipulation, handling, caressing or hitting and stroking, which may vary enormously from time to time according to the mood, atmosphere or nature of the circumstances. This view of sex is opposed to prejudices, idées fixes, planned operations, or anything which is at all self-conscious and egoistic. The next evolutionary step will bring with it the freedom to have this natural and receptive intercourse, which hopefully will become prevalent in the next century.

Sexual fantasies which spontaneously arise in childhood and become more elaborate and defined during adolescence, are of great significance because they are the product of one's inner feeling, one's natural dreamlife. Desires implicit in these fantasies are repressed by the majority of people, who have allowed themselves to be socially conditioned. With the 'normal' individual (anyone who has not been able to resist social pressures to conform) another, different kind of sexual fantasy may develop later in life, during puberty, and this kind of fantasy which comes from the ego

relates only to the external world, to 'outer' conditions, and 'outer' desires. Very often, particularly with voy males and with dard women the 'outer' fantasy replaces the 'inner' one which was repressed as soon as the wish to be 'normal' asserted itself, usually between the ages of 7 to 14. The 'inner' fantasy of a voy or 'vey' boy, for instance, might have been that he was captured, bound and undressed and despite his screams, protests and struggles overpowered, or beaten, or prodded, or made to do, or having done to him all manner of things. The sexual emotion derives from fear, a feeling of 'awe', the thrill of being possessed by someone who has power and is in control in this case. In his 'outer' fantasy he masturbates, or 'makes love' to girls who do not become involved with him on a serious or deeper level. His 'inner' fantasy is set in a natural environment, whereas his 'outer' fantasy invariably has the bleak and flimsy, artificial atmosphere of the modern world. We would like to quote the following account, given by a voy young man, after having had a 'wet-dream' about masturbating a really nasty type of girl who had just killed someone in a church for no reason. The interpretation of this dream we suggest is that the church stands for the dreamer's 'higher' or serious feelings, his receptivity, whereas the girl and his attraction to her imply that he is not at one with his 'higher' and 'inner self'. In the same dream the girl was reading during the sexual experience, a left-wing newspaper called 'Warfare'.

Q: "What do you think of your heterosexuality after dreaming about these violent and destructive undercurrents?"

A: "I think it is something which has to be kept firmly under control. It is a combination of compulsion and unrelated fantasy, unrelated to my better feelings. It is inhuman and causes a division in me, which has the germ of schizophrenia. I think that this phenomenon is common enough today. I have, through waking up with this dream still fresh in my mind, become conscious of something in myself which underlies a great deal of extreme behaviour like hooliganism, violent demos and fashions like punk".

Q: "Why should this heterosexuality be associated with violence? Why should it be disconnected from love?"

A: "Because it is caught up with 'the Outer' and has nothing to do with my 'Inner feeling'. It is connected with the things I hate, unlovely things, the ugly, modern world, everything which threatens my tender feelings which crave for protection. The girl in this ugly world is an object, not a real human being. It is all a question of what you're aiming at in life. You can either allow yourself to be soft and sincerely love someone who can give you a feeling of security, of being protected and allow yourself to be spontaneous and real, or you can give in to your 'mechanical' side which is supported by everyone you know, the whole of society. You then become weaker, less alive and healthy, less human, and you end up 'asleep', a complete robot. One has to be ruthlessly objective and you can only do this by remembering what you really feel: Do I really want this bar of chocolate, girl, cup of coffee or cigarette (whatever it happens to be), or is it my imagination playing tricks on me? If you *really* want to be *whole* then you have to give up or at least come to terms with your compulsive and perverse aspect, the 'devil in you'".

Imagination can be used in two ways, 'rightly' and 'wrongly'. In the right way it truly reflects what someone feels, wrongly used the fantasy becomes furtive and unhealthy. It may become lurid and artificial, an obsession unrelated to the rest of someone's life and what he actually is and feels. The fantasy becomes enmeshed in lies, deception and confusion. Christian institutions have a lot to answer for, as they have made people feel guilty about the 'right' kind of fantasies, those essential for their inner growth. A very common 'right' kind of fantasy (much more common than anyone would think) is that of a man who wishes to discipline, punish and possess boys. Conversely some voy (vey) boys wish to be disciplined and given sexual punishment as a necessary therapeutic treatment. These boys, the wild and voy example we used, for instance, need to be held back, pushed back into themselves and sometimes sexually treated as if they were wilful animals. A great many soldiers, guardsmen* and sailors are amongst these. Under present conditions this creates a kind of social hornet's nest of unhealthy attitudes. The reason is that a type of man who becomes a barrister, judge, MP or civil servant may respond in an entirely natural way to sexual stimuli transmitted by a guardsman. Should he give in to this he runs the risk of a scandal and of losing his position in society. The alternative is a hypocritical denial of what he really, truly and actually feels. In healthy and natural circumstances the MPs or judges and the guardsmen would be able to experience each other freely and mutually benefit from a contact both 'sides' subconsciously crave for. The barracks would provide a kind of 'mènage' where the MPs etc. could watch their favourite guardsmen being put through their paces, before having sexual intercourse in a safe and uncontaminated way.

One envisages a light and agreeable place where dard types can sit to watch the voy types, the guardsmen's display of drill, acrobatics and the like. Here in a receptive atmosphere the participants, knowing quite openly that sexual feelings are aroused, without any embarrassment or fear, can relax and 'receive' what is necessary. However bizarre and absurd, obscene or perverse this may seem to many people in our present-day world, a future, spiritual society will support this type of 'release', where mutually beneficial contact is made by people who are socially, culturally and spiritually divided. The MP and the guardsman will be able to enjoy each other safely and because of spiritual guidance realize exactly what they can do for each other, what will unlock something extraordinary through a sexual encounter. Without any danger from bad reactions 'horseplay' can become magical, where the brute,

*These voy types are attracted by the highly disciplined life in a guard's regiment; the many rules and the tightness of the way in which everything is ordered gives them a sense of security and relief from any responsibility. These types yearn for guidance.

216

animal, potentially destructive force is harnessed and subdued. The Virgin riding the Bull who is under control is inspiring*, the bull killing the virgin is a gruesome image. One is the archetype for ℧ ✳, the other for ↑ Φ. The encounter between the MP and the guardsman is that between ✳ ℧, the Head, the Master, and Φ ↑, the body, the Slave. The guardsman who is often one of two voy types: ✳ ℧ ↑ Φ or ℧ ✳ ↑ Φ, could also be: Φ ✳ ↑ ℧, the opposite of the usual ↑ ℧ Φ ✳ male politician, another voy type which identifies with Φ ↑ and ↑ Φ. In these worlds there is no consciousness and outwardly there will be nothing to suspect the inner motivation. This is to submit to and obey the disposition of the Master. In their

'normal' state such types can be negatively in ↑ Φ (the Warrior), their opposites in ℧ ✳ (the Angel). The resulting conflict is harmful to both; the guardsman must submit to fulfill himself, the MP** be respected, including his desire for guardsmen.

We can safely make this dogma: sexual encounters in which the partners relate with their 3rd elements are bad; the only valid relationships are in terms of the last elements. Voy types who have ✳ or ↑ 3rd and relate to masculine types with Φ or ℧ 3rd in this way – which usually happens in a marriage between a voy man (playing a masculine role) and a dard woman (playing a feminine role) – are neither doing themselves nor their partners any good. This also happens often where the dard husband has his ✳ or ↑ 2nd (the element supressed or 'in the box') and is unable to assert himself over his ✳ or ↑ 3rd wife, who then becomes a devilish tyrant and may cause his death, to probably regret it afterwards. Many homosexual relationships, particularly where an older man

*Europa and the Bull – a Greek Myth.

**Please note, in this case, we have used the position of MP in an almost archetypal sense, i.e. representing the MP as a particular (dard) psychological type and the guardsman as a particular (voy) psychological type. In actual, real life some MPs *are* this type and so are the guardsmen, their opposites.

is attracted to younger men, or boys, can be disastrous in this way. The cases of Oscar Wilde and Verlaine, the 19th Century French poet, should be well-known. Oscar Wilde was dard and probably ↑ Φ ℧ ✳, fulfilling himself in the Patriarch ✳ ℧, his boyfriend Lord Alfred Douglas was voy, probably ℧ ✳ ↑ Φ, fulfilling himself in the Slave: Φ ↑. It was Douglas's ↑ 3rd behaviour, his rashness, egoism and 'playing with fire' which caused the trouble. The friendship between Verlaine Φ ↑ ℧ ✳ and Rimbaud ✳ ℧ ↑ Φ (a typical example) also perished in the blazing inferno of ↑ 3rd. Both Douglas and Rimbaud should have been 'taken down a peg or two', given special treatment, restrained and brought back to themselves. In a future society this will be understood and such feminine types will be given the discipline they crave*. We need a supporting social structure to contain this wild fire and hold it in. Conversely with ✳ 3rd we get a detached, or icy superiority, pride and conceit.

There are 6 types of sexual relationships: 1. Conquest and Surrender, 2. Domination and Submission, 3. Observation and Display, 4. Abandon and Restraint, 5. Penetration and Absorption, 6. Manipulation and Sensitivity. The first two belong to the Nomadic group and are motivated by the animal forces, they imply Aggressor-Victim and Master-Slave relationships; the second two belong to the Urban Group and are motivated by the mineral forces, they imply a desire for independence (which is what a voyeur wishes to maintain) and the freedom to break with restrictions (expressed by the 'flasher' or exhibitionist). Men who have a tendency towards exhibitionism – which is no more 'unnatural' than any other type of sexuality – would fulfil themselves in the Fool and are ℧ 3rd and ↑ last. The Gods Pan and Dionysus and the Fool in the Tarot were often drawn with large erections. The last two types of sexual relationship belong to the Agricultural Group and are motivated by the vegetable forces; they imply the total compensation of the feminine ℧ Φ and Φ ℧ for the masculine ↑ ✳ and ✳ ↑. This is what characterizes the heterosexuality of Judaism (and that of Christianity which was derived from it) and which is now regarded as 'normal', 'natural' sex. What is forgotten is that in other cultures, other traits are, or were, selected as 'normal'. Male brothels, which

*Heterosexual examples of this phenomenon are that of Socrates and his wife Xantippe and in Shakespear's play 'The Taming of the Shrew'.

are unknown in our society, were common in Eastern countries, and so was temple prostitution; even the temple in Jerusalem was surrounded by the 'Houses of the Sodomites' until these were closed down with the tightening of Judaistic, 'fire-conscious' laws. The three sexual groups also relate to three types of economy: these are by conquest (theft), by barter (exchange), and by token (money). Theft, exchange and money may again have sexual implications in rape, 'wife-swopping' and in prostitution: Nomads take what they want, their economy is based on conquest, moving on, to them ownership is a transient notion; they certainly have no concept of owning land. Settlers in an agricultural society grow and make things which they can exchange for other goods from other places. In an urban society, such as ours, money becomes ALL IMPORTANT and alienates and isolates people from each other. Fetishism can be more easily understood in the context of these three groups with their six sexual variations: the meaning of the horse and the bit or bridle as a sex symbol is totally obvious in the case of the King or Patriarch's fantasy; he wishes to reign in*, to control his fire third opposite, as was explained earlier. Dard types who fulfil themselves in the Warrior (↑ Φ) have fantasies about explosives – they need to 'blow up' the icy detachment of their ✳ 3rd opposites. Those who fulfil themselves in the Fool (↑ ℧) wish to shock or 'bring down' the Patriarch in their ✳ 3rd opposites and will fantasize about that which shocks (running around naked with an erection in the street). Those who fulfil themselves in the Observer wish to remain impassive (✳ Φ) and not react in any way to the ↑ 3rd of their opposites who fulfil themselves in the Actress (℧ ↑, the Lover) and are given to dramatic outbursts, creating scenes and passionate demonstrations.

In a future society there will be places for sexual liberation: circuses, theatres, baths, playing fields and stables where anyone could find the fulfilment of their fantasies, where people will be able to relieve themselves. If we could transport ourselves 100 years into the future we would find a world totally shocking to many

*This applies to dard types with ℧ 3rd and ✳ last, whose opposites are ↑ 3rd and therefore tend to be rash, extravagant and careless, fulfilling themselves in Φ ↑, the earthy world of animal warmth; to them the thought of being turned into a horse may, once they are in touch with their 'psychic body', appeal greatly.

The four elements in sex

modern eyes, but utterly delightful to those who love nature and the human soul. It will be the world of our dreams in which the terrible emotional thirst and sexual hunger of our own day has long been forgotten. Over-population will be a thing of the past, because sexual gratification will come in ways which would now, by most people, be thought of as abnormal. Why otherwise – apart from the need to procreate – should we have sexual emotions, desires and fantasies? If these are objective and true, such feelings must become an aid to discovering a deeper part of ourselves, apart from being helpful to those to whom we are attracted. In our present society the extent to which we are able to express our yearning for our opposites is very limited and constantly in danger of being exploited. A woman may lure a man to a poky bedroom where he gets his watch and wallet stolen; a boy may pick up a man in order to blackmail him, have him tripped up and assaulted or robbed by his friends or ambushed in the local park or wood (so-called 'queer-bashing'). Society, instead of aiding the men who naturally long to possess their 'fire-third' opposites and would give them exactly what they need in order to get 'through to their earth', encourages the criminal. Neurotic 'fire third' is given every opportunity to do its worst, the ubiquitous vandalism, mayhem and crime in our towns and cities are there to prove this.

Sexual expression which is motivated from the psyche will, in the future, in a spiritual society, have the blessing of the Graigian Church, or 'Salubriat', and sexual intercourse will no longer be thought of as normal only within the terms of marriage. Procreation will be the last, not the first, purpose to which sex is to be put. A far more fluid view of sex and love will prevail, a view which would mean sexual fulfilment for a great many people, who have no chance of experiencing this under present circumstances. Such

a wonderful state of affairs becomes possible with a generally objective and receptive approach to life, when in fact the message of Jesus Christ is put into practice and goodwill prevails amongst all men. Only a new religious teaching, that of Graigianity with its discovery of Natural Psychology, can bring this about, not Christian dogma, or materialistic, polluting industrial growth. The violence of our present day world will have to be curbed, the rubbish of our affluent society thrown out. Sex has become perverted to violence, but this violence in turn can be converted into a great sexual power which can transform, heal and liberate.

Sexual freedom is often connected with a silly licentiousness, unwanted pregnancies and venereal diseases, but this is merely looking through 'Fire-Conscious' eyes. Most of us are condemned to such a limited vision by our education; a static, disconnected, so-called 'realistic' way of looking at life. The future will undoubtedly embrace 'Water-Consciousness' for inevitably we will reclaim our birthright and will have again the intuitive, dream-like vision of a Gypsy or fortune-teller: An imaginative, symbolic interpretation of things, in which life has meaning because of lovely and beautiful, not miserable and ugly, associations. This Water-Conscious world is of misty woods, cooing pigeons, the stars shining above a bonfire burning in a open space, the sounds of insects and of wild animals hunting, the strange patterns in wax, tea-leaves, ink or sand which reveal what is to happen: A poetic and romantic world.

With the upsurge of Water-Consciousness and a generation of children growing up in a permissive atmosphere, used to seeing men and boys with long hair and accepting the possibilities of expanded consciousness and self-development, sexual freedom will become the norm and there will no longer be any need for suspicion, guilt or fear. The television will show 'pornographic' or 'blue films' which will be objectively and attractively explained, so that viewers will learn to understand the psychic reasons for various sexual desires. This pornography will be beautiful, like the drawings of Beardsley, not harsh and garish as it normally is today. As a result of this approach sexual hunger will abate and people will no longer be obsessed by their terrible need. Women and girls at present are fairly free in talking and thinking about sex, and one suspects that many enlightened *tête à tête* conversations are about their expectations, frustrations and fantasies. Men on the other hand connect sex with pride and prowess and are very frightened of being despised by other men, or boys, for 'not being good at it'. Many male chauvinist expressions are really frightful; for instance, one hears of wanting to 'pull that bird' or 'lay that chick' or 'screw this bit of fluff' which suggest a violent, tortuous experience connected with contempt and hatred. We do not imagine that the majority of females really enjoy, or wish to be, pulled, layed or screwed. This unimaginative, ugly, hard and bleak attitude is in sharp contrast to the sexuality conjured up at the beginning of this century (when in cultured western European cities there was a short-lived flowering of Water-Conscious art and literature which floundered with the First World War) by Beardsley, Bakst, Klimt, Wilde and Proust: An act, a subtle game of looks, glances, touches and *svelte* movements; a fantasy world in which anything is possible. One can imagine a room straight out of the *Arabian Nights*, the princess, 'la Sultane Bleue', is reclining on a sofa covered in embroideries and silken cushions: A curtain of shimmering crimson, mauve and black beads in front of the curved Arabesque doorway, a marble fountain playing, the sunlight broken into intricate patterns as it falls through the tracery of sandalwood, the turquoise and lustred tiles, the soft, red Eastern carpets on the floor. A feast is laid out by a young negro boy in pantaloons, a decorated waistcoat and a feathered, jewelled head-dress; there are musicians playing strange tunes on stringed instruments, dancing-girls and boys and the lover is let in at a secret door.

This romanticism of the *fin-de-siècle* and the first decade of this century with its *art-nouveau* has been revived during the last 10 years*. Such a revival is unique in our history; women's fashions, lettering on shops and on posters, furniture, lamps, book illustrations and wall-paper have returned to the styles of 60 years ago, as if half a century had not happened at all. We regard this as highly significant. Never before have the fashions of the grandchildren returned to those of their grandparents; it is as if we are continuing

*This was written in 1976.

a cultural trend which was interrupted by 60 years of an alien anti-culture, of the bleak modernism of the period between the two world wars, with its hard, brutal political doctrines, its repressive regimes in Germany, Russia, Italy and Spain and its manufacture of frightful weapons. All this has served as a model for African, Asian and South American countries which are now copying their European examples of this inter-war period. While we write this we have in front of us an *art-nouveau* silver buckle of exquisite workmanship decorated with blue, turquoise and green enamel which is suggestive of a beautiful pool of water in an enchanted forest.

There are clearly two opposing trends in the world today, the Fire-Conscious trend (as seen on television) which is now taking over the 'Third World' with all its frightful machinery, gadgetry, mass-production and uniformity, and the Water-Conscious one which has become 'trendy' in the cultural centre of the future world: London NW1, 3 and 5.

While Africans and Asians aspire to nylon suits made in Hong Kong and pre-packed American food, the *avant garde* fraternity sit cross-legged to eat brown rice or sweet potatoes and proudly show off an Arab ceremonial wedding dress. Wholefoods and organic living are gaining popularity and for this reason alone our prophecy must be taken seriously*. What was thought to be daring, 'modern' and chic in the 1930's is now commonplace; it follows that tomorrow's world will be that of today's 'cranks' and 'hippies'. Thus a healthy interest in sex, taking it seriously and allowing the motivation to arise from natural rather than contrived emotions will be inevitable. In the future it will be quite common for a voy (or vey) boy — knowing himself to be this, which is generally recognized and respected — to have several easy-

*Even in the 1950's vegetarianism was thought to be wildly eccentric.

going friendships with voy girls, while owing absolute and total allegiance to his devoted, dard true-love, whether this is a man or a woman. He will want to behave and dress in a feminine way, as a dard, fulfilled woman will want to in a masculine way. Once the 'penetration myth' has been exploded, the understanding of Natural Psychology can reach people generally and sexual education is enlightened and enlightening, girls will only become pregnant by choice. If a girl is dard and unmotherly she will be able to give the baby to her voy boyfriend who then becomes a mother. It will be normal in the future to see babies brought up by boys whose dard 'husbands' will be acknowledged as the spiritual father, and there will be homosexual and lesbian couples with children.

What we are really emphasising is that with the development of true vision relationships will be seen for what they really are and spiritual, true love will be honoured and respected, whereas a purely physical arrangement (the average marriage of today) based on antiquated ideas about male and female rôles will not be glorified and made out to be something which it is not. The dependency in the girlfriend/marriage trip will be a thing of the past when girls and women go for 'sex-therapy' to a masseur or 'healer'; a 'communicator' with special, spiritual powers. He might be a voy male dressed in a green, or blue, robe. In a bathroom there will be, on wooden, unpainted shelves, an array of herbal preparations, on the window-sill sweet-smelling plants. There will be a kind of magic; its purpose is either to cure physical ailments, to relieve tensions or to release sexual energy, which in young girls today can find no safe outlet, except in masturbation. The Communicator, an alchemist, is able to 'receive' what the girl in question needs and becomes the ideal on which the girl can concentrate her needs and longing without any risk of these being rejected, misunderstood or abused. Any girl going to this Communicator will know full well that she can that she can never own him or lay claims to him. He will belong to his dard friend and there will be no need for a denial of this fact.

The scene is set in a bathroom because we are concerned with purification. When the girl enters the Communicator talks to her to find out what she feels or what is wrong while she is bathed. There is no secrecy or false shame. He is constantly – because he is able to live in his psychic body, his Ʊ and Φ – registering the sensations communicated by her and thus he can tell what he must do to help her. He uses his scents and unguents to create a particular atmosphere – he might sing or hum or say magical words. This is a sexual experience accompanied by caresses and kisses and it serves a healing purpose, bringing relief and joy. Nothing in this situation is forced, inorganic or inhibited by notions of 'craziness' or 'lunacy'. Fear still comes in 1994 like an evil shadow between the partners in a sexual experience, making them nervous of each other, unable to feel secure, to relax and be receptive. This fear is of rejection and persecution, of the interference by those who were themselves blocked when they were young. In the same way that many terrible plagues and fatal diseases were defeated in this country and social injustices and filthy living-conditions abolished, so the repression and frustration, the psychic ailments, unhappiness and sexual mess, the trash of our 'throw-away' society, will be relieved and cleared. The sun will surely shine from behind the heavy clouds and it will be on an island where sexuality is no longer hemmed in by laws and repressive social morals – an infliction from a dark and prejudiced past – which do not reflect in any way the will of Nature, what people really feel inside. All this will be so if the human race survives.

Aids, or H.I.V., caused a frightful reaction against homosexuality by the gutter press and gave a chance to its retrograde and bigoted devotees, who have been waiting for such an opportunity to inflict their vile and stupid prejudices on the 'general public'. The virus is

a symptom of soulless mechanicality promoted by these very bigots and came about through the impurity and superficiality of this modern period. It was not homosexual intercourse which brought about Aids and spread it, but the atmosphere of present-day America. In Ancient Greece, in the Roman world and in Arabia for thousands of years homosexual relationships were an integral part of the social structure without any venereal diseases at all. These cultures were – apart from the decadence of the Roman Empire – beautiful and pure. The impurity of the modern, American world was not created by homosexuals, but by a competitive and insensitive industrial society, which allowed nature to be replaced by polluting artificiality. We can prevent Aids from spreading by spirituality and self-purification, by making the changes that are advocated in this book. No end of 'jiggery-pokery' in laboratories will help, e.g. giving the disease to monkeys so that these poor animals have to die for our 'sins', which are nothing to do with our sexual inclinations, but with tolerating a horrible, artificial and superficial atmosphere.

The age of Pisces, which began approximately 2000 years ago and has now come, or is coming, to an end, was characterized by division, two fishes swimming in opposite directions, 'a man is this and a woman that'. With the age of Aquarius and Natural Psychology, the knowledge of dard and voy, sex will be better understood and therefore with a more honest and conscious approach to it people will consider the consequences of their actions. This is what we mean by conscience. Aquarian spirituality will not be a denial of sexual feelings, but an imaginative and truthful expression of these. Many young women and men will want to live together under a master (a guru), a dard type who can help them to develop themselves. A new kind of monastery will be established everywhere. The difference between the physical sexes will be less emphasized as time goes on and the deep psychological and spiritual difference of dard and voy will become marked in a natural and flowing dress and behaviour. Voy youths will, in the future, consciously dress to excite, as girls now do. It will not be unusual to see them almost totally nude in summer, or in long, light robes and barefoot. They will show off their bottom and legs deliberately in tight hose, because they consciously wish to attract the attention of dard men and women. The fashions of the next millennium will revert to the timelessness of those of the Middle Ages, or like those of the East and of Antiquity, which were simple, elegant and graceful. Only when humanity gives recognition to what is deeply felt and becomes natural again can its survival be a certainty. Our culture and that of all the world will then become unchanging and beautiful, as it was before a restless desire to explore and conquer took it to the ultimate of ugly artificiality and of potential total annihilation. The image of Aquarius is a youth emptying an amphora of water, which must symbolize the 'collective unconscious' of mankind. A flow of water which we associate with 'Deeplake' (℧ Φ).

When Christianity came here in the first millennium it opposed a world ruled by warrior gods like Thor and Wotan in which life was short, harsh, dark and rough. Now 1400 years later, we have a world in which tricksters rule the roost and life, accordingly, is empty, meaningless and totally devoid of taste. A new counterbalancing religion has to be of our deeper feelings, ℧ Φ, Deeplake, to bring back sensitivity and sensing, or 'receiving'. Christianity brought ℧ ✳, Dawndew, the Angel and the Virgin, to these lands and the image of the Annunciation is the essence of Mediaeval

religiosity. ℧ ✳, the surface of the water, reflects the sky, the clouds, the sun, or moon and stars at night, it is (unless polluted) pure. Down in the depths of the water, ℧ Φ, all sort of rubbish can collect, but when this is clear and purified an astonishing variety of life-forms can be seen; such were the true beginnings of all that lives and grows. The Christian religion has been the agent of 'conditioning' in which, particularly sexual, feelings were repressed. Natural Psychology is about natural behaviour.

Christianity is the religion of ℧ ✳. It reconciles, at its best, the body and the head through love in reflective thought and imagination. This the Christians call 'Heaven' and is above. Below us is the earth and sex and all that grows and by means of receptivity and goodness, this can be now made into 'Paradise'. Because ℧ ✳ and ↑ ✳ both have AIR in common, there is no psychological conflict, at all, between reflective imagination and inventiveness, and the Christian world has been quite happy with tastelessness, an unbridled rule of Sparklewheel (↑✳) with pretence and games, and a riot of invention and fantasy by which no one could express their actual feelings. In this artificial world and 'fire-conscious climate' any form of sex which differs from what is officially sanctioned together with the mention of natural functions became socially forbidden.

The most soulless and hideous urban environment that could possibly exist has been erected in the last hundred years, shops sell all that is grotesque and shoddy and entertainments on television are frightful, yet the same people who subscribe to all this evil are shocked by words which denote our private parts and sexual activity. ℧ Φ does not conflict with ↑ Φ and in a world which embraces truth, magic, true love and taste, the 'dirty' words and 'foul' language of today's 'morality' will be used like any other words, or language.

CHAPTER 7.

CRIMINALITY

HERE are only two ways possible in which our civilization may develop: it can either become more inhuman or more human. Both trends are apparent and present in our society; the first receives a remarkable amount of money and backing. The popular newspapers and a great many television programmes exist to boost the mentality behind it and to propagate the vision of a totally hard, ugly, metallic and plastic way of life to which our children and their children are to be condemned. Right through this book we have compared fire with water-consciousness – the hard, shallow and masculine with the soft, deep and feminine. We have also said that this is nothing to do with one's gender or sex. A gentleman is presumed to be gentle and a fish-wife rude. A human future is one in which society as a whole becomes more feminine, gentle, natural and compassionate. An inhuman future is one-sidedly masculine, taken to such an extreme point that our environment becomes totally artificial. and human beings hardened to its soul-destroying propensities: Criminality will thus be given full rein, because there would be no conscience.

The criminal mind is possessed by desire: for money, for revenge, for power over other people in order to exploit them. It is vindictive, full of hate, contempt and indifference. It is also unbalanced and full of contradictions. The criminal is mentally sick for he has denied his true nature and his soul has become polluted, his mind no longer registers what his conscience, his reflective and intuitive, feminine and sensitive, objective self would tell him, if it could. He hates himself for any feminine weakness, for any sensitivity he may have. His reflective, receptive self has been lost and he is inwardly as impure as a cesspool. Society, because it constantly reinforces his manly virtues, wants him to stay like this. His tastes and his amusements are reflected in the vulgar ostentation of the world he lives in, in the West-End of London, in Hollywood movies, in all the hideous artificiality which most people have come to accept as normal. A soulless environment and crime go hand in glove, and the more soulless our environment, the more criminal it becomes. Before 1960 Chicago was the most soulless place on earth* and it was also the most advanced in crime. Since that date European cities have copied their American example and thus they too are becoming unsafe. There were, of course, always hoodlums and footpads, pickpockets, burglars and thieves; in the 18th Century they were hanged at Tyburn and in the 19th Dickens put them in his novels; in days before the railways came there were highwaymen and before that outlaws with bows and arrows in the woods. There were always hard and heartless men who cynically, and without any conscience, robbed and ill-treated and killed their victims. In the Middle Ages there were barons who did this, and later on Ivan the Terrible, who amongst a host of other despots in the world's history stole and murdered, lied and cheated much as, or more than, Hitler, Himmler and all the other criminals in authority one would wish to name.

In a world where only the fittest survive and the strongest, loudest and biggest rule, where the Archetype for ↑ Φ (Fire and Earth), the Warrior, is God, where there is no mercy, it will be common

practice to take what you want from anyone who can't defend himself and to try to kill him if he does so. This is called the law of the jungle and it is by this law, which is the basis for war and competition, that the present-day political scene was set: Savage hordes of fast, furious Vandals, Vikings, Visigoths, lashing their horses into a frenzy, overpowered like a dreadful hurricane the countries before them, pillaged, burnt and devastated all the land, the towns, the monasteries and the churches. Terrible fleets of billowing ships, their great sails

*This may also have had something to do with the number of slaughterhouses there.

roaring in the wind, galleys rowed by suffering slaves, cruelty without measure, crossed the seas to conquer. The invaders killed the natives and ruled the land, thus the Celts came to Britain, the Romans, the Anglo-Saxons, the Normans and thus the white man came to America, to Africa and the Indies. Like a wind which blew from the East to the West, like a rising tide beating upon the shore, wave upon wave of conquering hoodlums, bandits, terrorists, poured out of the steppes of central Russia over Germany, over Britain and from there – in time – over the continent of North America, over the great Pacific Ocean, until the entire globe was permeated, polluted and petrified by the Western way-of-life, the worship of powerful machines; a mechanical, unfeeling, skyscraper mentality dressed in the same trousers and jackets all the world over. This is not as some might misguidedly see it, the advance of Christianity, but in fact that of the God Wotan, relentlessly progressing with his warlike counterparts Thor and Odin and all the rest, not forgetting Mars, of course. It was the grafting of Latin, square-bashing ingenuity on to Germanic thoroughness which gave birth to the preoccupation with technology and industry which characterises the Anglo-Saxon, whether in England or in the U. S. A. The first machines were made for warlike purposes and a warring, competing hardheadedness has manned, maintained and made more of them ever since.

When a group of people settle down on land which was cleared or conquered and begin to cultivate their fields and gardens, they require laws to protect their interests and rights. That is the second type of law, which is associated with custom and with order. A great many of these laws are a matter of convenience, an agreement that people behave in a certain way to avoid accidents, collisions and congestion. Such laws have no moral base; transgression against them is a- or anti-social and comes from foolishness, or ignorance or carelessness. A person who drives on the right hand side of the road in England is a menace, and someone who disturbs the peace in a public park, who is 'drunk and disorderly', who runs in and out of the library and upsets things in the High Street, causing people to drop their shopping bags is, although perhaps funny, a nuisance. The third type of law is a moral or ethical code and is associated with religion, that which is generally believed to

232

be true and right. This in the case of our own culture and society is sustained by the 10 Commandments which were given to the Jewish Nation by its founder who was inspired by a patriarchal god on top of a mountain. Our moral code derives also from the missionaries and evangelists of Christianity. Transgression against these laws is known as sin. In the Western world there always ex-isted a dichotomy between Church and State, Pope and Emperor. The first was there by virtue of its mission and its monasteries, its ability to convert heathens and establish learning. The second had established itself in a violent way, by means of winning battles and subduing the native people. The laws of the State were usually repressive and only concerned with ethical or religious considerations in so far as these aided this repression. The inquisition was always very popular with the state, witch-hunting, for instance, created terror amongst the common people and helped to keep them 'in their place'.

Since the 14th Century in this country, by degrees, the townspeople won themselves privileges and made themselves free from the tyrannical, warlike landowners who had originally acquired their estates, their houses and slaves or serfs by means of conquest. These fighters were what we now would consider to be criminals – the barons who fought with William the Conqueror – ruthless, ambitious, cruel men who were only kept in check in so far as they could be frightened by fear of damnation and hell-fire. Their power was replaced by that of wealthy merchants who created a new kind of serfdom, that of the exploited factory workers who, by uniting in endless agitation, have in their turn emancipated themselves. The laws we now have are the outcome of this process, they are concerned with three things: one, the protection of property; two, the safety of the individual; and three, the maintenance of (mostly sexual) morality. Parliament has, particularly during the second half of this century, become less patriarchal and our legal code has become more 'permissive' as a result. In spite of this the laws of our country are still largely aimed at the promotion of Fire-

Consciousness* and it is preoccupied with divisions which keep the Establishment intact. For instance it is assumed that the nuclear family is the only possible social unit and that the husband is 'ipso-facto' the head of it. Communes, homosexual or lesbian relationships and one-parent families don't enter the official consciousness. Any view which is genuinely humane but emotional, poetic, or artistic is accorded little validity in a court of law. For instance, anyone who loves a tree, a place or an animal and may have done so for many years has no rights to protect these against damage or harm, yet someone who owns them by some quirk of fate, although he might not care a fig for them, has the law on his side. There are still laws to inhibit the free expression of feeling, laws against certain forms of sexual contact and behaviour which are considered to be 'irregular' or 'improper'. The authors of this book would think of only actually harmful behaviour as criminal, behaviour which causes pain or suffering to other people or to animals; which deprives them of their human rights or of proper conditions.

There are two images of the devil: one is that of a horned beast, of a dragon, a mindless monster, and the other that of a schemer and a deceiver, who with his clever arguments will trick you into selling your soul. These are the two fiery Archetypes, the one representing in his positive aspect courage, daring, action, determination and confidence, the other resilience, skill, inventiveness, resourcefulness and wit. They are represented by a blazing inferno and hot, scintillating air. In the denial of their opposites ♉ ✳ and ♉ Φ, the Virgin or Angel and the Lady of Mysterious Depths, the gentle mist on the reflecting surface and the flowing undercurrents of the water; (surrender and kindness, receptivity and truth) they become negative, violent and cynical. Their abode is hell, whereas the Angels live in heaven. This is not merely a Christian way of looking at things, this imagery is universal and belongs to the *Collective Unconscious* of mankind. The evaporated water, the clouds float up above us in the delicate blue of heaven, whereas

*Fire-Consciousness is the result of thinking without feeling – thought which is disconnected from any intuition or instinct. It is therefore artificial and contrived and has to be taught, induced, instilled into a child in spite of, or irrespective of, any natural feelings, which then become subconscious.

234

The Pope, Hierophant or King of Heaven, the archetypal father figure governs the law and is the supreme judge, but is also a spiritual shepherd and therefore carries a crook. Behind Him are the elm tree which is associated with this archetype and a fir tree in a snow landscape associated with the elements air *and* water; ice *and* frost.

below us in the earth there lurks an inferno of molten lava which bursts out of volcanic craters with devastating violence from time to time. We associate the first with our conscience and day dreams, our poetic feelings, and the second with our pulsating, passionate blood, carnivorous passions and lust. With its philosophy of self-sacrifice, reflective thought, prayer and forgiveness, the Christian religion attempted to counteract the barbarous, 'devilish', blood-thirsty behaviour of the 'heathen'. Likewise it opposed 'worldly' excesses in everyday Mediaeval life and the criminality which persisted in spite of churches and monasteries. But heaven and hell were totally irreconcilable, 'the world' and its archetypes: ↑✶ and ↑Φ; the playful deceptiveness and the greed of the fire were always at loggerheads with ℧✶ and ℧Φ, the reflective tranquillity and the mysterious depth of the water, the inner world represented by the church. Christianity was too subjective, too intolerant, the Christian too hung up on his principles, his struggle with 'temptations', his sexual repression, to reconcile these opposites.

Fire, the potentially criminal element, can be reconciled with water only through detachment and objectivity, through being impassive and impartial. The archetype is the Observer, ✶Φ, space, distance, stillness, the absence of reactions. Fire feeds on reactions, but when it meets with a blank space, with a neutral, a silent endlessness the colour of this paper, it can only turn back on itself. The Christian sees himself as a 'miserable sinner' and is obsessed with his sinfulness, just because he has a bloodstream and a pair of buttocks, a penis and guts. We deliberately use the masculine gender because Christianity has always been a Patriarchal (✶℧) and masculine religion. It was, like most of the world until our own age (at least since our history began), not interested in nature and only feminine in so far as it included the Virgin Mary and the Angelic Host, which, although endowed with female looks and propensities, were nevertheless thought of as pretty boys, led by Archangels who are clearly men. God, the archetype for ✶℧, the bearded Patriarch, was cold and just, but had no truck with his female opposite Φ↑, the suckling, warm, cosy, earthy mother whose place is by the fireside, down below. Because Christianity has been so one-sidedly masculine, crystallized and full of judgements and condemnation, because the Christian is forever beating his breast, because he cannot see that this kind of emotionalism will not help to make the world more peaceful, a happier place to live in, that guilt-mongering cannot make us happy and that happiness is the only way to a less violent and destructive social organisation, it has only managed to keep alive a code of 'decency', but it has done little to cure the world of crime.

There are certain potentially criminal types: Types with ↑3rd, particularly those who have their ʊ 2nd, 'in the box', repressed. This includes one type which isn't ↑3rd, but Φ3rd (↑ʊΦ✳). Most successful men in our society belong to this type, who unconsciously, quite automatically identify with the Hero Archetype, the Warrior (↑ 1st, Φ3rd); our political leaders, Churchill, Bevan, Kennedy, Kruschev, all heavy-jowled, forceful, dynamic men, heads of large concerns, nationalized industries are of this type*. They have the Observer ✳Φ as their ideal** which gives them the ability to be fair-minded. Although certain types are psychologically predisposed towards behaving in a particular way, the conditions under which we grow up, the way we are brought up and influenced, the quality of our environment give us the outlook, the mentality and the degree of refinement we acquire. Greed, waste and mess are basic to a criminal mentality and create the loveless and brutal environment in which children grow up without guidance, kindness or even care. The parents had been shouted at and were thrown out on to the street... and they treat their children in the same way. Large, plastic toys become a substitute for any real affection or understanding and a greedy, careless, gripey dissatisfaction with life takes over. Thus the boys become part of a gang who spray their pseudonyms on walls and doors, break saplings in half, or destroy telephone boxes. They go 'nicking' in supermarkets and later on start 'casing a joint' and 'doing jobs'. Nothing in their en-

*The Φ3rd, that is to say their identification with being earthy, friendly, realistic etc. makes them acceptable to the majority of people in this, the age of the common man. (To be common is to be earthy).

**With the 'ideal' we mean that aspect of our 'personality' in which we find fulfilment, many people will see it as that which they most naturally are, others will realise that it is what they have grown into, what they have developed in adult life or are still unable to attain and need to become; it is always admired.

THE GRAIGS ON T.V.

vironment encourages them to behave in any other way. The fire rages unchecked – there is no water to put it out. Society as a whole is alienated from nature and no longer recognizes what is valuable and beautiful; its values are based on foibles which change according to the fashion. The old institutions of Church and State aimed at keeping standards apply only to the middle class and to the countryside, they were never effective in the 'slums' of our great cities, and anyway these standards are not always helpful. The whole structure of modern society has become amoral and untrustworthy. Materialists at the lower end of the social scale admire and envy those who have got to the top for their ability to reap their harvest by dubious and devious practices. In a criminal world, the *only* crime is being found out! Nevertheless, because of an overlaying ethos there exists a rift between the 'upper' and the 'lower' classes which, although material gains are held out to be the only worthwhile pursuit throughout conventional society, divides people in the way they think about acquiring their riches.

The upper-middle-class director of a company with his public school code of honour (thou shalt neither steal nor lie) may have no idea at all of what Johnny, the caretaker in the basement, is up to. The lower classes are free from hypocrisy and accept themselves as they are and will therefore quite naturally, given the opportunity – for acquisition is survival – 'nick' what they can. Lying too, of course, is part of 'the game' and this is commonly accepted. But the criminal world has a matiness and a solidarity which gives it its own code of honour: 'Grassing' – giving away your friends to the police – is considered to be as bad as stealing in the 'straight' world. If you are part of a 'dodgy' set up you can easily get 50 feet of free copper piping from the Gas Board, or a load of ice-cream in return for a few pounds or a favour. The criminal mentality exists because of Fire-Consciousness, because of competition and exploitation, because one man is rich and many others poor, because of a long history of selfishness and unkindness, because the newspapers and the other media promote the idea of ugly, material wealth, but most of all because children are not helped and encouraged to express their better feelings, because love and loveliness are nowhere made into public examples.

If kindness, compassion, and Water-Consciousness (which includes boys kissing each other) were promoted and given good publicity, if children were taught to share and not to compete with, or hurt each other (or animals or plants), then at last heaven would exist on earth. This is not an impossible dream – there *are* a few heavenly places where saintly (not unctuous), artistic, imaginative, free and cultured people live; painters, musicians, sculptors, poets, who have broken away from conventional society, or simple people who have never been part of it, where magic prevails and a real fairy or elfin world exists, where there are carpets of wild flowers in lush meadows, where the turtle doves gurgle and where solid, simple wooden furniture glows in a white interior and the soft colours, the reflections in picture-glass speak only of love. These places should be shown regularly on television, more and more articles about them should appear in the Press. Ordinary people should be allowed to know about them as they know 'Crossroads'* or some other serial about conventional ugliness, the hell they are used to. Beautiful examples may at first infuriate people with their unfamiliarity, but eventually they will be accepted and copied.

Heavenly conditions do exist and Utopia is already here with us on earth. Some of us were lucky enough to grow up in Paradise; we were privileged and fortunate enough to have had great-grandparents in the 1850's, who, being cultured and rich, could afford to

*This may have been replaced by 'East Enders', 'Neighbours' or 'Brookside'.

239

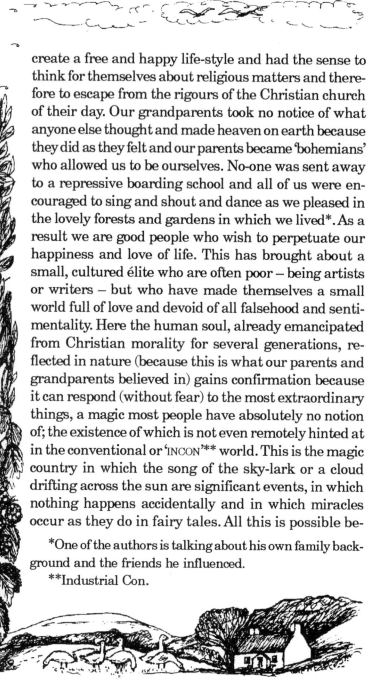

create a free and happy life-style and had the sense to think for themselves about religious matters and therefore to escape from the rigours of the Christian church of their day. Our grandparents took no notice of what anyone else thought and made heaven on earth because they did as they felt and our parents became 'bohemians' who allowed us to be ourselves. No-one was sent away to a repressive boarding school and all of us were encouraged to sing and shout and dance as we pleased in the lovely forests and gardens in which we lived*. As a result we are good people who wish to perpetuate our happiness and love of life. This has brought about a small, cultured élite who are often poor – being artists or writers – but who have made themselves a small world full of love and devoid of all falsehood and sentimentality. Here the human soul, already emancipated from Christian morality for several generations, reflected in nature (because this is what our parents and grandparents believed in) gains confirmation because it can respond (without fear) to the most extraordinary things, a magic most people have absolutely no notion of; the existence of which is not even remotely hinted at in the conventional or 'INCON'** world. This is the magic country in which the song of the sky-lark or a cloud drifting across the sun are significant events, in which nothing happens accidentally and in which miracles occur as they do in fairy tales. All this is possible be-

*One of the authors is talking about his own family background and the friends he influenced.

**Industrial Con.

240

cause it is outside the Fire-Conscious establishment, because it has escaped. Now the time is drawing near in which this Water-Conscious land, this magic country, this strange élite of our friends will grow and become strong and be recognized. On a programme like 'Any Questions', Enoch Powell, Katherine Whitehorn and Co. feel compelled to say that Utopia is nowhere, impossible, and non-existent, something to make a bad joke about, that to them our present world, with all its bloodshed and horror is the only possible reality. Our Water-Conscious world, being a threat to them – because it would force them to become different, to surrender to love – cannot be allowed by them, and therefore, as far as they are concerned, does not exist. Some of us have been through experiences which turned us into quite different people from these personalities on the radio and the television who, unfortunately, still lead public opinion. Their days are numbered, however, a world which they have no conception of will grow larger and larger, until it can overcome the present establishment and a new species, a new kind of human being takes over.

It is very noticeable that the most criminal element in society is also the most deprived. Children who grow up in a very poor and bad environment perpetuate the neglect they have suffered, but likewise children who grow up in loveless stately homes, or were sent to repressive boarding schools pass on their lack of freedom and joy. Neurosis is caused by neurotic parents and means an inability to feel confident and happy about

one's natural, real self. Animals which have been treated with kindness and understanding become beautiful and plants which are
well looked-after thrive. A human being who is free to be himself
and loved for what he really is, who is allowed to love and to be
what he naturally wants to be (and for many boys this will mean
loving a man and being feminine) becomes lovely. If you are growing a field of corn or are looking after lambs, the sowing of that
seed, the rearing of those sheep can either be an act of devotion or
not, out of reverence for nature, part of the rhythm of the seasons,
or meaningless and part of nothing but money-making. Those sheep
and that corn are growing because of you, through your care, are a
reflection of you and that explains why under identical conditions
a bad man's livestock will look mangy and miserable and a good
man's happy and healthy. To the hard-headed factory-farmer this
will appear to be 'airy-fairy' nonsense and ditto to the Ministry of
Agriculture, Fisheries and Food, but you cannot deny the psychic
or spiritual world (the magic country), without denying all satisfaction, love and beauty and without actually encouraging crime.
What is the difference between a good and a bad man? What is the
difference between love and hate? In a world where love is the rule
(that Water-Conscious land) we sacrifice ourselves to our inferiors,
co-operate with our equals and honour those above us. In a world
of grinding hate we despise our inferiors, are indifferent to our
equals and are afraid of those above us. A good farmer is content
with the number of cattle, or sheep or fields he can manage, because you can't love what you can't cope with, it becomes too much
for you, and wears you down. He is sensible and knows each sheep
individually, he is satisfied to keep his farm on a small, personal
level. If a sheep fall ill he knows the reason why, whereas the bad
farmer, who is just a businessman, delegates to some incompetent
nincompoop who does not care about his work... and if one sheep
falls ill, will inject the whole lot.

An ideal society is one in which there is sacrifice, co-operation
and honour, where people communicate with each other, around
the lamp on the table, in the corner-shop, or the village store, where
there is a sense of community. Whereas in some areas there are
signs that this sense of community is growing, in others there is
nothing but division, self-centredness and discord. The television

sets blare out horrific films on war, murder and devastation watched by the children upstairs, while their parents are gazing at the television downstairs. These people shop in a supermarket where an atmosphere of greed and suspicion prevails, where closed-circuit television, store detectives, private policemen standing guard in brown uniforms with peaked caps and terrifying security cash-collectors, robotically filing out of an armoured van, create the impression that only criminality exists and nothing else is at all possible. Perhaps children growing up under such conditions look forward to life in prison as at least a chance to communicate with their fellow men. In the other kind of society, the Water-Conscious world, criminal activity is confined to just a few eccentric deviants who are known by everyone to be a bit loopy. This is a society of small-holdings in the countryside, or rehabilitated Victorian and Georgian (or even older) districts in the towns. In such places, in North Wales, in North London, in parts of Scotland, the new world is gradually coming of age, when it will grow like a plant with many tendrils, like bindweed all over the conventional establishment. The land of fairytales will spring into reality, a land of medieval market-towns, of whispering trees and magic incantations. Unfortunately in the minds of only too many people this will be confused with 'Disneyland' and 'Good News' day on an American

Architect's Bazaar

243

Radio Station, some artificial tourist dump, or something else with a vulgar, sentimental, cloying appeal. This is how far too many people have deviated from any natural and honest appreciation.

In the 15th and 16th centuries, until the landlords enclosed common land and the resultant vagrant population became persecuted, an ideal world nearly existed, had it not been for cruel injustices, religious persecution, bad medicine and plagues. We have more or less done away with these four evils, at least in our country, but meanwhile the towns and the countryside have been lost to us. This means that the circumstances of human existence have improved in some ways, we live longer, we are comfortably housed and there is no abject poverty*. Human society is evolving towards a better state and in this process certain stages have to be passed, one of these was technology, the next one will be psychology, the way to a harmonious development of ourselves and our environment. We are prophesying that mediaeval towns will be resurrected and restored and that the countryside will be reclaimed, that a Water-Conscious society (what we mean is a society in which the balance between fire and water has been achieved) will make the fairytale world of the later Middle Ages real and good. William Morris pictures this future in 'News from Nowhere', that his message is devoid of any psychological and sexual reality characterizes the time in which he wrote and worked. His vision is through the haze of rather stiff, pre-Raphaelite romanticism and the ethos of his day. William Morris believed naïvely that a world of socialist equality was also a world in which there would be no criminals. In many ways the hygienic, clean Welfare State he wished for has come about, for we have forgotten the grime and soot and misery he saw in the streets, but what would he have thought of the cars and the council estates? What would he have thought of the way in which the romance of crime is extolled? A book on the adventures of a criminal gang is reviewed on every conceivable radio programme, films on banditry have immense popular appeal and even start off fashions: Crime is Big Business. Why in the face of all this popular support should it cease? The majority of people follow the fashion, they have no independent minds. There seems to be no

*This was in 1976, in 1994, after 15 years of 'Thatcherism' this may sadly no longer be the case.

social stigma attached to being a criminal, in fact quite the opposite! On the other hand the slightest suggestion of mental illness can mean the loss of all your friends. If this situation could be reversed then the *'Sainsburys'* policemen and *'Tesco'* store detectives would have to look for more creative work and the television would be obliged to put on the plays *we* might enjoy watching and listening to.

UBLIC life, the media and parliament are dominated by a specific group of people in this *day and age* – to use a fashionable phrase – who pander to popular fashions (e.g. 'Punk'*) and in whose interest it is that whatever is promoted should appeal to a majority and sell. Thus the public is constantly conditioned to and fed with what it is supposed to 'want' (that is to say, has got used to). There is absolutely no morality in this and therefore the basest instincts, the most revolting tastes have to be catered for and these become the real life religion** of the masses. Crime rates highly in all this because it has the fascination of being rebellious and destructive and is therefore a release for frustration and bad feeling. It is really nothing but a big punch-bag for negative emotions, bad atmospheres (literally 'stink') and violent reactions. The demons of unresolved situations, stupid choices, unsuitable marriages and work which fails to satisfy, which lead to a joyless home, are everywhere in evidence and rule most people's lives. One obviously cannot lock up one third of the entire population of Britain. If we are really seriously concerned and wish to counteract a criminal society, we must organize ourselves to do this. In every street, community or block of flats, once a week, a meeting must be held presided over by an Inter-Communicator. These meetings are arranged by the Communicator for the area who has trained the Inter-Communicator in social, psychological and spiritual work.

*This was written in 1976; in 1994, is it 'Post Punk'?

**A religion is what people believe in; in this case it is a kind of hedonism which goes under the banner of 'freedom'.

245

These young women and men fulfill the role of teachers in really happy, imaginative schools, of playleaders and social workers, but they are also Graigian priests*. In Communication there is no division between the spiritual, artistic, scientific or political aspects of life. As has been said before by us there will be Institutes of Natural Psychology, run by male and female monks dressed in green robes and cloaks, in converted country houses and at universities everywhere in Britain. These are the Mentates referred to earlier where Communicators are taught. Criminality will be regarded as a kind of sickness and like any illness its prevention will be preferable to its cure. The trained Communicator is a nurse or a doctor who is able to bring people back to themselves, often just by listening, by introducing exercises ('Activation')** games, discussions, nature walks, slide and film shows, lectures, readings and other sessions. In these groups people who have criminal leanings or intentions can discuss these openly. They will be understood in a group context as the group becomes more supportive and understanding. The prime object is to gently push people back into themselves and to give them confidence in their own true feelings. Crazy talk which takes them away from real experience, belief in 'other worlds', Martian and so on*** will naturally die down.

The spread of an urban life-style with unnatural, bourgeois values has reached its zenith, and even small villages in remote places here and in far-off countries like Arabia, which remained the same for thousands of years, are now changed overnight and suffused with all the paraphernalia of civilization e.g. Walkmans and breezeblocks. A criminal mentality thrives on this ugliness

*Please don't confuse Graigian priest(esses) with any kind of priesthood you may be familiar with. Graigians are an entirely NEW PHENOMENON; totally unconventional, natural and spontaneously *awake* people, *not* unctuous moralists. For instance, they use four letter words and bathe out of doors in the nude.

**Since 'Activation' takes place in 'Hallowhalls' and is to do with purification, it could also become known as 'Hallowing'. At present this exercise is practised in 'Subud' and is known as the 'Latihan'.

***We are referring here to the kind of escapist fantasy exploited by film producers, so called science-fiction and the like, which serves to alienate people even more from their natural environment than they already are.

and this is emphasized by daily news bulletins about violent attacks by 'terrorists', maddened not by political idealism so much as by their lack of integrity. These terrorists are nearly always a particular voy type: $* \cup \uparrow \Phi$, fully explained in a former chapter. What this type needs is discipline, firstly by confinement in the care of their opposite types $\uparrow \Phi \cup *$ or $\Phi \uparrow \cup *$ who, secondly, wish to give them the natural therapy they long for, even before they get a chance to hijack or kidnap. In other words this suggests an understanding arrived at by an extremely clear mind. The degree of perception and lack of prejudice which is required to 'receive', that is to say intuitively understand and objectively feel what the inner needs of a person suspected of criminal intentions, or of a convict, are, would belong to a Mediator of our future society. Usually this kind of mind has been associated with holy men or women; with sainthood.

Holy people, spiritual people, good people, have always existed, but have been driven underground by the malevolent conditions of society. At the moment they are sad or confused and hide away in their rooms, always seeking the *'Shangri-La'*, the little cottage in Ireland, the 'Ivory Tower' where they can secure the peace, stillness and serenity of mind which they value so highly, the abundance and lushness of living a spiritual life in a natural setting. Such people will come out of hiding in ever-increasing numbers, like water trickling through a dam and in their green and brown robes, green cloaks and brown hats they will be seen and heard everywhere, bringing with them the freshness of the country air and purity of the water. They will bring with them the knowledge of Natural Psychology: 'In the midst of the street of it and on either side of the river there was the tree of life which bare twelve manner of fruits, and yielded her fruit every month and the leaves of the tree were for the healing of the nations'. They will give hope to the despondent, courage to the weak, understanding to the confused, forgiveness to the

stupid, companionship to the lonely, health to the sick and whole-someness to the artificial. They will come into schools, universities, colleges, community centres and cafés like a swarm of bees. They will be angels with kind faces, clear eyes and shimmering hair, initiated on the Holy Mountain of 'Anelog'*, where in all sincerity these ideas have been received. This is the sacred land where in 1965 the Green Movement** started and for which after 12 miraculous years the "Save the Vale of Anelog" campaign was launched. Mount Anelog looks over to Bardsey, the island where 20,000 saints are said to be buried and which in 1978 was bought to be made into a wildlife sanctuary. The Vale of Anelog, which is the far end of the Llŷn*** Peninsula will, if goodness prevails, be cut off from the rest of Britain by a frontier, to become a spiritual haven with its heart at Graig, our home on the mountain. Our green people: (the 'angels' referred to) the monks, the Rangers, Inter-Communicators and Communicators will be known as 'Graigians'. Y Graig – Er Grige, as in tide – means 'the rock' in Welsh.

Just as greed, waste is another component of criminality: Say you have just stolen a million cigarettes or a thousand biros. Because you have a glut of these goods, you cannot respect them, you start throwing them around or selling them for an absurdly low price at which they have lost any value. A kind of inverted inflation takes place, if you can see it that way. Without respect, self-respect, esteem or regard, life becomes cheapened and devalued. If you have a *'fuck you'* attitude to the World you no longer care for anything but your own selfish comfort, you no longer look after things, clean them or care for them, you do not sort out your rubbish or even bother to get rid of it. Depressed, criminal, city areas are characterised by rubbish and mess. Few plants or trees can grow there, which brings us back to our constant theme of natural growth and human

*Near Aberdaron, North Wales. Pronounced àNelog.
**This was by the first group of people with 'Green' ideals to produce a Green Manifesto.
***Also spelt Lleyn

integrity: Everyone must be given the chance to have a small plot of land, or an allotment, or to keep animals. Unfortunately, for such ideas to be put into practice at the present time there is not yet enough opposition to the antiquated way in which the established, conventional world functions. In that respect we do not live in a free society. For instance, the politician, the comedian who imitates the politician and the audience who laugh are all fulfilling a totally automatic rôle, they are all doing what is expected of them and in that respect they are conforming to the expectations of the establishment. The only organ of dissent is a magazine called 'Private Eye' which, although it was probably founded with the good intention of counteracting hypocrisy and big-headedness amongst politicians, businessmen and royalty, has degenerated into a comic for cynical – but intelligent – people. The only really successful 'underground' newspaper 'IT', unfortunately floundered through sloppiness and degenerated into a comic, disappeared for a decade and was then revived, but may have disappeared again.

In a Spiritual Society which must come into being – unless we are to sink into a pit of apathetic gormlessness, which is unlikely, because, just like the weather, the *Zeitgeist* changes – the law will be administered very differently from the way it is now. At present the Police carry out investigations, interrogations and arrests in a heavy-handed way, rush about in screaming cars and are popular only with 'tre-lopers'*. They seem more interested in arresting hippies who smoke cannabis (less harmful than alcohol) than in catching burglars and have a black, ugly image (anyone who disagrees with us is invited to spend an afternoon in the average police station) and although one should sympathise with them really for doing a difficult job there is no reason except that of habit why we should have to go on paying for an inefficient, prejudiced and insensitive force. Its place will be taken, as has been the theme all through this book, by a green force of social workers: Communicators, Inter-Communicators and Rangers, the first two are spiritual ranks whereas the latter are their lay helpers. Another constant

---

*A term we use to describe a certain type of extremely 'stick in the mud', repressive, conventional person who had his heyday in the first world war, covers everything in concrete and obstructs or lops anything in the least alive and free. It developed from 'tree-lopper', because it was misread.

theme which we have used is that of the living, tangible, good example; the Rangers look up to and love their friendly guide, their Communicator, the Communicator derives spiritual guidance and practical advice from his/her Nominator and Mediators, all of whom may be monks. This changeover will not mean the creation of a lawless or anarchistic state by any means and it is quite possible that the Rangers would have, in the event of the Police Force being dissolved, their own department equivalent to the CID. Rangers would be assisted, whenever needed, by the Positive Force. It must be remembered that these soldiers will be quite unlike the ones we have today: they will be openly aware of their femininity and passionately devoted too – that is to say truly in love with – their spiritual ideal. This will give them a kind of voluptuous, submissive sexuality, a feminine caring, a wholesomeness quite unknown today amongst these kind of boys. We realise that a number of our readers will find what we say objectionable, just as the Pope objected when Galileo stated that the earth revolves around the sun, and yet what we say is true and will happen. Archaic, Fire-Conscious prejudices will go down into the grave with the people who hold them, whereas what is new and young and fresh will live! Nature has decreed that many young men should be voy and Nature is bound to triumph!

There will be, to counteract the criminal backlash of centuries of Fire-Conscious conditioning (that is to say a long history of male chauvinism), a wide range of interesting and socially useful jobs for young people, a whole spectrum of social help and community services. This 'New Age' will demand a great emphasis on respect for humanity and particularly to those least able to help themselves: the old, the lonely, battered mothers and children, the avalanche of mentally ill, ex-prisoners, drug addicts and those who have been misunderstood. The ranks among the Rangers might be called after trees, the equivalent of a Police Constable could be called a Willow Ranger, the Sergeant, an Ash Ranger and the Inspector, an Elder Ranger; the Chief Commissioner of Police would then be called the Oak Ranger. The symbols of rank may well be designs of these trees embroidered onto the cloak or smock, as a silver pendant, or a badge worn in the hat, of warm brown felt, high-crowned and narrow rimmed. All the Rangers carry a whistle, and also wear beads, because they are the kind of people who in the late 1960's became squatters, hippies, drop-outs, and took an interest in the Tarot-cards, are strict vegetarians and became the devotees of an Indian Guru. Much of their work will consist of walking the streets, visiting people and talking to them, becoming involved in the life of the district, like a priest, and keeping a watchful eye on everything going on. The Rangers and Inter-Communicators are the eyes, ears, hands and voice of the Communicator and it is essential that the Communicator loves them and gets on with them well.

The subject of Mediation has already been dealt with. At present the courts of law are stuffy and the procedures cumbersome, the court-rooms were usually built before the Second World War and the system has not changed much since Victorian times. The court is more often than not presided over by a stuck-up, doddery magistrate, or judge who owes his position to recommendations, his ability to make the right impression, to repress what he feels deep down and to say and do what is expected of him. It is quite possible that he hides the kind of sexual fantasy we described in a previous chapter while sentencing a pathetic wreck of a man to years of imprisonment for some, so-called, 'sexual offence'. What happens in a Court of Law is regarded as a game in which everyone is more or less expected to lie. The barrister defends the accused by any trick he can muster and the prosecutor – who is also merely putting on a show – will try and pick holes in the defence. If you have knocked someone down for instance, or committed some other crime, you must never admit it, you must make excuses or blame someone else. If you did admit responsibility this would be used in evidence against you and you would not stand a chance, you would have to plead guilty. In the West we are conditioned to be subjective and we are taught to justify ourselves at all costs. We fail to be objective about ourselves and do not accept the consequences of our own actions. In this legal subjectivity, the truth is lost, for truth can only be revealed in sincerity and in a receptive atmosphere, in a place where there is stillness, purity, a peaceful acceptance and integrity. Under the present legal system judges go by hidebound principles, jurors do not know their own rights, let alone those of the accused, the Police twist the evidence any way they like, the barrister is motivated by the fee he is paid and yet this is considered to be the best of all possible legal systems. We promise the reader that a better one lies ahead.

A Mediator who has graduated not just at a University, but through the ranks of social work and who has dedicated her/himself to a spiritual way of life will be able to see through a pack of lies and intuitively understand what is going on below the surface. Rangers and Communicators who are socially motivated will want to help the accused and meanwhile protect the rest of the community from potentially dangerous persons*. In an objective and sensitive atmosphere the truth will always prevail and hypocrisy, vindictiveness and sentimentality have no place. It is a question of a certain refinement predominating, a refinement and a purity which are nevertheless down to earth, in touch with life and without any affectations. Against this any falsehood will show up as clearly as a gate post in the snow. Crime must be dealt with in terms of human suffering, that is to say the harm done to human feeling and the emotional loss which is suffered. A great change will come in the attitude towards ownership which will be regarded as commitment (caring for something) or responsibility (to be answerable for it). Ownership will no longer be a 'carte blanche' to abuse property and animals or to hurt children. It is very monstrous that babies are battered, children treated badly, dogs abandoned, that any vandalistic owner can do what he likes with his house**, his

---

*There has been a great deal of hysteria in the last decade (1984-94) about 'child-abuse', much of it imaginary (like the witch's 'league with the devil' in the 17th century). If such 'abuse' really does take place with actual harmful effects on children, it should certainly *not* be dealt with by policemen, come to Court, be allowed to fortify prejudices and destroy a teacher's, vicar's or scoutmaster's life.

**To some extent planning laws counteract the worst abuses, but still the red concrete-tiled roofs proliferated in London's Victorian districts; an ugly fashion like this could be discouraged, but the appropriate propaganda is not put out and laws have not been designed to counteract this kind of deterioration.

trees, his land, and that the proverbial villain, the factory-farmer was allowed, even encouraged to pull down hedgerows and ancient earth walls. Ownership will be conditional, implying proper care, welfare and maintenance, so that old cottages can no longer be defaced by picture windows and suburban front doors, old farm buildings allowed to fall into ruin and old farmhouses covered in 'snowcemed' pebbledash and surrounded by suburban gardens with conifers and wrought-iron embellishments, quite out of keeping with any tradition whatsoever.

It is terrible to think that many young criminals have never had understanding parents, do not know anything about animals or plants from a real, first-hand experience and have not found it

possible to be creative in an imaginative way. So often children living in a rough environment who want to paint or make things have their work destroyed by other children and are thus discouraged. The reason children are destructive is that they are misdirected and bored, they have no access to their inner life because everything around them, from the garish wallpaper to the incessantly ejaculating T.V. set in the corner and the general hub-bub and din of entertainments (pop music etc.) takes them away from themselves. Any sensitivity is seen as 'queer' and honesty as 'stupid', school-work as a result means little to them, they do not respect their teachers and cannot identify with the alien academic world because their parents and neighbours are opposed to it. We are here confronted with two sets of values, one 'bright red', the other 'deep blue'. There are two ways of healing the breach, the first one is discipline, the second is silence, a space between the red and the blue, the fire and the water. Children need and want a certain order and regularity, they need to be told that toads are different from frogs, that plants do not like being walked on, that rabbits do not eat boiled sweet. By discipline, we mean enlightened guidelines which the children are given and can apply to themselves later in life, we are not talking about unnecessary restrictions or pointless punishments. The cults of 'Batman', or 'Bionic', or some other mechanical man need to be counteracted instead of indulged; the tribal rituals these gods prescribe must be given an antidote, the way into a new world. Criminality is born out of the sterile boredom of enforced conformity to negative fashions, the 'gang syndrome' of 'Skinhead', 'Punks', 'Rockers' and their equivalents. This needs to be broken with another force, that of water.

Rootlessness is another one of the major factors in the creation of criminality. The more uprooted and alienated people are, the more 'lost' and bewildered they become. So-called 'mugging' for instance is most common in areas like Brixton (South London) where a great many immigrants from the West Indies have settled. West Indian negroes have a long history of being uprooted. Firstly they were herded like cattle and made to work under duress, they were treated with contempt and forced to live in strange places under terrible conditions. Twice their roots have been left behind, first in Africa and then in the West Indies. If we are to take the effects of rootlessness seriously – just as we have been able to rid ourselves of malignant and dangerous diseases, such as leprosy and more recently diphtheria, by inoculations and other precautions – we will have to treat the conditions which give rise to crime and mental illness. These conditions are a direct result of the colonial expansion which West-European countries perpetuated since the discovery of America, roughly since the beginning of the 16th century. That is why South America and Africa have become the worst places on earth. It happened unavoidably as part of our evolution, part of the process by which civilization travelled from Egypt to Crete to Greece to Rome to Britain and so on. It had to be so, this consciousness had to be evolved and technology developed. Mankind was compelled to explore the external world and with rockets shooting into outer space this has been accomplished. There is little more to be discovered outside ourselves by the usual mechanistic, scientific methods. The cure for cancer, the answer to the riddle of the universe lie within and the arts and sciences that will come about in the future will tell us what we do not yet know or understand by exploring the inner depths.

The flames of fires flare up on a broad wall, built of old plum-coloured London bricks. The arched gates are guarded by fantastic soldiers who themselves look like the flames in yellow ochre uniforms, striped with red and orange. They are obviously most contented, voy and pink-faced, for there is no inner trouble with them. They resemble in their costumes ballet dancers, or late Mediaeval lancers. Behind this wall is a sacred place, which for many of the young stalwarts living there is a prison, but to the girls and girlish-looking boys (one can scarcely tell the difference) in their wide-flowing dresses – these dresses might be better described as ' robes ', they are of an entirely new style – it is a paradise. The fires are burning rubbish, the garbage of the city, the accumulated trash of the second half of the 20th century: All sorts of things made since 1950; anything that can be burnt, like shoddy furniture, things made of useless lumber, but *not* plastic, which needs to be recycled or dealt with in some other way. Whoever enters this prison, or this Paradise, is to have all her or his rubbish burnt, not only ugly and inappropriate possessions, but metaphorically, also all their affectations, bad ideas and idiotic concepts, all the egoistic, destructive and cynical theories and philosophies which, for instance, would condemn what we are writing on this page. This fire is the first purification, the second purification is by water. In the centre of the sacred city in a walled garden, there is a shallow round pool made of bricks which is a font below a weeping willow, surrounded by red and white rambling roses, linden trees and a large elder bush. In what was once a comprehensive school the boys are trained to become members of the Positive Force. They are prisoners selected from the Special Zones (referred to in Chapter II, Re-orientation) who have certain qualities and are the right kind and of the right type. They will be made to surrender to the Life Force and to submit to a discipline which will make them obedient, strong, useful and constructive, instead of perverse, weak, useless and destructive. After serving in this prison for a year they will be allowed outside to do duty elsewhere, except for a few of them who have developed in a way which makes them indispensable for certain functions in this new and sacred city. We must remember this is an extraordinary spiritual centre, like a Vatican or a Potala and thus such duties would be of a religious nature, like that of bringing in the braziers of burning branches in the second act of the Moonday celebration which is held at midnight in the Salubriat.

In the bad old days lunatics were chained up in Bedlam to be watched by people for a penny, like animals at the zoo. We still confine convicts in Victorian prisons, guarded by 'screws' and convey them in 'sweat-boxes' to other places. Some of these are Open Prisons which could actually help to make a criminal better, because we have to look upon a convict who is justly sentenced as someone in need of help, someone who is inwardly crying out for a particular kind of treatment. A receptive, sensitive doctor, a Mediator will be able to sense what this treatment is to be, what the prisoner needs to get better, to become whole. Should he be beyond this, so bad, so incurable that he will always be a menace, then like the chronically ill he will have to be looked after for the rest of his life. The moment someone is sentenced he is put into care. Until he has found a way to live successfully, a place to live, something to do, a position in society, he should be cared for. In the near future the care prisoners receive – and there will be many more of them, because of the colossal increase in crime – should consist of all kinds of therapy which to modern eyes would look strange, like certain forms of massage, the use of certain aids, exercises and sensitively applied restraints and treatment to develop good feelings. The criminal must be studied as we now study the physically or mentally sick. He would have to get the food which will help him to become healthy and good, also the recreation and work he needs. A great deal of this work would be connected with Reclamation (Chapter I).

There will eventually be half-way houses for children who want to leave home, a house set aside in every area where children can 'run away to' and where their problems will be sorted out by experienced, trained, loving people. There will be many more homes for battered or misunderstood mothers and their children, who will be helped to make a new life for themselves. Everyone must have a purpose, an aim in life, even if it is a small one like keeping one's home nice and fresh, or looking after a rabbit. There will be no reason for anyone to feel lonely or unwanted, there will be enough for everyone to do in a creative, spiritual world, in which our work is our evolution as human beings towards fulfilment and nobility. The monks, Rangers, Inter-Communicators and Communicators will be 'Angels' in human form, come down from Heaven (Heaven or Paradise refers to the special areas with their Salubriat, Hallow Hall and Mentate, the Sacred City or Prison, described earlier in this chapter) to heal, care for and guide a sick, confused and lost people and to bring happiness to us all.

"And he carried me away in the spirit to a great and high mountain and showed me that great city, the holy Jerusalem, descending out of heaven from God, having the glory of God and her light was like unto a stone most precious, even like a jasper stone, clear as crystal; and had a wall great and high and had twelve gates and at the gates twelve angels and names written thereon, which are the names of the twelve tribes of the children of Israel: on the east three gates; on the north three gates; on the south three gates; and on the west three gates. And the wall of the city had twelve foundations and in them the names of the twelve apostles of the lamb".

APPENDIX I.

Agribusiness and Rural Renewal

If you had flown over the countryside of Britain in the year 1920 you would have seen a spectacular, jewel-like 'patch-work' quilt of fields with wooden or wrought iron 5 bar gates, interspersed with a plethora of commons, woods and ponds.

Criminal use of fertilizers and weed killers, the grubbing-up of hedges, the chopping down of whole lines of ancient trees, *none* of this had yet happened. There were neither tractors nor J.C.B's and the farmers worked with sturdy horses and wooden carts. In some very remote places there were still old shepherds who carried lovely bone-handled crooks and wore exquisite smocks... each smock-design being particular to a village or area.

If you were to fly on the same route today, 74 years later, you would see a landscape changed beyond all recognition; instead of barns (some of them 500 years old) for storing grain you would notice towering, silver silos; instead of horses you would see tank-like monstrosities, gigantic wheels front and back and blazing head-lights below a remote glass cabin with a bored, unthinking, unfeel-ing clodhopper in it: An Φ 3rd lump, who follows the frightful fash-ion without a conscience. The Leviathan he manoeuvres compresses and compacts the soil, inhibits the billions of earthworms and bac-teria which keep the earth in good working order, apart from mak-ing noise, smell and pollution.

But the *greatest* change of all would be in the way land is owned and used; 10, 20, 30 fields have all been conglomerated into *one*, enormous, American-style prairie. All the hedges and trees which used to be home to countless songbirds and small mammals have vanished. All that remains is an uneasy silence, a memorial to a land of once magical loveliness.

What, one may ask, is grown on these fields? The sad, doleful answer is, apart from wheat and other crops like rapeseed, they grow silage grass. This grass is *not* the sweet yellowy green grass of old meadows, but a horrible strain of rye grass, dark emerald in colour; it cuts your legs as you walk through it and it is used to make a disgusting mush called silage which is fed to cattle. The advantage is, to the farmer, that you can harvest this grass with a huge lawn-mower/hoover-type contraption *twice* a year whereas the traditional hay harvest can only be done *once*. Also getting in the hay is a labour-intensive task; much of it involves several operations over a period of time which also depend on warm, sunny weather. The modern, money-mad business tycoon does not want any of *that* and considers the time-honoured methods of using scythes and wide wooden rakes, or even the horse drawn implements of the 30's, to be *nostalgic*, foolish and 'romantically' starry-eyed. For spiritual and psychological reasons, however, it matters greatly that anything 'nostalgic' and 'romantic' is revived if we don't wish to create a soulless hell on earth, a hell in which the little of real value we still possess is threatened by crime, madness and despairing cynicism.

Urban people today, on the whole, no longer relate to the reality of the countryside and don't know what silage is and how harvesting is done. They have *ideas* about fields and meadows which are kept alive by commerce with pictures on jars and packets depicting an idyllic scene which no longer exists. Farming and its effect on the landscape have become a mirror of the psychic mess the 'space age' created and perpetuates in order to be 'viably productive'. In spite of all the talk of being realistic, the consuming public is deceived into thinking that ploughing is done with horses (on pickle jars), haymaking continues in the meadows (on tins of bedtime drinks), corn is bound in sheaves (on the wrapping of mass produced bread) and cows are milked by hand (on packets of butter), even wallpaper is sold by means of such illusions.

The dreadful fact is that the piles of shiny, black plastic bags which have replaced haystacks are liable to have some escape and these are blown about to pollute the earth, together with poisonous chemicals, when the factory-farmers and their bovine minions have finished with them. The bags are trodden and driven into the ground, particularly along the tractor tracks and wave about in bushes and from trees vying with flags of polythene. In case the reader is unfamiliar with it, bin-liner type bags are used to preserve the silage (grass-cuttings) in an air tight condition and are stacked up in an ugly pile under a net, weighed down by car and lorry tyres.

Silage making is justified, like all other labour saving 'improvements' which are part of 'progress' and 'modernization', or 'rationalization', by its cheapness. The price we will have to pay, however, will be of an unexpected kind, but far greater than anything saved by such a deplorable method. Just as a hole appeared in the ozone layer and polluted air and water threaten our health and safety, so will the increased indifference to anything which may have moved them, the apathy and superficiality which the majority of people passively have allowed to rule their lives, deprive them of their sanity. A disfigured countryside, the phantasy that replaces it and the soul destroying conditions of urban life will take their toll. Many more people than are mad already will end up with drugs, drunk, or in a lunatic-asylum.

Factory farming must be abolished, just as the slave-trade and slavery was. Examples should be set to show how sensitive husbandry can be an advantage to our mental health and doesn't belie the way food is advertised. This is what we all love, the adorable (from adore) country lane bordered by cowparsley, campion and buttercups like bright, amazing stars, the beautiful, bright cock in the farmyard, plump carthorses drawing marvellous, wholesome, painted carts. Farmers in J.C.B's or tractors are in complete conflict with the countryside in May and violate this spiritual, sweet and soft world. The traditional ways are fitting and by their slowness healthy and peaceful.

Farmers who are able to feel deeply (who are not types with water second and 'in the box'; see Chapter V, Spirituality) should plough with horses, gather hay with these and use straw bedding for honest manure. The thousands of people, now living aimless, desperately empty, despairing lives should be able to work on the land and be given hope and beneficial influences and then there will be plenty of hands to divide the work. Harvesting in the time-honoured way is good, meaningful and *lovely*, like the cornflowers which once grew amongst the rye; but one youth listening to pop-music through earphones on top of a monstrous, combined harvester in a glass cabin on a field of 50 acres is depriving two dozen people of work and the nation of a moving and stimulating experience. Why should the spiritual content our lives are yearning for be condemned as unpractical and uneconomic?

Instead is it totally uneconomic to 'set aside' and 'diversify'. Because with intensive farming too much devitalised food is produced, land has to be wasted in the most unimaginative way possible: just a long strip growing thistles beside the silage field. Efforts to 'diversify' end up by being unsightly and inappropriate: One farm has a yard full of plastic furniture or toys, another has fishponds for a local club, where people are treated like pets, allotted a square, tarmaced space to fish from in the newly dug pond and another space on a tarmaced area to park their car where there was once a public footpath. This is the domestication of nature in which lawns have to be hoovered with rotary mowers and verges cut with strimmers. Nothing as irregular as a wildflower is allowed to exist in this suburban, bourgeois environment. Farmyards, concreted over, become sterile laboratories for experiments with cattle and the dead, strimmed and stilted atmosphere will have a disastrous effect on the 'eco-diversity' (to use a fashionable phrase): Children growing up in this boring world will become pale and unhealthy. We must fight to keep sub-urbanisation out of the remaining real and beautiful countryside. All the grants and subsidies paid to bolster up 'set aside' and 'diversification' should go to the conversion of intensive farming to organic and traditional ways. The European Common Agricultural Policy is to blame and *must* be changed. Many sensitive farmers can't compete with this mass-producing, brutal big-business, which erodes and spoils the soil for future generations and besides causes rural communities to suffer as these farmers and their workers are forced off the land.

If you want to eat fresh, organically produced food *every day* at a price you can afford write to your M.E.P (Member of the European Parliament) or M.P. today and tell him, or her, that you disagree with the system of set-aside and do *not* want farmers in this country to be paid to let good land go to waste. Names and addresses of M.E.P's can be obtained from your local council or library. For more information: SAFE, 21 Tower Street, London WC2H 9NS (0171-240 1811) or: Farm and Food Society, 4 Winifield Way, London NW11 (0181-455 0634).

In Praise of the Fat Carthorse.

A powerful, young stallion or gelding Percheron, Suffolk or Dutch carthorse lumbering along a flowered country lane or rutted track is an inspiring sight, marvellous, exciting and fitting. Its ample buttocks invite the whip, or a flat stick to force it into straining uphill or to break into a trot. Even this possible cruelty, or disturbance of the peaceful atmosphere is no violation of it, as modern machinery is.

Although a programmed readership will not understand this, those horses are intensely sexually evocative. Big buttocks serving a practical purpose are somuch to be preferred as sex objects to pummel and spank than those of young women. Who wants to think of their mother as a once sex object, a focal point of sexual excitement made to parade boobs and buttocks like a slave? Why should human females constantly be the target for erotic slapping and smacking and advertise their fundament for such activity with the likely consequence of pregnancy; adding one more probably unwanted and unloved child to an already overpopulated world?

Carthorses, bred to pull, or be sat upon, naturally make submissive slaves and don't have the mind to object to it. We have a duty to care for them, to feed them well, to give them oats and allow them to graze in sweet, lush meadows, full of herbs necessary for their health, so that they should retain their glossy hide and be strong.

Essentially there is no need for hurry at all. We will all live longer and better if we surrender to the lifeforce and open ourselves to what our senses tell us. Then it will become obvious enough that our true feelings were buried below prejudices, phantasies and fables, ideas about life which we swallowed like so much pap or porridge. The influences we were subjected to have made us frightened of the very thing that will make us really happy: The truth of actual experience, the realization that what we always deeply felt and gives us a warm glow is the truth, is real and good. So many people have grown up in ugly, depressing, loveless, tasteless, inappropriate, unimaginative, boring and even hideous surroundings, backed up by all kinds of religious compulsions and fixed ideas, that they lost any sense of what is truly theirs in early childhood. For them a release is overdue. In this way they will realise what they have missed in all that pressure, tension, speed, haste, competition, artificiality and our subjection to machines. For this reason alone we need to relate properly to the land, and to return to farming which is done lovingly, slowly, organically and modestly, WITH CARTHORSES, powerful, plump beasts showing us their private parts shamelessly below their flailing, docked tails. Such earthiness is a necessary antidote to all the plastic and flimsiness that has surrounded us for too long, and if we can listen to what our blood and our belly tell us we will know that these horses, stamping, snorting and steaming, have an appeal and attraction which stinking, noisy tractors have not.

As they pull those wonderful wooden carts, made carefully by craftsmen, the plough or old fashioned iron implements, the simple machines of 50 or 60 years ago, they fertilise the land with their droppings, which is the most excellent manure. Unlike tractors and J.C.B's they reproduce themselves and they eat the hay and the oats which is gathered or grown with their labour and is not finite like petrol or oil.

APPENDIX II.

Coping With Crime

EARLY twenty years ago, in the first draft of this book, we predicted, you may remember, that the cynical obsession with 'progress' and 'growth', then 'all the rage', would lead to a dangerous escalation of crime. Soulless conditions bring about a mental climate in which people go mad, become psychotic, violent and uncaring. Perhaps *now* it is obvious to many more people that what we *then* predicted is happening. If we wish to rid ourselves of criminal behaviour and no longer live in fear of burglary, muggings, shootings, rape and robbery we must do something about the conditions which breed crime. At present such conditions are perpetuated by the *cupidity which rules our country* and is the rule amongst what is considered 'normality' in all the world. Repressive measures, more police and prisons will do nothing to alleviate the problem, even judges and prison governors say this nowadays.

There are a number of factors which create a criminal world; an impersonal environment – a 70's housing estate – is one of these, the lack of *wild* open spaces is another: Places where we built 'camps' or 'huts' when we were young and saw bats in the dusk of autumn evenings swooping overhead have been 'developed', adding to the characterless modern townscape. Children are increasingly *deprived* of natural influences and watch television and videos, or play computer games. Such distractions are designed to take them 'out of themselves' and lose whatever contact they may have had with their true feelings. All kinds of desire become paramount because this 'wanting', this voracious appetite for clothes, objects, cars, drugs and so on and forth is fanned by all they see and hear. A roaring fire takes over which demands to be fed and has no patience and neither care nor compassion for anything or anyone else. In art, in architecture and music any old idea and novelty or nastiness has been prized by fashionable opinion above what until the 60's still counted as 'fine' or valuable. This 'outer freedom', this creed of 'anything goes', this speedy 'living for laughs' and looking for thrills has given those who grew up in the last 30 years the impression that nothing really matters and that there is nothing to live for but sex, money and a 'good time', or 'living it up'.

When in 1973 we, the authors, were involved in the running of a community centre (designed by a group headed by Anelog) built by Camden Council on a housing estate, we said that there were *two* enemies, the yobbos who vandalised the building and the trendy 'starry eyed' idealists who thought 'self-expression' was everything: "The moest mawr-vellous things happen in places where all the windows get smeashed!" said one lady (at a committee meeting) aptly called Wilde! With such attitudes in control it is *obvious* that the flames will leap higher and higher. We call this the inevitable result of 'fire-consciousness'.

What Can Be Done?

Fire is put out by *water* or *earth*. The earth will keep it within bounds and the water extinguishes it. Thus we need a restraining earthy influence to contain crime. If we picture a house which is in total disorder and where chaos reigns, we can only clear it up and bring sense into it by doing this systematically and wholeheartedly. We must start in one corner of one room and the rest follows (In Chapter 4. we described how). A large city like London needs to be divided into 'villages', real places with a centre, or heart, not stupid, nondescript, impersonal boroughs like *Camden* which were fabricated in 1965, but Kentish Town, Hampstead, or Highgate Village, places which are real and mean something to the people who live there. These places can be compared to the house which is divided into rooms. As we have already said Kentish Town, our own 'village' has 3 parts, West and East on each side of the Highstreet and North above it where the ancient Highway forks. Each of these can again be divided into neighbourhoods with their tenants' or residents' associations giving support to an 'empowered' 'COMMUNICATOR'S OFFICE'.

We described how this office has a force of a new kind of social-worker/police-officer/psychologist attached to it, say 3 to 6 such officers, depending on how problematic the neighbourhood is. These highly trained workers know Natural Psychology and have done the Anelog course in 'living from the Inner'. They would be called

·A GRAIGIAN HALLOWHALL·

'Inter Communicators' and 'Rangers' and owe allegiance to the Communicator who is a Graigian priest(ess)/inspector /functionary/official who makes it her/his business to know everyone in the area. He/she is concerned with the whole community and makes sure that everyone in need receives their social benefits and spends the money on essentials, so that children don't suffer for their parents' bad habits. In fact she/he looks after his/her flock, rather like the old fashioned mediaeval parish priest.

This is the earthy aspect,
which can only come about by *true* Socialism,
which is *Social Care.*

The 'watery', psychological, feeling aspect, the spirituality of the INNER SELF comes into its own once the channels through which the water can flow are made. Because of centuries of repression and negation (and we mean real *oppression* from the State) during which horrible male monsters with their murderous FIRE CONSCIOUSNESS had their way (think of hanging, flogging, fighting and conquering, the slave trade, so-called British justice, witch hunting, public schools: 'Dotheboys Hall', and deprivation suffered by children generally), many aspects of WATER CONSCIOUSNESS are hardly known at all. We have a surfeit of technology, but *no understanding* in everything children are presented with. It is, for instance, always supposed that 'feelings' must be subjective. It is a fact though that 'psychics' can receive information about people or places which is quite accurate, i.e. objectively true. Anyone can develop their 'psychic', inner self, but needs to be 'opened' to it. We can live *objectively in our feelings* and realise the truth about ourselves and our life. This is called 'self-realisation' and must replace normal, dogmatic, opinionated patriarchal religion if we wish to create a non-criminal society.

NCE someone is 'opened' to their deeper feelings she/he changes and begins to live from the Inner Self, thus he/she will acquire a conscience by reflecting on what he/she hears and sees, bringing a new awareness of her/his surroundings. In order to live in this way people surrender to what comes up from within without prejudice or fear of condemnation. Even grown up schoolboys must talk about their feelings and give way to the emotions which come up and be moved to express them, weep, lament, sing and dance spontaneously from the inner. They must tremble and shake, fall down on the floor like a Muslim in prayer and bow to the inevitable truth to which they must submit. Once sensibility (the use of the senses) has become an ordinary part of life people will form good relationships. Loving parents living in a caring environment are not likely to breed hoodlums.

If we wish to rid ourselves of crime we must re-organise society to this purpose. Our point of view should be presented on T.V. and the resulting reaction should be on the front pages of the popular tabloids. Soap operas should contain episodes in which our solution to criminality is presented. Issues like those of over-population, sexuality and spirituality should become popular subjects for discussion and be imaginatively put before the general public. If no-one can be found with such an imagination in the normal journalistic and media-world, why not ask us, the authors of this book? We Graigian Green Monks have abilities which most people are quite unfamiliar with, as they are with the Work of Gurdjieff, with the Subud Latihan, with Anthroposophy and anything else censored by established and conventional attitudes. Crime will disappear forever when stuffed shirtism is no longer in control, when our Graigian values become the rule and knowledge which is inwardly liberating, true, fair and wise can be taught.

Criminal behaviour is often a reaction to repressive circumstances, to a lack of sensitivity and understanding, goodwill and kindness. Many people living in harsh surroundings have no access at all to anything but Christian sects of a rather extreme nature: No access to understanding which could help them with a different outlook from the terrible one they are accustomed to. It is so important, so vital that a new attitude to life is put forward. This we have defined by the slogan: 'TO GRAIGIANISE IS TO HUMANIZE!' It contains a very simple and promising idea. The robin on the badge

means a friendly and cheerful spirit. To humanize is to make the world around us more human, for people to have examples put before them of how to become caring, kind and considerate. When one wears the badge one is saying this to every one.

As we have said in previous chapters, Y Graig is Welsh for The Rock, like crag. It is pronounced 'er grige', the *i* as in 'tide'. A rock is solid and enduring; the good humanizing spirit must be born of solidarity and endure! By standing our ground, by being as solid in our united resolution as a rock, the greed, prejudice, dishonesty and malice all around us may be overcome. We must be rockhard in our endeavour to humanize the world. When we face a common enemy, differences of opinion, of religion and beliefs are forgotten and everyone can unite. The common enemy of our future life on earth is wasteful and cynical selfishness. This can be fought by making it to be socially unacceptable.

Wear the badge and tell others what it means! In our own neighbourhood we Graigians have created an example of what a humanizing spirit is able to do. We talk to our neighbours without any self-consciousness or negative attitudes. We try to be as helpful as we can; by sweeping the road off the constantly accumulating litter, looking after trees along the pavements, feeding pets when their owners are on holiday, giving neighbours lifts in our car and not being disappointed when someone does not express gratitude. On sunny days we sit on our doorstep with our lunch or tea. We take our own and other people's paper to the recycling centre and any other rubbish that can be recycled. We collect wood, furniture and clothes we find in skips, or are given to us and pass these on to anyone in need, hold jumble-sales outside our garden gate and pick up plastic in the countryside. After persisting like this for 34 years, our neighbourhood has become a very pleasant place to live in. The York stone pavement has been preserved and trees have been listed through our intervention.

The administration of the Graigian Society, which publishes a quarterly newsletter to which over 300 members have subscribed, is run from our monastic house in North London. If you wish to receive a badge (20p each + 30p postage) or would like some more information (please send a stamped, addressed envelope) or become a member (£3 unwaged, £5 waged or £7 joint-membership a year) please write to the Secretary:

**The Graigian Society
10 Lady Somerset Road
Kentish Town
London NW5 1UP**

GLOSSARY

The Four Elements:

- ✳ Air, thought, consciousness, a symbol of light, a star.
- ℧ Water, feeling, emotion, a symbol of fluidity, a chalice.
- ↑ Fire, energy, action, a symbol of force, an arrow.
- Φ Earth, matter, solidity, a symbol of substance, a seed.

Anelog Work:

A dynamic and effective system of 'Self-Development' which is an amalgam of wisdom and experience derived from 'Gurdjieff Work' combined with the revelation of Natural Psychology, plus practical tasks and art-therapy.

Archetype:

Just as a psychological type is defined by four elements in various sequences, so an archetype is characterised by the image resulting from combining two: Φ ℧, mud; ℧ Φ, water on earth, a lake, sea or river and so on. 'Lady Deeplake' stands for our feelings and was called by Jung the 'Anima', the opposite of the 'Trickster' ↑ ✳, hot air or wind. Archetypes appear in mythology and fairytales and were originally defined thus by Jung.

Communicator:

A Graigian priest(ess)/inspector/functionary/official who looks after an area (like a parish priest) and makes sure that those in need receive their social benefits at the Communicators's Office, or have their problems dealt with.

Community Holiday:

A holiday used as an introduction to 'working on oneself' and learning to relate constructively to others. Its purpose is to become more natural and 'awake', i.e. aware of oneself.

271

Dard:

A word coined by the Venerable Anelog to describe a person, male *or* female, who fulfils him/herself in the masculine elements of fire or air. We call this 'fire last' or 'air last'. Last meaning the 4th. element in the typology.

Fire Consciousness:

First used by Richard Gardner to identify the ruling consciousness of the contemporary world. It is associated with Patriarchy, is masculine and hard, for it excludes feeling. Fire consciousness was first developed in the Middle East (±2000 B.C.).

Graigian Monk:

A man, or woman, who dedicates the WHOLE of his/her life to monastic devotion... and to Graigian, humanitarian, Green ideals.

Graigian Society:

The Graigian Society is an environmental & spiritual organisation with a community of monk-artists at its core. It was founded on May 12th 1983 by the Venerable Anelog, Green Brother Sebastien and Green Brother Hereward.

Graigianity:

The 'religion' of the 'Graigians'; those who identify with the meditations, rituals, dress and customs of the Graigian Monastery. The Graigian colours are soft-green, warm-brown and off-white: Those of the bracken on Anelog in spring and autumn and of the cottages and rocks on this hill. The 'Graigians' have no beliefs in anything super-natural (life after death etc.), no God other than the 'Divine Inner Self' and no creed other than Natural Psychology.

Green Movement:

This is an extraordinary, dynamic spectrum of hundreds of organisations and societies throughout Britain. The movement ranges from animal welfare groups and countryside conservation through to the Graigian Society and on to extremely large associations like the National Trust. The Green Movement, in Europe, as a novel, political/cultural/spiritual concept was started by the Venerable Anelog (plus some 'SUBUD' friends) on Mount, or Mynydd, Anelog in the summer of 1965. It was initiated as a REACTION TO SOULLESSNESS AND CONSUMERISM..... The 'Keystone' of the Green Movement is to reduce, for *less, not more*. Unfortunately this point-of-view, especially regarding the world's population, has *not* yet been taken seriously. The colour 'green', a deliberate 'identification' with the beauty & freshness of Nature, was introduced by the 'Graigians' in 1971, when they were called the 'Green People' in a local paper.

Gurdjieff, George Ivanovitch (circa 1867-1949):

Revolutionary philosopher, psychologist, mystic, born in the Caucasus. He settled in France where he ran an 'Institute for the Harmonious Development of Man' near Fontainebleu and founded the concept of 'Gurdjieff Work' which he continued to teach from a flat in Paris until his death.

Hallow Hall:

A hall or a converted church where the Latihan, now called 'Hallowing', is practised.

INCON:

The INCON world is that of the industrial, conventional, conservative, con-merchant ('Smart-Alec') who runs everything in the business world. 'IN' comes from *in*dustrial, 'CON' comes from *con*fidence trick or *con*sumer.

Inter-communicator:

A new kind of social worker/police officer/psychologist who owes allegiance to the Communicator.

Inner Self:

Usually unconscious feelings which upon reflection can become part of one's awareness. The part of onself from which dreams and true love emanate.

273

Jung, Carl Gustav (1875-1960):

Doctor, psychiatrist, professor and psychologist who originally studied with Freud with whom he had a profound disagreement. He founded psychotherapy and coined many words which are now part of the language, such as 'intro- and extravert', 'the collective unconscious' etc. Through his profoundly imaginative work he had a DRAMATIC EFFECT on how mankind sees itself.

Latihan:

A psychodynamic exercise, or dance, practised by members of SUBUD, usually once a week, in a special hall. 'Latihan' means exercise in Javanese.

Mediator:

A rank equivalent to magistrate, or archdeacon.

Mentate:

A classroom, a study place with comfortable chairs and stools around an open fireplace... a sympathetic place to sit in and learn, in an informal atmosphere. The name comes from the Latin 'mens' – mind.

Natural Psychology:

The scientific understanding of the Four Elements combined to give us 12 'Worlds' and their Archetypes. Natural Psychology has been developed from 1956 to the present day. Initially it had strong connections with Jungian psychotherapy.

Nominator:

A rank equivalent to a bishop, or High Court judge.

Nominator Princeps:

A rank of *great* eminence equivalent to a prince(ess), king or queen. He or she presides over one of the countries of Britain and is a person of great taste, sensitivity & spiritual worth.

Opposite Type:

The 'opposites' are those, both male & female, who have their elements in more or less the opposite order to yourself. These opposites are the persons to whom you are emotionally, spiritually, intellectually, sexually and physically *attracted*. These persons may well be a business partner, admired friend, priest, guru, teacher or mentor.

Original Green Manifesto of 1965:

A document of Everest-like stature written by a friend/colleague of the Venerable Anelog: James Adler. This document, albeit brief, was the first DEFINITE REACTION to the greed & pollution of this industrial age, the 'effluent society'. James, known universally as Jimmy, did a considerable amount of research yet could find nothing AT ALL prior to the summer of 1965 which pointed away from gross consumerism. He was a journalist & craftsman and killed himself out of despair in 1970.

Positive Force (The):

The 'army' of a future Graigian State or Spiritual Government. The 'soldiers' have no dangerous weapons and carry staves (or lances) instead of guns. Their duties are confined to useful demolition, construction work and guarding vulnerable places. They also serve on parades dressed in a most fantastic and exciting way. The training for this force is character building yet liberating for the kind of youth who makes the streets unsafe in this 'day and age' through boredom and misguided identification.

Psychological or 'soul' type:

A totally immutable 'quality' of psyche. There are 24 such types (not 8 as proposed by Jung) defined by the 4 elements in various sequences, e.g. $* \circlearrowup \uparrow \Phi$ which type has $* \circlearrowup$, the world or archetype of judgement and authority as his/her essence or nature. The first element $*$ corresponds to Jung's 'thinking type', the second element $\circlearrowup$, in this case, is repressed. The third, $\uparrow$ with this type is the centre of gravity; the element he/she identifies with and the last, Φ is his/her fulfilment which he/she wishes to develop and looks for in his/her opposite type.

Ranger:

A new kind of police officer who has a social conscience and dresses in a flowing & feminine way, like the modern 'hippy'. He/she is in the service of the Communicator.

Salubriat:

The meditation or shrine room, temple or chapel of the Graigian, Green Religion (Graigianity).

SUBUD:

A spiritual organisation (originally brought to England in 1957 by J.G.Bennett), started in Cilandak, Jakarta, Indonesia by 'Bapak' (Pak Subuh). Many practitioners of the Gurdjieff Work in the 1950's and 1960's were involved in this movement. The name 'SUBUD' derives from *Susila Budhi Dharma* (The Path of Living according to Truth).

Tre-loper (from treelopper):

A term we use to describe an extremely 'stick in the mud' repressive, conventional person who had his heyday in the First World War, covers everything in concrete, obstructs or lops anything in the least alive or free and constantly forbids, or complains about, what he deems to be irregular or abnormal, like honest Anglo-Saxon four letter words, whereas he himself lives in abysmal ugliness and condones factory farming and the transportation of live animals for slaughter.

Voy:

A word coined by the Venerable Anelog to describe a person, male *or* female, who fulfils him/herself in the feminine elements of earth or water. We call this 'earth last' or 'water last'. Last meaning the 4th element in the typology.

276

Water Consciousness:

Used by Richard Gardner to identify intuitive awareness, reflective thought, imagination and sensing or receptivity; the dreamworld. It is miraculous and gentle and existed before 'civilization'. Magic is practised by all indigenous so-called 'primitive' peoples and comes from water-consciousness.

Work on Oneself:

This simply means self-development, i.e. becoming aware of one's shortcomings and by various exercises developing what is lacking in one's character: Seeing things about oneself and becoming open to change.

Y Graig:

(Welsh for 'The Rock') is the name of a small house in Gwynedd, North Wales, whose natural beauty inspired the owners to start a society for environmental protection, 'Green' activity & spiritual growth. These owners are the authors of this book.

Natural Psychology
summing up

☀ air	↑ fire
∇ water	⊕ earth

4 Elements
corresponding to 4 states: solid, liquid (feeling), gaseous (thought), energy.

6 Dimensions
length breadth height density volume time

12 Archetypes
furthest biggest highest lightest emptiest fastest
nearest smallest lowest densest fullest slowest

Observer Hero Father Wizard Trickster Fool
Lover Angel Mother Peasant Madonna Old Woman

each Archetype has 2 elements:

☀⊕ ↑∇ ☀∇ ☀↑ ↑☀ ↑∇
∇↑ ∇☀ ⊕↑ ⊕∇ ∇⊕ ⊕☀

24 Types
Each one has 4 elements in different orders:

1) first element + 2nd = one's nature, basic inclination

2) second element = what is avoided, repressed (all 3 aspects)

3) third element = what one identifies with (all 3 aspects)

4) last element = what one idealises, for instance

Earth (⊕) last + Fire (↑) 3rd: warm earth, the hearth, cosiness relaxed solidarity

12 Voy and 12 Dard types
pertaining to the Mother archetype

The last element determines whether one is Voy or Dard. There are 6 types with earth, 6 with water, 6 with air and 6 with fire last. Earth and water are feminine, Fire and Air masculine. We fulfil ourselves in our last.

3 Groups

Animal
Nomadic

This group consists of types with Earth/Fire and Fire/Earth or Air/Water and Water/Air as their 1st and 2nd or 3rd and last.

⊕↑ ☀∇
☀∇ ⊕↑
etc.

Vegetable
Rural, Agricultural

This group consists of types with Water/Earth and Earth/Water or Fire/Air and Air/Fire as their 1st and 2nd or 3rd and last.

∇⊕ ↑☀
↑☀ ∇⊕
etc.

Mineral
Urban

This group consists of types with Earth/Air and Air/Earth or Fire/Water and Water/Fire as their 1st and 2nd or 3rd and last

⊕☀ ↑∇
↑∇ ⊕☀
etc.

SUPPLEMENTS

Cleaning up the countryside

Where ever you go, in every country lane in England and in the greater part of Wales, there is litter; rubbish and discarded objects lying about, disfiguring the landscape. Broken television sets, cookers, doors and furniture thrown carelessly into the hedges and thickets (where these have not been removed, torn out to make room for factory farming) demonstrate a total disregard for nature. The same applies to open spaces in cities and towns; wherever vegetation grows wild, there the plastic blows in the wind amongst the dog roses, the ragwort, the mallow and the elderbushes. Blinded by television and other distractions passers-by are not inclined to pick up rubbish and the borough council employ men who come with strimmers and other machines to destroy the wildflowers, revealing and often leaving the litter.

The Graigian Society wishes to initiate a campaign with the slogan "To Graigianize is to Humanize, leave the 'weeds' and remove the rubbish", painted on a board over a litterbag hanging between two poles on legs.

A group of Graigian members, all wearing a robin badge and green or/and rust brown clothes go to places where litter has accumulated to pick it up. Passers-by will be interested and ask questions, which is an opportunity to talk about the Graigian Society and give out leaflets. The members may call themselves 'The Graigian Volunteers' and carry long rods, which can be lengthened by fitting them together, with hooks at one end to tear plastic and polythene 'flags' out of trees. Thermos flasks and cups of tea with biscuits can make this into a social occasion, a Graigian picnic on the wayside with the Graigians entertaining some of the more interested and serious bystanders, who may join this event.

Thus this lighthearted way of purifying the countryside and open spaces in the towns will bring people together and give them an opportunity to discover the truth about the woods & fields around their hometown, both what remains of the lovely and how the vandalism of factory - farming and a criminal, careless, loveless attitude have made nature into a desert interspersed with a sad and dreadful dumping ground.

A man who figures widely in the press, a multi-millionaire renowned for his grandiose enterprises was given a vast sum of money by Mrs. Thatcher, a number of years ago, to initiate a project called U.K. 2000 which was to tidy up our environment. What happened to all this money? It was certainly not spent in such a way which would make a difference to the dumping and scattering of trash. Why was a totally unsuitable person chosen for a purpose which demands serious dedication? We must not forget this outrage. There is nothing more disgraceful than the lack of reverence for our natural environment shown by the churlish louts who have inherited it, nothing more characteristic of consumerism than the way country lanes are disfigured. May the Graigian Society achieve what several million Thatcherite pounds given to a high flyer did not!

To instill respect and reverence for our universal Mother, the earth, the sleeping, cossetted, conventional mass of people in their upholstered press-button way of life need to be bombarded with propaganda, as there is for God, but about our endeavours this time. This book: 'The Future Will Be Green' must replace the Bible. You, who have been moved by what we have said must help us to sell it and propagate it. You must dress in soft green and warm brown, the colours of nature, and stand on a street corner with leaflets and pamphlets about this book and this society. You must write to us and we will send you what you need. Be confident that nothing in us, the three Green Monks, wishes to spend any money at all on any of the vulgar and ostentatious indulgences of the flaunting millionaire!

Membership of the Graigian Society entitles you to a quarterly newsletter, an invitation to a tea party in October, one in December and one with a puppet play in February. You will have the right to join our fortnightly Sunday group (talks on Natural Psychology and Anelog Work, participation in self discovery through art and mask making). There will also be the performance of masked mime and phoenix events. You will be able to join our community holidays on Mount Anelog and stay at our cottage Tai Bwlch no.2 for £39 a week on the same hill at the far end of the Lleyn Peninsula (it sleeps 5).

The Graigian monastery was bought in 1979 when 4 years of converting this Victorian corner house began. In that year Y Graig Anelog was also acquired for the society. From 1983-1985 the monastic life was initiated with the new spirituality which this entails. In 1985 the Graigian Society started a membership drive with its campaign to buy Bron Orion, the 65 acre field in which it was intended to put the ancient earth walls, flattened in 1976, back. It was, however, not possible then but it is still an avowed aim of the society to buy this land and make an example of restoring it to its original condition, to be farmed in a traditional and sensitive way.

Another intention of the Graigian Society is to open Graigian shops. These sell Graigian products and have a cafe where drinks, wholemeal cakes etc. are for sale. The products are Graigian T shirts, beads called 'chanters', books and booklets, pottery, badges, Batiked scarves, pictures, address labels, postcards etc. All made with a distinct Graigian character.

To publicise 'The Future will be Green' phoenix marches will be organized with the phoenix on top of a car, participants giving out leaflets and selling the book from the boot. A masked mime of the 12 Archetypes will be devised as street theatre and eventually produced with musical accompaniment on stage.

the Anelog

Hu Man or Machine Man

Every manual activity has its own rhythm: When you trim a hedge with a billhook you get into the rhythm of it after a while. You become aware of the way you are standing, moving and swinging. At any point you come across something; a thick branch, a difficult manoeuvre which has to be made and needs considering, this makes you pause and become aware of what is around you: Aware of your work as a whole, not just the part you are cutting back but also flowers, berries, sounds, smells, the birds in the sky and waving tree tops. When you are doing something by hand you know when you are tired and want to stop. You remain in touch with yourself and your surroundings. This is an Inner experience which working with a machine denies. Because you are doing a job slowly it is done with feeling and is an experience which enriches you, it gives you life. If you love it and therefore are in harmony with everything around you, you have struck a balance between yourself and nature. It becomes a creative activity and akin to painting a lovely picture and like a picture it will give you a wonderful feeling every time you return to admire it.

A man operating a mechanical hedge flayer smashes everything apart and thereby destroys life. Small mammals will hide away and if its done in the spring birds nests will be decimated. This machine-man loses touch with the earth. He is surrounded by the noise of the engine and suffers its jarring vibration. If he is in a glass cabin he is physically isolated from his surroundings. What it does to him physically is bad enough, but when he looks at the ugly result of his work it is devastating for his psyche. This bad result leads to unhealthy consequences which may shorten his life. There is an astronomically high suicide rate amongst farmers, mainly due to the demands of agribusiness which rates profits higher than life. This is part of the vicious cycle of having to use machines to economise on time and manpower to meet with the higher demands.

As I get older the more I value the importance of Inner sustenance. The psyche needs feeding, just as the body does. Everything done by hand unselfconsciously expresses feeling and these manifested feelings give Inner nourishment to anyone, whether they are conscious of it or not.

Green Brother Hereward

The Role of the Artist in Society

Visual art has become stagnant. Why? Because we have not progressed from Dada... and Surrealism was never developed seriously. Damien Hirst still flies the Dada flag. In 80 years of art nothing has changed. This is a terrible indictment of our Western culture.

Artists can be split into two groups: Those who can use their talents to serve other peoples needs, like portraitists and illustrators, and to some extent landscapists, and those who create pictures out of a sense of compulsion. This includes artist from all sorts of schools formed since the 1920's: Abstract, cubist, imaginative art and later pop, op and minimalist. Apart from imaginative art the general trend has been to reduce art to its bare basics as if the artist was trying to redefine his work. A lot of people seem to be stuck with this idea of art and any new work has to be more shocking, banal or ridiculous than the last and the artist will go to extremes to do this, hence Dada still lives.

But now, on the edges of public awareness, are emerging a small number of artists who use their time to create serious works of art based on their deeper feelings and their observations of the world around them. They are freely exploring their own Inner processes and are drawing up images directly from their unconscious. They often have heightened or mystical experiences. This group, which I call Symbolic or Mythic Artists are yet to be recognised and be seen as vital to society because they can show what is happening on an unconscious level. The unconscious is what motivates life. It expresses itself through feelings. Nowadays it is recognised that someone can go astray when they are leading their life contrary to their deeper feelings and need to change dramatically to reach a feeling of well being. Just as people lead individual lives, society has a collective existence. It too can go astray when it is bamboozled by greater forces and therefore needs guidance to bring it back to itself. The Mythic artist can provide this guidance by being a social barometer of its collective psyche. They are like visual Shamans who express themselves in symbolic imagery. Mythic artists should be respected and paid generously for their valuable contribution to the cultural health of society.

Green Brother Hereward

How you can be more Green

Rather than being schoolmasterish & didactic & saying 'This is what you MUST do - whether you like it or not', I am simply going to give a few examples of how we Green, Graigian monks live:

We only wear clothes of 100% cotton, wool or linen - nothing at all, EVER, of nylon or polyester. We patch the clothes endlessly until they drop off us with age!

We try, all the time, to keep our lifestyle as SIMPLE AS POSSIBLE - e.g. we have a car for long journeys... & three old bicycles for short ones... & that is it!

We only holiday & travel WITHIN THE BRITISH ISLES... this saves a fortune on package tours to Ibiza!

We work, sleep, rest & live all within the SAME BUILD-ING, the monastic house; this saves the astonishing amount of time, energy & money most people expend on endlessly shuttling between home... & workplace.

Whether it is shoes, bicycles, candles or books we ALWAYS BUY QUALITY GOODS - if something is of GOOD QUALITY & IT LASTS... then, in the long term, we will save money!

O.P.D. (Own Personal Drama)... GET RID OF IT ALTO-GETHER! O.P.D. includes bad relations with your parents or siblings, disastrous & silly love affairs, stupid arguments, mad investments, badly-planned journeys, hopeless court-cases, fisti-cuffs with the Police, unbelievably expensive divorce settlements etc. etc. 'ad infinitum'. Being 'awake', attentive & self-aware is the only method of eliminating O.P.D.

Reduce, Re-use, Recycle... by being very careful, nay Scrooge-like, with all the hundreds of things you use throughout your lives (in the house, flat, bungalow, garage, workplace, cottage, dinghy, yacht or potting-shed) a huge SAVING in time, money, energy, metals, electricity, oil, petrol, water, plastics can be achieved.

We only go shopping ONCE A WEEK... coming back laden with huge boxes of groceries, fruit & vegetables... this saves a mammoth wadge of time... & temper!

We only eat vegetarian food (plus a little bit of fish & dairy products)... this is kind to animals; it is also kind to your purse.

We always put our leftover food into the 'fridge... this cer-tainly saves money... we also eat EVERYTHING on our plate!

We grow our salad vegetables (Permaculture style!) on a small flat roof-garden... why not try & do this yourself? Its even possible to grow a small nursery of seedling-trees... which can be used to replant desecrated & desertified parts of the British countryside.

Alcohol! We make all our own wine & all our own beer too. The equipment & materials for this are inexpensive & the taste is 'out-of-this-world'. Home-made wine & beer is free of tax so it only costs a few pence per pint.

We studiously avoid ecologically-wasteful, consumerist habits - e.g. we buy as few BATTERIES as possible; they are an expensive & 'materials-costly' way of getting electricity. Radios, tape recorders & other household products can be cheaply run on a plug-in transformer (240v down to 9v).

Presents! Presents! Presents! When we give presents we always give a painting or a pot we have made ourselves... or something of real practical use like a T-shirt, a house-plant or a shopping bag. WE AVOID EXPENSIVE, WHIMSICAL FRIPPERIES!

Green Brother Sebastien

286

SELECTED BIBLIOGRAPHY

BENNETT, John Godolphin:
Concerning Subud London: Hodder & Stroughton 1960.
Deeper Man London: Turnstone Press 1985.
The Dramatic Universe (4 vols) London: Hodder & Stroughton
1956-66; Charles Town (USA): Claymont Communications 1987.
Energies: Material, Vital, Cosmic Charles Town: Claymont
Communications 1989.
Gurdjieff: Making of a New World London: Turnstone Press
1974; New York: Harper & Row 1976.
Gurdjieff Today London: Turnstone Press 1973.
Hazard Santa Fe (USA): Bennett Books 1991.
Idiots in Paris Sherborne: Coombe Springs Press 1980.
Needs of a New Age Community Santa Fe: Bennett Books 1990.
The Sevenfold Work Charles Town: Claymont Communications 1979.
Witness: An Autobiography London: Turnstone Press 1974;
Charles Town: Claymont Communications 1983.

CAVENDISH, Richard: *The Tarot* London: Michael Joseph 1975.

GARDNER, Richard:
The Purpose of Love Rigel Press 1970.
Evolution through the Tarot Rigel Press 1970.

GURDJIEFF, George Ivanovich:
Beelzebub's Tales to his Grandson;
Meetings with Remarkable Men;
Views from the Real World: Early Talks of Gurdjieff as
Recollected by his Pupils;
All London: Routledge & Kegan Paul [many editions].
The Herald of Coming Good Paris 1933; New York: Weiser 1970.

HOPCKE, Robert H.: *Jung, Jungians and Homosexuality*
Boston (USA) and London: Shambhala Publications 1989.

HORNEY, Karen: *Neurosis and Human Growth*
London: Routledge & Kegan Paul 1951.

HUTTON, Alice: *The Cards Can't Lie* Jupiter Books 1979.

JUNG, Carl Gustav:
The Archetypes and the Collective Unconscious
Modern Man in Search of a Soul
Psychological Types
All in London: Routledge & Kegan Paul [many editions]
Memories, Dreams and Reflections [Autobiography]
London: Collins (Fontana Library) 1961

KAPLAN, Stuart R: *The Encyclopedia of the Tarot*
U.S. Games Systems Inc. 1978

MICHELL, John: *View over Atlantis* Thames & Hudson 1969

NICOLL, Maurice:
Living Time London: Vicent Stuart 1949
*Psychological Commentories on the Teaching of G.L Gurdjieff and
P.D. Ouspensky* London: Vicent Stuart 1952

OUSPENSKY, Peter Demian:
The Fourth Way;
In Search of the Miraculous;
A New Model of the Universe;
Tertium Organum;
All in London: Routledge & Kegan Paul [many editions].

PETERS, Fritz:
Boyhood with Gurdjieff London: Victor Gollancz 1964.
Gurdjieff Remembered London: Victor Gollancz 1965.

RAKOCZI, Basil Ivan: *The Painted Caravan*
Le Hague: L.J.C. Boucher 1954

SALZMANN, Jeanne de: (Foreword to *Views from the Real World*)
[See GURDJIEFF].

SHUMACHER, E.F.:
Small is Beautiful Hutchinson 1993
A Guide for the Perplexed London: Jonathan Cape 1977

WALKER, Kenneth:
Venture with Ideas Neville Spearman 1951, 1973
A Study of Gurdjieff's Teaching London: Jonathan Cape 1957, 1973